P9-DOE-185

LIVE IN GRACE, WALK IN LOVE

LIVE IN GRACE

◆

WALK IN LOVE

A 365-DAY JOURNEY

BOB GOFF

NELSON
BOOKS

An Imprint of Thomas Nelson

© 2019 Bob Goff

All rights reserved. No portion of this book may be reproduced, stored in a retrieval system, or transmitted in any form or by any means—electronic, mechanical, photocopy, recording, scanning, or other—except for brief quotations in critical reviews or articles, without the prior written permission of the publisher.

Published in Nashville, Tennessee, by Nelson Books, an imprint of Thomas Nelson. Nelson Books and Thomas Nelson are registered trademarks of HarperCollins Christian Publishing, Inc.

The author is represented by Alive Literary Agency, www.aliveliterary.com.

Thomas Nelson titles may be purchased in bulk for educational, business, fund-raising, or sales promotional use. For information, please e-mail SpecialMarkets@ThomasNelson.com.

Scripture quotations are taken from the Holy Bible, New International Version®, NIV®. Copyright © 1973, 1978, 1984, 2011 by Biblica, Inc.® Used by permission of Zondervan. All rights reserved worldwide. www.Zondervan.com. The "NIV" and "New International Version" are trademarks registered in the United States Patent and Trademark Office by Biblica, Inc.®

Any Internet addresses, phone numbers, or company or product information printed in this book are offered as a resource and are not intended in any way to be or to imply an endorsement by Thomas Nelson, nor does Thomas Nelson vouch for the existence, content, or services of these sites, phone numbers, companies, or products beyond the life of this book.

ISBN 978-1-4002-0378-9 (eBook)
ISBN 978-1-4002-0377-2 (HC)

Library of Congress Control Number: 2019939195

Printed in Germany
20 21 22   CPIG   20 19 18 17 16 15 14 13 12

LIVE IN GRACE, WALK IN LOVE.

Come to me, all you who are weary and burdened, and I will give you rest. Take my yoke upon you and learn from me, for I am gentle and humble in heart, and you will find rest for your souls. For my yoke is easy and my burden is light.

MATTHEW 11:28–30

I remember learning to ride my first bike, but my favorite bike memories are when I taught my kids. Without fail, at the beginning, the front tire would wobble back and forth more and more wildly just before one of them bit the dust. And they all bit the dust. Sometimes they would try again; sometimes they would call it quits. Learning to ride a bike at first is completely unnatural. Once it clicks—the balance, pedaling, steering—it's hard to imagine *not* knowing how to do it. With enough practice, you don't even think about riding a bike anymore. You just do it.

Jesus talks about taking up a challenge to live differently. It's sort of like riding a bike. He wants us to live in grace and walk in love, but at first it is a gangly, wobbly wreck. We might even get banged up a little. Then, after a while, you just know how to do it. The Bible describes it as a rhythm, like breathing itself, where we are taking in grace for ourselves and holding out love for others. It is not natural, and it takes some practice. But Jesus showed us the way. Maybe one day we'll look a little more graceful and pull off some cool tricks—hop a couple of curbs, do a wheelie or a bunny hop. Not unlike Peter and John, who healed a man in Acts 3, Jesus wants us to stick with Him through the awkward learning parts so we can learn to ride like He does. He wants to take our mind off of falling so we can pedal more fearlessly. Sure, there will be some scratches and scrapes. But we can pick each other up and help each other get back on for another go.

What habits and rhythms do you need to practice to help you naturally experience God's grace in your life?

JANUARY 2

PLANS WORK OR THEY DON'T. LOVE ALWAYS WORKS. GO WITH THE SURE THING.

The entire law is fulfilled in keeping this one command: "Love your neighbor as yourself."

GALATIANS 5:14

What is it about January 1 and making New Year's resolutions? I think they're terrific because they get people inspired to move toward the person they want to be. Later in January, I go around asking people if they made any resolutions—it gives you a window into what their hopes and dreams are. One predictable recurring theme is friends who want to go the gym on a regular basis. They say their gyms are like ghost towns in November and December, then January hits and they get as busy as a New York City subway. They also say the crowds begin to trickle down as the month goes on, and by February they're back to the familiar faces they see throughout the year. If only we could make our commitments surefire bets, right? Here's the thing. Plans are a toss-up: sometimes they work out and sometimes they wither. Love always works. What if we simply commit to love?

Don't plan on doing it or make a resolution to do it the way people hope to go to the gym. Just do it. No plan, no agenda. Just Jesus leaking out through you into the world. Our lives are a series of positive experiences and more than a few negative ones. Make your life about people and you won't regret it. There's no gym to join, no pounds to lose. Our hours and minutes are what make up our lives, and God never intended relationships to be an afterthought. Make this year about people. We won't give our friends the love they deserve if we try to work them in when our lives slow down. We'll wake up one day and realize we never really got to know the people we bump into every day, even if they're the ones who sit across the dinner table from us each night. If you have to choose between your plans and your loved ones, go with the sure thing and choose love.

Who do you need to focus your love toward today?

JANUARY 3

GOD HOPES WE'LL DEVELOP A GREATER
FEAR OF INACTION THAN OF FAILURE.

Even though I walk through the darkest valley, I will fear no evil, for
you are with me; your rod and your staff, they comfort me.

PSALM 23:4

Have you ever heard a plane break the sound barrier?

About 768 miles per hour—that's how fast you have to go to outrun sound
itself. Modern planes can do it pretty easily. Around World War II, though,
scientists and engineers thought Mach speeds might be impossible in a manned
aircraft. Their hesitance had everything to do with what happened at 767 miles
per hour. Just before a plane breaks the sound barrier, all the created energy
is pushing against the plane. Think of riding an old, rickety roller coaster in
midair—all the shaking, jerking, and rattling made more than a few pilots
throttle back.

When we're chasing our dreams, all the turbulence we face shouldn't scare
us into pulling back, though. The shaking, jerking, and rattling in our lives are
telling us we're getting close to the breakthrough.

If there's anything to fear, often it's pulling back, not pressing forward.
Is fear of failure holding you back from breaking your personal barriers? You
might be at 767 miles per hour. Throw the throttle down, because once you
push through fear produced by the rattling, you find the next-level experience
you've been hoping for. God hopes we'll develop a greater fear of inaction than
of failure, because then, we'll experience with wide-eyed excitement what it's
like to cruise, doing what we were made to do.

Where is fear holding you back right now?

LIVE A LIFE OF CONSTANT ANTICIPATION.

[Abraham] did not waver through unbelief regarding the promise of God, but was strengthened in his faith and gave glory to God, being fully persuaded that God had power to do what he had promised. This is why "it was credited to him as righteousness."

ROMANS 4:20-22

The city where I live is known for one of the best fireworks shows on the planet. It's no secret either. People from all over fly into San Diego to witness the spectacle. The city loads four barges down with munitions, parks them in different parts of the bay, then synchronizes the launch with music as hundreds of thousands of people assemble to watch an hour of explosions. Thousands of fireworks are put on display. It's a pyromaniac's dream. The question isn't whether the show will burn your retinas a little bit but if you'll get there early enough to get a parking spot and a good seat.

One year, instead of a perfect symphony of pyrotechnics and patriotism over the course of an hour, someone made a mistake and hit the wrong button. Every single firework went off at once. It was all over within thirty *seconds*. It was nine o'clock at night, but the sky was as bright as noon for a brief moment as thousands of fireworks all exploded on the decks of the barges. It was *awesome*! More than a few people in San Diego lost their eyebrows that night. The people with the best view were the dudes who pushed the button. Sure, they lost their jobs, but I bet they thought it was worth it.

When we're really walking with Jesus, our lives look just as expectant as people in San Diego do now every Fourth of July. There's no question that something awesome is going to happen. It might be a big success or an epic fail; the only question is how close you'll be when all the fireworks go off.

Live a life of constant anticipation. Is it possible your big idea will blow up? You bet. Do it anyway. Trusting Jesus is like watching a lit fuse; it's only a matter of time before He's going to do awesome things in your life. Quit playing it safe. Press the button.

Where in your life are you playing it safe? What could you do to press the button?

DON'T LET WHAT YOU'RE AFRAID OF KEEP YOU FROM WHAT YOU WERE MADE FOR.

[Be] confident of this, that he who began a good work in you will carry it on to completion until the day of Christ Jesus.

PHILIPPIANS 1:6

Before Bill Gates was one of the richest men in the world, he was a Harvard dropout with a failed business. He cofounded a business called Traf-O-Data. Have you heard of it? Of course not. Me neither. It was started in the 1970s, and this company generated reports about roadway traffic to help cities know where to put traffic lights or which roads needed improving. It was far from a head turner. Here's why it's interesting. The company and its ideas crashed and burned.

Bill Gates was born with a gift, though, and he didn't bury the gift just because his first attempt was a failure. He and his business partner learned from their mistakes, started Microsoft, and changed the world.

Failure tops the list of greatest fears for most of us. It's vulnerable to put our passions into action because we can't play it cool if it crumbles. If others see us go all in, they'll certainly see us if we fail. We'll be embarrassed, broke, and our friends might be awkward in the way they handle it all. What if they see that our best wasn't enough? What if we hear that dark voice inside us again that says, *You're not enough*?

We can't win the game from the bleachers. We'll never succeed unless we get out on the field and go for it. Whether it's starting a business, putting music to your poems, or braving rejection from the girl who makes you lose your words, you won't get the gold if you're too scared to work the mine. God created you with unique gifts and ignited the passions He put in your heart for a reason—don't let fear steal your opportunities and leave you on the sidelines wishing you'd tried. Do what you believe you were created to do. Is it possible it won't work? You bet. Fail trying, don't fail watching.

What do you need to hear or believe from God in order to find the courage to step out on a big dream you have?

QUIT WAITING FOR A PLAN; JUST GO LOVE EVERYBODY.

Dear friends, let us love one another, for love comes from God. Everyone who loves has been born of God and knows God.

1 JOHN 4:7

Have you noticed a surge in the number of workout programs out there? It seems like every time I pick up a magazine, a new study says the key to weight loss is to avoid carbs, or only eat carbs, or eat only free-range llama eggs. I'm still looking for the workout plan that pushes popsicles, cake pops, and Pop-Tarts as the key to getting ripped. It would seem the only thing we love more than dieting is talking about dieting.

I'm not one for diets or workout plans, but I do know what it's like to spend too much time coming up with a plan instead of just *doing* the plan. The same holds true with our personal plans. It's tempting to sit around dreaming about what we would do if only we had the money or the time or the unique opportunity. But all that planning for the future takes us away from the one thing all of us can do right now: love the people around us.

God isn't dazzled when we go across an ocean. He delights when we go across the street.

It's great to map out a plan to use your gifts to make the world a little more beautiful or functional, but try not to forget that you're already where you are. Go change the world from where you are, while you're moving toward where you wish you were. Changing the world turns out to be easier and harder than we tend to make it: it's easier because it doesn't take as much money or time as we think it will, but it's harder because, like the workouts we avoid, it takes courage, commitment, and sacrifice in the moment.

If you're a planner, terrific. Go do loads of planning. If you were wired to be spontaneous, do plenty of that. By all means, keep scheming up plans, but don't forget there's a big difference between always preparing and actually being ready to start.

What is it that you've been planning without starting? You don't have to take all the steps—just the next one.

DON'T LET ANYTHING BUT JESUS DISTRACT YOU.

When you pray, go into your room, close the door and pray to your Father, who is unseen. Then your Father, who sees what is done in secret, will reward you.

MATTHEW 6:6

I read that the average person spends one out of every five minutes on social media. It's literally taking over our lives, minute by minute. To minimize the distraction, software companies have developed apps to keep you off for twenty-four hours, no matter what. Some apps are designed to restrict your internet access completely, and you can't turn your computer off and on, restart your internet, or do anything to get around it. This is how serious our distractive habits have become, and I know it personally. We all have our weaknesses. For some people, it's sports or fashion or cars. Me, I can't stay off social media when friends of mine start posting their kids' back-to-school pictures or Halloween costumes. How are we supposed to be productive when we see four-year-old pumpkins with superpowers?

It's easy to get distracted by everything else; what takes a little more work is to only get distracted by Jesus. When it comes time for praying or reading about Jesus, it's easy to feel like we're wasting time. We get fidgety. Our minds start to wander. Our fingers reach for our phones to take a quick peek and see what our friends are doing. With all the stuff on our to-do lists and all the opportunities to connect with others, it can feel forced to stop, be still, and be silent.

We're not wasting time on God. It's actually the best use of time to spend time with the One who created time in the first place. He knew we would need to eat, sleep, work, and brush our teeth, yet He still asked us to pray. He urged us to spend time with Him because He knew it would actually change everything.

Sure, it's good to guard your time, but it's even better to guard your heart. Don't keep such a tight grip on your time that you miss out on Jesus. Take some time today and decide to only be distracted by Him.

What's your plan to be distracted by Him today?

JANUARY 8

GOD USES UNCERTAINTY TO CHASE US OUT INTO THE OPEN WHERE WE CAN FIND HIM ALL OVER AGAIN.

In all this you greatly rejoice, though now for a little while you may have had to suffer grief in all kinds of trials. These have come so that the proven genuineness of your faith—of greater worth than gold, which perishes even though refined by fire—may result in praise, glory and honor when Jesus Christ is revealed.

1 PETER 1:6–7

When we pray, it's easy to get a little tongue-tied. We don't always know what to say or how to do it "right." But when there's a crisis, sometimes we turn into world-class orators when we pray. We know exactly what we want, right? Whether you're driving through a hailstorm with your kids in the back seat or going through an unwanted career change with no opportunities on the horizon, difficult things can make us feel small. They make us feel so needy. They help us realize our absolute need for God to help us. These are the moments we find ourselves whispering panicked prayers as if our lives depended on them—because, in fact, they sometimes do.

It would be great if we could recognize how dependent we are on God in the high times, too, when we're healthy or have a little extra in our savings account. But the discomfort brought by fear and uncertainty in our lives can become blessings. Here's the reason why: comfortable people don't need Jesus; desperate people do.

I heard the other day that a lot of the buttons we have to push don't actually do anything. I don't know if it's true or not, but we've all had our suspicions. Like the button to change the traffic light so you can walk across the street or the one to make an elevator door close faster. They put those buttons there so we *feel* like we have some control over our lives, when we actually don't. We might think we've got everything in hand, but the reality is that it's only an illusion. Here's the thing: we encounter God all over again every time we're desperate enough to realize we're not actually in charge.

Fear and uncertainty launch us toward God, and He's always there to receive us when we arrive. When all signs tell us there's no way out, we find God in the uncertainty, and He always makes a way. Take confidence in this. Realize you're terribly needy. It's a good thing.

**What are you feeling uncertain about that
you can bring to God in prayer?**

DON'T WORRY ABOUT ALL THE STEPS. BEGIN.

Do not be anxious about anything, but in every situation, by prayer and petition, with thanksgiving, present your requests to God. And the peace of God, which transcends all understanding, will guard your hearts and your minds in Christ Jesus.

PHILIPPIANS 4:6–7

Have you ever run a marathon? Me neither. I have some friends who have done it, and I've learned a lot about life from what they experienced. They say that they feel like their bodies are going to shut down at multiple points in the race, so they keep moving when they stop by tables with water or orange slices. Some say they get a little delusional at certain points and sometimes feel an unexplainable sense of euphoria. All the friends I've asked say they couldn't think too far ahead when they felt like they were falling apart. In other words, they couldn't think about mile twenty-two when they were on mile twenty-one because it was just too overwhelming. They had to focus on putting one foot in front of another, and repeating this, until they finally crossed the finish line.

I think the same is true for most of us when we start a new project or pivot to a new direction in our lives. We can do our best to plan and train, but once we're in the race, all we can do is be present in the moment. We won't know what needs to happen at mile twenty-two until we get there. Some people delight in this, but most spend too much energy feeling anxious about a mile marker they haven't yet arrived at. Does that sound like you? Usually the things we worry about the most don't happen anyway. We fear there will be disaster only to find balloons when we arrive.

Take heart. If we're diligent and thoughtful each step of the way, we don't have to fret over contingencies down the road. Don't worry about what may or may not happen; stick by Jesus and trust He will work it all out in the end.

What's your next step? When will you take it?

WHILE YOU'RE FIGURING OUT WHAT GOD'S PLAN IS FOR YOUR LIFE, JUST GO LOVE EVERYBODY. THAT'S THE PLAN.

As God's chosen people, holy and dearly loved, clothe yourselves with compassion, kindness, humility, gentleness and patience.

COLOSSIANS 3:12

You know what's delightful? Catching up with someone in their fifties or sixties and finding out they're making an enormous career change. It reminds me we can always change and grow.

We tend to leave the risks and big life changes to college students or young professionals as if skinny jeans were the gatekeeper. The problem is this: most of us spend our whole lives trying to figure out what we're supposed to do with them. At some point we thought we had found our callings, so we ran toward them. Then we rethink whether we'd be better off using our gifts to serve in business instead of ministry, or as a social worker instead of a dentist, or as a Disney greeter instead of a banker. Because we're given so many options and opportunities, it's easy to spend so much time trying to find the ideal career that we miss our life. What comes from a good place doesn't always lead us to a good place.

We all want to use all our gifts. That's a good thing. There's nothing wrong with taking time to figure out the path that complements your ambitions and capabilities. We get into trouble when we become more concerned with all the potential paths we could take than we are about the people right in front of us.

Don't get wrapped around the axle thinking about God's "will for your life." God already showed us what it is. He wants us to love Him and love one another. It's that simple and that hard. He doesn't seem to have a strong opinion about the context in which we do it. He just wants us to give our love away freely.

While you're trying to choose which road to take when you get to a fork, be sure to keep your focus on the things you can be certain of. God wants us to love others the way He loved us. That kind of love will free you up to choose any path with a confidence you may have been lacking.

What do you need to do to refocus on the simple things today?

NO ONE IS REMEMBERED FOR WHAT THEY JUST PLANNED TO DO.

Do not merely listen to the word, and so deceive yourselves. Do what it says.

JAMES 1:22

Have you ever settled into bed at the end of a long day only to realize you forgot a family member's birthday? We've all experienced making the call of shame the next day, the apologies, and reassurance that we meant to call and that something special (very special) is on the way.

We've all been told, "It's the thought that counts!" But there's a difference between hearing someone meant to send flowers and the excitement of hearing the knock on the front door. There's a difference between a kind text message and a friend who's actually beside us when we get the phone call from the doctor with bad news.

It's so much easier to love people with our intentions than to love them in real life. It's exciting to scheme ways to make the world a little more beautiful. We can Google the details of our plans and tell our friends what we dreamed up. We can blog about it to raise awareness or have a Kickstarter campaign to raise money. Often, though, this is just brain candy. While it makes us feel good, it doesn't do much to move the needle in people's lives. No one is remembered for what they just *planned* to do.

Just like great characters in films are remembered by what they *do* and not by what they merely think about, we're known for our actions. The power of love is in the sacrifice and commitment it requires. Sacrifice and commitment always travel with love and action. Love looks like showing up with hands to help even when we don't know what to do. Love looks like stopping by even if we don't know what to say. Simply put, love doesn't just think about it; love does it.

Who have you been "planning" to demonstrate love to? What can you do today to follow through on that plan?

DON'T JUST DO WHAT YOU'RE ABLE TO DO; FIGURE OUT WHAT YOU WERE MADE TO DO, THEN DO A LOT OF THAT.

This is why it is said: "Wake up, sleeper, rise from the dead, and Christ will shine on you."

EPHESIANS 5:14

I've always had a soft spot for the kids on sports teams who seem to put the jersey on to please their parents. I look at those kids and feel myself melt with compassion. I want to tell them they are awesome just the way they are, no home runs required. I want to tell them God gave them unique gifts and passions, and they're free to run after all of them, whether they come with a jersey or not. They don't have to stick to kicking soccer balls just because it makes the people around them happy. I want them to figure out what sparks life in them and throw themselves into it without caring whether anyone is watching.

We all have capabilities. For example, I'm a lawyer by training and have loads of states I can practice law in. But just because I'm able to be a lawyer doesn't mean I'm made to be a lawyer. We don't need to do what we're merely capable of doing. The trick is to figure out what we were made to do and then make some changes to keep current with who we've become. We're all constantly changing. We're new creations. It's supposed to be this way. Don't resist the change. Go with it. Don't be limited by what you excel at. Ask God to show you what the newest version of you was made to do.

Kids who are pressured too much to fit into a box that doesn't fit who they are turning into will let you know about it. Many adults don't, though. We tolerate jobs no longer meant for us. The truth is, too many of us are a job or two behind who we've turned into. You may have picked your career path because it's something you were competent at in college, but it's not you anymore. Some of us are still crunching numbers because our parents did it and they sold us on the idea of a certain kind of career success. They helped us get a "good job" when what we're looking for is an epic life.

You not only have the freedom to make the changes you need to make; you must. With the urgency of a rock in your shoe you haven't stopped to take out, act on the ache you feel when you see someone else living out the story you always wanted—the story you were made to live.

It's never too late to do what you were made to do. You didn't make a wrong turn before; you merely turned into someone else. Go with it. It might mean a career change, or it might simply mean shifting your schedule to prioritize your newfound passions. Whatever it looks like at this stage of your life, figure out what you were made to do and then do a lot of that.

> Forget who you've been and what you've done. If you
> had to claim it right now, what are you made to do?

IF YOU WANT TO FLY, YOU HAVE TO FAIL. DON'T BE TOO HARD ON YOURSELF WHEN YOU DO.

Though the righteous fall seven times, they rise again, but the wicked stumble when calamity strikes.

PROVERBS 24:16

I started an airline once. It sounds impressive, but it really isn't. Here was the idea. I live for part of each year far away from everyone in Canada. The nearest home is more than ten thousand square miles away. I thought it would be cool to have a fleet of amphibious planes that take off and land on the water to fly folks to mountain lakes and other inaccessible places like the place I live with my family. So I got a dock, hired some pilots, gave them fancy airline hats, and bought a bunch of official-looking pilot shirts with the gold stripes on the shoulders. I had everything in place except one minor detail—I didn't have an airplane. I'm not kidding.

I checked around, and buying an airplane that was already flying was too expensive, so we assembled our first one by picking over grounded planes—a couple of wings here, a fuselage there, a tire from that one—oh, and a propeller. We assembled our airplane from all the parts and stood next to it. The Wright brothers could not have been prouder. We put a Krispy Kreme–inspired paint job on it just so folks knew how serious we were. It looked delicious, if only barely airworthy. Simply put: we moved from thinking about this idea to trying it.

Chances are, you've started your own small airline before too. You've made a paper airplane, right? Then you've got one. Sure, it's a small airline, but who cares? The things that keep us from pursuing our dreams are often the failures and letdowns we've experienced in the past. Don't let who you were decide who you're becoming. The setbacks we all face can be big or small. We can spend all sorts of time carefully folding paper, hoping for the coolest-looking plane, or we can throw it into the air and see if it flies.

What if you decide in advance that failure isn't going to be a limiting factor in your life anymore? Strip from the past the power you've given it over your future. Imagine what would happen if you realized one of the most crucial steps to getting from where you are to where you want to go is to not be afraid of making a couple of mistakes along the way. You're never going to the land the plane in your life until you make enough mistakes to get your idea airborne. Will it work? There's only one way to find out.

What past failures have kept you grounded, and what steps are you going to take today to get back in the air?

DO A CANNONBALL WITH YOUR LIFE.
IT'S OKAY TO GET A LITTLE WET.

When [Jesus] had finished speaking, he said to Simon, "Put out
into deep water, and let down the nets for a catch."

LUKE 5:4

When we play Monopoly at my house, everyone races to land on Boardwalk first. If you've played the game, you know Boardwalk is the most valuable property on the board. It can win you the game, but you have to take on some risk to buy it and build there. In Monopoly, you can't earn big money without risking a lot. If you only put a little on the line, you won't see much of a return. Sometimes you've got to go big to achieve your goals.

The same is true about us and the character we want to develop in our lives. Maybe we're skimping on our relationships, playing it safe and staying on the sidelines. Maybe we're coasting in a job because it pays the bills even though it bores us to tears. What if you were to flip it around? What would it look like to go all in with your life? Don't put your toe in the water; grab your knees and do a cannonball. Push all the chips to the center of the table. I know you'll be scared. Do it anyway. It's where the good stuff happens.

Forget buying Boardwalk. What would it look like to say yes to vulnerability in big ways? Tell someone you trust what's really going on inside of you, not what you wish were going on. If it's fear you need to move past, blow past it like it's not even there. Are you willing to risk failure, hoping you might be surprised by success? If it's learning to love a group of people you don't understand, what if you left the comfort of your easy relationships to build a couple of new ones with people you know might be a little more difficult but would stretch you?

There's no shortcut to big change; it always comes with big risk. Are you willing to take yours today? Don't make a list; make a call. You just might be surprised by the life you find on the other side of what's holding you back.

What vulnerable step do you need to take next?

DON'T LET OTHER PEOPLE DECIDE WHO YOU ARE. ONLY GOD GETS TO NAME US.

I no longer call you servants, because a servant does not know his master's business. Instead, I have called you friends, for everything that I learned from my Father I have made known to you.

JOHN 15:15

The nicknames we were given as kids often stick with us our entire lives. Sometimes the nicknames are given to us in jest and bear no resemblance to us. For instance, the basketball center called "Shorty" or the football linebacker called "Tiny." Other times they can be spot-on.

When we're most innocent and vulnerable, we sometimes latch on to the worst labels, then carry them with us wherever we go. These aren't labels others give us in jest, they're names we give ourselves through our pain. For some of us, it's self-effacing names we gave ourselves about our weight or our intelligence. For others, it's about where we lived or how much money our parents had or didn't have. So many of us were labeled by whatever it was that made us stand out, and the label stuck to us like duct tape and continues to define us today.

Our Creator cleared it up for us, though. When Jesus called Peter a "rock" after he had failed, He demonstrated that many of these labels we've given ourselves just aren't true; they're lies masquerading as reality (Matthew 16:18). When you find yourself calling yourself by a name that just isn't true, remember what God calls us—He calls us His beloved.

We're all different. Not just a little bit different, but wonderfully and sometimes dramatically so. God chose to put different parts of His image inside every single person, so we all reflect Him in unique ways. Not so we would ricochet off of each other, but so we could refract His light in us in wonderfully colorful ways. What made you stand out as unique might be the thing God wants to use to show what He looks like to the rest of the world. What people used to tear you down is something God wants to use to build you up.

The swirls that make marbled stone so unique are also the points of greatest weakness. Don't let your uniqueness break you. Don't let your failures define you. Don't give or receive names God never had for you.

The critics don't get the final word in God's kingdom. God gets to tell us who we are, and He says we're loved. Not just a little, and not for a while, but from here to eternity and back. The next time you hear the old tapes that make you feel unworthy, remember that the God who spoke the universe into existence, who hears the thoughts you don't speak out loud, says you're beloved and you're His. That's His name for you.

What nickname have you given yourself or been given by others that has hurt your sense of worth?

JANUARY 16

WHEN WE SAY WE'RE WAITING ON GOD, WE'RE PROBABLY JUST STALLING.

Follow my example, as I follow the example of Christ.

1 CORINTHIANS 11:1

Sometimes when someone says they're waiting on God, really they're just stalling. We're all prone to that more often than we'd like to admit. It can happen when there's a big decision before us and our gut has already given us an answer. Instead of making moves, we make lists. It can happen when the Bible gives a command but we rationalize why we should wait. We say we're waiting on God, but this isn't what's happening.

We'll pray more often and go on retreats to listen closely for God's voice. We'll talk it over with friends and Google our options late into the night. Maybe we'll give it a rest to see if the thing we know we need to do eventually resurfaces, telling ourselves, *Then I'll know it was from God*. But when we say we're waiting on God, He's often waiting on us.

In the life of Jesus, we get an example of how we're to live in the world. We know we're here to welcome people who look like strangers. We're here to offer places in our homes for those with nowhere to go. We're here to be friends with the lonely, the ones who were told they weren't worthy of love. The Bible is constantly talking about care for widows and orphans, the most vulnerable in society. You don't need another Bible study about the "will of God"; perhaps you need to decide you will simply do something.

If we're waiting on God to find out whether or not we should live a little more like Jesus, don't waste any more time—the answer is *yes*. We don't find many answers tied to the dock; we find them when we go all in on love. If you're feeling stuck, don't create a safe harbor by saying you're still waiting for God. Cast off the lines, point your boat toward the open seas, and set sail. There's a good chance God's waiting on you to make the next move.

What message have you been waiting to hear that you need to act on instead of waiting longer?

WHERE WE SEE HOLES WE'VE DUG, GOD SEES FOUNDATIONS HE'S MAKING.

Whoever conceals their sins does not prosper, but the one who confesses and renounces them finds mercy.

PROVERBS 28:13

Up in British Columbia, I like to dig holes in the ground for different projects. There are excavators and tractors and drilling rigs, and I like to put them all to good use. It's a paradise for a guy who likes to make things happen. I built a chapel and a barn, and we blazed some new trails to the mountaintops. We built a bridge to cross a ravine I couldn't quite jump.

More than anything, though, I enjoy the surprised look on Sweet Maria's face when she finds out what I've been up to with all the diggers, tractors, and dynamite. For my latest project, I got a little wild with the dynamite, blew a big hole in the ground, and filled it with water. Once the new lake was done, I took Maria to have a look. I wanted to give her the naming rights. When we were getting close, I asked her, "So, what are we going to name the lake I'm taking you to?" She answered, "What lake?!" Now we have a lake named What Lake. That'll be fun to explain to the grandkids.

God does that with all the holes we make in our lives. We think we've blown it again, but He points to them and says, "This'll make a great spot to pour out My love." Sometimes He makes lakes for us to dive in and other times He makes foundations for building our character on. No matter what, God finds us in the holes we've dug for ourselves. Where we see our failures, God sees foundations He's making.

**What hole do you have in your life that God can
use to build deeper character in you?**

WE CAN'T BE NEW CREATIONS IF EVERYTHING STAYS THE SAME.

"Martha, Martha," the Lord answered, "you are worried and upset about many things, but few things are needed—or indeed only one. Mary has chosen what is better, and it will not be taken away from her."

LUKE 10:41-42

Ask a few folks how they're doing today, and I guarantee you at least one will raise their eyebrows and say, "Busy!" Whether it's a mom juggling soccer practices and gymnastics, or a college student keeping up with classes and running for student government, or the person working at Arby's slicing the roast beef, everyone has their head down and their plate full of activity. It's not surprising that we often find our identity in the things we accomplish. We let responsibilities and activities in our lives build layer by layer on top of us until we finally break underneath them.

A lot of beauty gets buried in that hustle. What most of us long for, more than anything else, is a community where we can simply be known and loved. We want to be seen for who we actually are, not what we do or the person we appear to be. And we want to see others in their vulnerability too. This is the deepest need we all feel, and it's the easiest to meet in one another when we choose to make ourselves available.

If your schedule robs you of the joy of simply being fully present with the people you love, then it's time to quit a couple of things. We can't be new creations if everything stays the same. Don't feel stuck in all your activities; bail on the few that are robbing you of your ability to be present with the people you love the most. Friendship and hospitality are central to our new identity, and we can't welcome people into our lives if we're too busy to be available to them.

Quit something today. A job, a habit, a hobby, or sport that is stealing you away from the ones you love the most. You've been given not only permission by God to prioritize people over projects but the agency to do something about it.

What activities are getting in the way of your experiencing deeper love?

GOD DOESN'T TRY TO ENTICE US WITH SUCCESS OR PUNISH US WITH FAILURE; HE WANTS TO CAPTIVATE US WITH PURPOSE.

I am convinced that neither death nor life, neither angels nor demons, neither the present nor the future, nor any powers, neither height nor depth, nor anything else in all creation, will be able to separate us from the love of God that is in Christ Jesus our Lord.

ROMANS 8:38-39

When we were kids, for many of us life seemed to spin on a cycle of rewards and punishment. Life was performance based. If we got straight A's or hit the home run, we could go out for ice cream or on that camping trip with the Boy Scouts. If we struck out in a relationship or failed a friend or embarrassed our family, we were grounded. It was as if love would be given and withdrawn like the movements of the tide. It was about what we did more than who we were. It was only natural to assume God worked the same way. Do good things and succeed and you receive love and approval from God. Mess up and love is withdrawn.

If only we could remind ourselves more often that God never cares about the grades on our report cards. He wants us to make it all about His love, not our performance, and He's a whole lot more concerned about our character than our accomplishments. He doesn't find joy in our success; He delights in our attempts.

God's response to our success is love, not merely approval. And God's response when we fail is massive love. Nothing will separate you from His love. Money and big houses and status aren't what God offers us if we behave ourselves, and He doesn't punish us with loss or sickness when we make a mess of things. Are there consequences when we fail? You bet. Often, in fact; but one of them isn't that God pulls away. The opposite occurs. He draws close to us. He wants us to put our passion into action because He knows it is in our pursuit of Him where we'll find our greatest joy. He wants us to be captivated with purpose, regardless of whether it looks like worldly success.

If you find yourself believing God stacks all your successes on one side of a scale and your failures on the other to measure how you're doing, remember that the only curve He grades on always tips toward His extravagant and inexplicable love.

What success or failure has been getting in the way of your experiencing God's deep love for you?

JANUARY 20

GOD ISN'T AFRAID OF OUR DOUBTS; HE'S WAY MORE CONCERNED WHEN WE FAKE IT.

Nothing in all creation is hidden from God's sight.

HEBREWS 4:13

My all-time favorite game to play with our kids when they were young was hide-and-seek. I would walk into the room and see two feet, a knee, a child-sized bulge under the blanket, or perhaps an ear sticking out from behind a curtain. The kids thought they would be hard to find when, actually, they were hard to miss.

I think that's how God sees us when we try to hide who we really are from Him. He knows the thoughts we're too embarrassed to mention and the feelings we can't articulate, and He knows about all our uncertainties. He hears the prayers we wouldn't have the courage to even whisper and knows our hopes that are still being developed.

Yet we still try to hide who we really are from Him. Perhaps we think if we just hide how we really feel, what we really want, and how scared we really are, He won't see us behind the curtains we've made. Hiding from God didn't work in the garden of Eden, and it still doesn't work. He asks us now what He asked Adam and Eve then—*Where are you?*

God isn't afraid of our doubts. He's not put off when we struggle to believe, and He's not surprised when we don't understand what a God who says He surpasses all understanding is doing. He's not keeping track of the number of days when we feel close to Him, nor is He docking points when we wonder if He's even there. Instead, He sympathizes with our fears that He might not be as good as He's promised.

It's the very reason God sent His Son, Jesus, to us. Jesus came to give us a living example of the God we couldn't see, because He knew we needed someone who would feel the weight of our weakness while still living authentically into both His deity and His humanity. His response to Thomas, who saw Jesus in the flesh and still doubted, wasn't a scolding; it was grace (John 20:24–29).

You pick any story out of the Bible and you'll find the same. This is still His response to you and me. We need to get real enough with Him about our doubts so He can be Jesus enough with His grace. Simply put, we don't need to hide anymore.

What parts of your life are you hiding from God?

IF YOU WANT TO DAZZLE GOD, BE YOU.

Accept one another, then, just as Christ accepted you, in order to
bring praise to God.

ROMANS 15:7

For many years, our family would invite a bunch of friends every summer up
to our lodge in Canada. We spent weeks getting ready, and when we finally
saw the boat bringing them in from several miles away, we would jump into a
boat and speed out to greet them.

One of the things I have loved most is that we host people from all walks of
life, from many differing worldviews, from every side of a debate, from places
locked in war with each other, and everywhere in between. People who usually
sit at different tables join my family for the week at the same table, laughing
together and dreaming some dreams.

Since when did we decide as a community of faith that having the same beliefs
and opinions was a prerequisite for loving, accepting, and welcoming someone? It's
not enough to just tolerate or be polite to people we disagree with and for them to
merely do this with us. We need to love each other without an agenda. Do it any
other way and we signal to each other that others need to be like us to be liked by us.
The cost of acceptance is way too high if it costs people who God made them to be.

Life is so much better when we get to be authentically who we are and
others get to be authentically who they are. All of this isn't part of a plan to
make other people change; it's all done in the hopes that we'll change. And
guess what? It works. The people I used to think of as difficult I now think of
as delightfully different. We don't just tolerate those who are different from us
at the lodge—we celebrate them! We delight in the way each person shows us
a side of ourselves or Jesus we hadn't quite seen until we met them.

Instead of implying to people that they need to change in order to be welcome at the table, let them know they're welcome just as they are. You don't
need to be someone else to be loved by God, and no one else does either. If you
want to dazzle God, go be you.

**Who's on the opposite side of the table from you in your world?
What's your first step to building connection with them?**

LOVE DOESN'T OBEY ALL THE RULES WE TRY TO GIVE IT.

My brothers and sisters, believers in our glorious Lord Jesus Christ must not show favoritism.

JAMES 2:1

My kids always made up silly games when they were young. I didn't understand *at all* how to play them, how you won, or what the purpose was. But that didn't matter because I loved being with my kids. We didn't need a set of rules or a clear winner for the time to be meaningful.

I think love works the same way: love doesn't obey all the rules we try to give it anyway. Sure, we might tell ourselves to take it slow, to play it cool; but love can't wait for us to get ourselves sorted out. I've heard the phrases "true love" and "tough love" used in an attempt to distinguish the kind of love we're giving or experiencing, but love doesn't come in flavors; it travels with us.

Just like little kids in a make-believe game, love finds its own way because it's never stationary. It lives on the move, not in containment. It can't sit still for long because it's too eager to find people to express itself to.

It's good to have boundaries in our relationships, but it's also okay to break the rules every now and again too. People will tell you not to give money if you don't know how someone will spend it, but sometimes love tells you to give it away anyway. People will tell you to turn off your phone to create space to reflect and recharge, but sometimes love answers the call. People will try to put principles in place to give order to our lives, and that's fine. But love doesn't obey all the rules we try to give it, so don't get hung up making them.

What "rule" do you need to break so you can be more loving to others?

GOD'S MORE INTERESTED IN WHERE WE'RE HEADING WITH HIM THAN ALL THE PLACES WE'VE GONE ALONE.

Many are the plans in a person's heart, but it is the LORD's purpose that prevails.

PROVERBS 19:21

I bet I've been to fifty different countries so far. I spend half my life on planes because I want to be where people are. Since people are everywhere, it kind of makes sense. Every now and again, I'll look at pictures and reminisce on past adventures. I get to remember all the people who have changed my life, even the ones who helped me grow a few gray hairs. Occasionally I'll come across pictures that make me a little sad, though, because I'll remember it was a time I tried to tackle something without God's help. Do you know what I'm talking about? Those times where you think to yourself, *Don't worry God, I've got this one*?

You see, God's more interested in where we're heading with Him than all the places we've gone alone. He's not that impressed with our flashy social media posts if those pictures tell a story of a life lived without Him. He wants to be in the mix of it with us. He wants to surprise us with unexpected joys and spread love to others through us.

The exciting part about looking through old photos is the transformation we can see: if I flip a few pages back in the scrapbook, I'll see how I moved from going at it alone to going with God. The moment we turn to Him, He sometimes throws a party—but not always. More often, He nods to us and moves with us to the next adventure.

What project are you working on without God's help?

OUR FAITH ISN'T ALL THE THINGS WE SAY WE BELIEVE; IT'S WHAT WE DO NEXT.

You, Lord, are forgiving and good, abounding in love to all who call to you.

PSALM 86:5

When we try to follow Jesus, grace always meets us when we fall off the wagon. No matter how far we fall, God is there to take us back the moment we turn to Him. We don't have to give a long acceptance speech to receive His grace. We don't even need to get our act together first—He scoops us into His arms when we're still covered in mud from head to toe and calls us beautifully His. Is this fair? Heck no. Don't worry about it.

What that also means is this: we can't count on yesterday's faithfulness on our part to carry us through tomorrow's problems. Since it's never been about us being good enough or having the right answers, we can't just ease into cruise control. God doesn't care how many Bible studies you've been to. He isn't wowed because we've memorized a couple of verses either. He only cares about what we do next with what we already know, and every day we all start in the same place.

Sometimes we get so carried away trying to be right that we forget to be kind. We forget Jesus didn't ask us to have all the answers. He also doesn't need us to be the hall monitors of other people's conduct. He had a few strong words for the people who appointed themselves as protectors of truth. Jesus simply asked us to follow Him, not to monitor who everyone else is. And following Him sometimes means identifying with and hanging out with the very ones the religious people rejected.

If we find ourselves more concerned with proving we have all the right knowledge about Jesus than living out the message of Jesus, we need to get back to where we started when we first heard about grace. Is this going to be tough at times? You bet. Our faith isn't all the things we say believe; it's what we do next.

In what ways have you been trying to prove your commitment to God instead of trusting His approval of you?

GOD ISN'T AS CONCERNED ABOUT THE OUTCOMES AS WE ARE. HE WANTS US TO BE HIS WHILE WE TRY.

"Come now, let us settle the matter," says the LORD. "Though your sins are like scarlet, they shall be as white as snow; though they are red as crimson, they shall be like wool."

ISAIAH 1:18

If you've never been to a kids' baseball game, you're in for a real treat when you go. At least one time a game, when a kid happens to connect the bat with the ball, I bet you'll see them dart toward third base while the fans erupt with applause. Meanwhile, there's at least one player sitting down in the outfield, picking dandelions and blowing them out like birthday candles. At the end of the game, the kids line up to give high fives and then, win or lose, everyone gets a free soda and everyone makes a mad dash, side by side, for the concession stand where snacks are waiting.

Those games always remind me of how God feels about us. He doesn't get wound up when our plans fail, and He's not thrown off when we run in the wrong direction. We're the ones who came up with competitions, winners and losers. These distinctions were never part of God's plan. And God never told us that success meant big accomplishments. Success with Him has always meant simply living in grace and walking in love.

Have you blown it? Me too. Next time you feel like you've missed the mark, go watch a kids' baseball game. Watch the kids who wander around the outfield with curiosity and wonder. God delights in their joy even though they don't always have their eye on the ball. He delights in you too. Look at their faces when they guzzle the postgame sodas and remember God isn't as concerned about the outcomes as we are. He doesn't care what jersey we wear. He just wants us to be His while we try.

How have you blown it lately? Are you letting that setback convince you that God thinks less of you?

HEAVEN'S LEANING OVER THE RAILS, WONDERING IF WE'LL BE AS COURAGEOUS AS GOD THINKS WE ARE.

It is by grace you have been saved, through faith—and this is not from yourselves, it is the gift of God—not by works, so that no one can boast. For we are God's handiwork, created in Christ Jesus to do good works, which God prepared in advance for us to do.

EPHESIANS 2:8-10

I remember when my daughter, Lindsey, took her first steps. She was my first child, so I had never witnessed the moment a person goes from the "not walking" column to the "walking" one. For a few weeks, she would crawl and find the edge of the coffee table. Then she'd pull herself up, wondering if she should give it go. One fateful morning, after weeks of backing down, she made her first wobbly steps. Maria and I were holding out our arms, cheering and yelling. You would think she has just won the Iditarod the way we were carrying on.

Have you ever seen a parent watching their child take their first steps, who folds their arms and says nonchalantly "I've seen better"? Of course not! They're over the moon. I think that's how God sees us. He's not disappointed that we haven't already taken big steps or made big moves. He's already a few steps ahead of us, holding out His arms. He's waiting to see if we'll be as courageous as He thinks we are. When we take the step, He isn't surprised when we stumble, nor is He angry when we fall. He rushes toward us and scoops us into His arms.

A lot of people make God out to be an angry dad. I used to think God's expectation was perfection and that anything less made me a disappointment. No matter how hard I tried, I never believed I made God proud. But over the years I've come to realize God is far more like the proud parent who celebrates the steps rather than one who fixates on the stumbles. God delights in our every move, every brave step, no matter how small. Go make yours.

What small steps have you taken lately that God could be proud of?

REAL FAILURES ARE SO MUCH BETTER THAN FAKE SUCCESSES. DON'T BE AFRAID TO PUT A FEW THINGS ON THE LINE.

We are hard pressed on every side, but not crushed; perplexed, but not in despair; persecuted, but not abandoned; struck down, but not destroyed.

2 CORINTHIANS 4:8–9

They say that for every one good idea a person has, they had to produce at least forty bad ones to get there. I'm pretty sure the numbers are skewed because my ratio's at least one hundred bad for every good one, but who's counting? Usually when I feel like I've failed, it's because my definition of failure is a little off.

Sure, we might have to shut the doors on an organization we poured into for years. A vacation we planned for the kids might devolve into a week of petty arguments and ketchup smears all over the car. We might have given our all to college only to find we weren't cut out for the classroom. It doesn't always mean we failed. Sometimes it just means it's time for a change.

We often use other people's metrics to define what was a success and what was a failure. Even when our plans fail, we usually realize a lot of people were loved in the process, which was our goal in starting. We ended up crossing paths with people we might never have met if we hadn't put ourselves out there. Sometimes these people even nestle their way into our inner circle.

Beyond my faith, the goal I have in life is to find people to share it with. Our ideas are a success if we have more friends when they end. Our failures make us more real too. They give us more in common with everyone else who has experienced frustration and loss. You never know: whether it's a small, private failure or a big, public one, the impact our lives will have is sometimes much greater in our failures than in our successes. Try something big. Dust off that big idea you've had. Stop waiting. Don't worry about if it won't work. Be concerned if you won't give it a whirl. I'd rather have a couple of ideas fail than a faith that won't try.

What failure in your life do you need to redefine?

FAITH ISN'T FIGURING OUT WHAT WE'RE ABLE TO DO. IT'S DECIDING WHAT WE'RE GOING TO DO EVEN WHEN WE THINK WE CAN'T.

Jesus replied, "What is impossible with man is possible with God."

LUKE 18:27

I love how much Jesus talked about kids when He taught. He spoke to audiences packed with people who had memorized entire books of the Bible, religious leaders who were the recognized authorities on religious truth, leaders in the community. I bet they expected to be commended by Jesus for all their titles and degrees and perhaps affirmed as the ones who should be the guides for everyone else. Yet this isn't how Jesus rolled. Instead, He pointed to a couple of kids and told everyone that if they wanted to find understanding, they would need to trade in their large, complicated faith and have faith like a child. In other words, it wouldn't be when we earn the extra theology degrees or enter into formal ministry when faith leaps forward. Jesus said our faith will grow when we regain a sense of childlike wonder.

Nothing is impossible to kids. Ask them what they want to be when they grow up and they'll tell you, in all sincerity, they're going to wear NASA suits and fly to the moon. Sometimes I wonder if the only reason more of them don't do it is because we adults spend the next few decades telling them they can't. It's like we have our hands on their shoulders as they sit and each time we tell them to get up and chance their dream, we also tell them why it won't work. With each of these words of correction, we push them down a little harder into their seats.

But faith puts reason in its place. There's nothing wrong with using the minds God has given us. When our heads tell our hearts that our dreams are too big, or that we should grow up and be more reasonable with our faith, this is just a reminder to go find your kids playing and park and watch them interact with the same world you're living in. Then take them to get snow cones with extra syrup, get it all over your shirts, and let them tell you about their big, messy, outrageous dreams. Children are the ones Jesus sent to be our guides because faith isn't figuring out what we're able to do. It's deciding what we're going to do even when we think we can't.

**What's an outrageous dream you've buried that
God might want you to dig up again?**

IF JESUS DIDN'T THINK WE COULD LIVE THE LIFE HE DESCRIBED, HE WOULDN'T HAVE TOLD HIS FRIENDS THEY'D DO GREATER THINGS THAN HIM.

They also will answer, "Lord, when did we see you hungry or thirsty or a stranger or needing clothes or sick or in prison, and did not help you?" He will reply, "Truly I tell you, whatever you did not do for one of the least of these, you did not do for me."

MATTHEW 25:44–45

In the Bible, there's a story where Jesus wiped some mud on a blind man's eyes, and the man saw colors for the first time. Jesus strolled up to a guy who had never walked before and said, "Get up, take up your mat and go home." Jesus felt the touch of a woman who'd been bleeding for twelve years, and He turned to her and said: "Your faith has made you well." And she became well.

Jesus showed up on the scene and healed people. But before He healed them, He saw them. He saw their immediate need, sure, but He also saw what was behind it, because Jesus was attentive to those most overlooked. It's hard to believe we can do greater things than Jesus when we think about His miracles, but it starts by taking Him at His word and then seeing people the way Jesus did. How can we go about healing people if we don't see them through a gaze of love?

Of all the things Jesus did, I'm struck by what a miracle it was that He always had room for more. He seemed to pick up friends wherever He went: some who were hungry, some who were hurting, and some who were on a hunt for a new identity. Wherever they were, when they came with humble hearts, He said they were welcome.

This is the life Jesus wants for us: to see people, feed them, and welcome them. He wouldn't have told us we'd do greater things than Him if He didn't think we could.

Who do you see in your life who needs to be met by the love of God?

MOST OF THE THINGS JESUS ASKED HIS FRIENDS TO DO WERE SIMPLE, BUT THEY WEREN'T EASY.

Follow me.

JOHN 1:43

Some people make faith seem really complicated. It's hard to know what words written in the first century mean for those of us living two thousand years later, and I used to feel like I needed a pocket dictionary when someone threw around terms they learned in seminary.

Jesus wasn't confusing, though. Most of the things He asked His friends to do were simple, but they weren't easy. He told them to drop their plans because He had new ones for them, and it meant they had to give up being in charge. They had to let go of their need to be in control. He told others to give away all their money like they wouldn't need it tomorrow. What's the point, He asked, in saving up all your money if you're not going to take it with you when you die? He said to give it away now, when people around us need it to survive. Jesus told His friends to welcome both the popular speaker and the weird uncle. He said to bring people—even strangers—into your home so you can share your food with them around the table. I love this because tables feel like a great equalizer. We all sit side by side at the same height, eating the same food, passing the butter, and knocking over the salt.

Next time your head starts to get foggy from all the big religious words, go back to what Jesus said. Not only will it be clear to you, but it will show you a clear way to grow your faith by radically loving the people around you.

What simple message is Jesus calling you to hear and obey?

GOD DOESN'T WANT US TO JUST BEHAVE BETTER. HE WANTS US TO BE HIS.

See what great love the Father has lavished on us, that we should be called children of God! And that is what we are!

1 JOHN 3:1

When I was a kid, it seemed the adults in my life—my teachers, community leaders, and, sadly, sometimes my parents—liked me more when I was good. I get it. Who wants bad behavior? I learned that if I could bring myself to sit still, stay quiet, and wait to pass notes when my teacher was at the chalkboard, everything went more smoothly. We didn't learn better behavior, just better tactics. When I hit the mark, I didn't feel like such a nuisance. I felt like I was wanted. And I wanted to feel wanted. Who doesn't?

That sense of pressure to perform is a real punk, isn't it? It wasn't intended this way, but these things confirm our biggest fears: that we're not loved for who we are but for what we do, how we act, how things appear. We're loved if we make life easier for the people around us. We're loved as long as we hide our mistakes. As long as we're not an inconvenience, then we earn acceptance and permission to belong.

That is what's warped about transactional love: we secure it as long as we hold up our end of the deal. Here's the thing: God already took care of it. He said we're loved and belong because we were born. God says it doesn't matter whether we lose the game with a strikeout or hit it out of the park for the win—we're loved. He's not keeping score in the game because he already secured the win for eternity.

God doesn't want us to just behave better. He wants us to be His. We're already in! Can you just receive that you're in without figuring out all the reasons you shouldn't be? You, me, and the people who get under our skin the most—God said we're all His. Now go live like it.

What would change if you believed what God said about you?

FEBRUARY

FEBRUARY 1

BIG LOVE DOESN'T NEED TO ATTRACT BIG ATTENTION.

Jesus sent him away at once with a strong warning: "See that you don't tell this to anyone."

MARK 1:43-44

"Go and tell no one." That's what Jesus said to people after He restored their health or even their lives with the wave of His hand. People came to Him covered with leprosy, cast out of their communities while they waited to die, and Jesus cleared it up with a touch. But before they skipped back to their families and friends, before they appeared healthy and ready to get back in the mix, He told them one last thing: *Don't tell anyone.* This was His plan for self-promotion. For His entire life, Jesus did His best work in secret.

I have to admit there have been times when I've made someone's day in a *much* smaller way, and I wanted a megaphone to tell everyone about it. I wanted the *New York Times* to put its best reporter on the story and for it to land on the Sunday morning cover page. I'm sure after all that work drawing attention to myself, I'd wave my hand and say something like, "Ah, it was nothing," just to cover the huge tracks I'd left leading to me.

These days, Jesus has helped me get out of the way. He's helped me realize that big love doesn't need to attract big attention. You know, there's something transformational about showing love to someone without all the glitter and spotlights. The people who understand this make joy their reward. Give it a shot today. Drop a check in the mail for someone who's running low on cash or slip a lollipop to the kid who's screaming on the airplane. Maybe ask the parent first—they'll have to deal with the sugar rush. Wherever you are and whoever you're with, make more room for love by getting your ego out of the way. Leave the applause for the circus.

What secret act of love can you do for someone today?

PEOPLE NEED LOVE AND ACCEPTANCE A LOT MORE THAN THEY NEED ADVICE.

Let any one of you who is without sin be the first to throw a stone at her.

JOHN 8:7

Jesus' friend John tells this story in the Bible that I bank on for peace at least once a week. Jesus heads to the temple for another day of teaching, when the Pharisees march in with a woman who had been caught in adultery. "The Law commands us to stone women like her," they say with a sneer. Then they ask what Jesus has to say about it.

Jesus doesn't answer their question, actually. I like to think He touches her chin, looks her in the eye, and turns to the crowd to say, "Let any one of you who is without sin cast the first stone."

John says one by one the Pharisees drop their stones and walk away. Then Jesus looks at the woman and asks where they went. "Has no one condemned you?" He wonders aloud. "Well, I don't condemn you either."

He didn't shame her. He didn't ask if it was true. He didn't outline a path to recovery. He didn't even use it as a teachable moment to tell the people around Him about repentance or forgiveness. He simply embodied love and grace and let His actions speak for themselves. It was like He drew a circle around them both and said she was in. Grace does that.

It can feel uncomfortable. It can feel absurd. It can feel scandalous, right? Most of us have had moments where we felt a person in the wrong deserved punishment. But if we want to live like Jesus did, we have to default to a reaction like His. Most people who have failed don't need information. What they want is a hug. People need love and acceptance a lot more than they need advice.

Who is someone you know who might not "deserve" love, but God's inviting you to love anyway?

FEBRUARY 3

LOVE ISN'T SOMETHING WE DO.
IT'S SOMEONE WE BECOME.

Everyone who hears these words of mine and puts them into practice is like a wise man who built his house on the rock.

MATTHEW 7:24

Next time you meet someone, listen for their "I am" statements. It usually comes when we ask what they do and they say, "I am a _____." They're an attorney or a pastor or an actor or a college student or a stay-at-home mom. With that one piece of information, we can imagine the broad strokes of their life. In other words, the details of someone's life flow out of who they think they are.

I think love works the same way. When our identity is based on who we are as God's beloved kids, we start to live like we're just that. Beloved kids. We don't have to give ourselves pep talks just to visit a friend who's a little lonely, because our instincts begin to look like love. When we see people through a filter of love and imagine them as worthy of love, we can't help but snag a seat in their fan section.

This isn't the same as having an identity based on a religion. A lot of people say they're a Christian before anything else, but it quickly spirals into these same people thinking they have "the truth" everyone else needs. This may be true, but here's the problem: it morphs into an identity rooted in having answers rather than being love.

Jesus didn't tell us to become religious. He told us to be like Him, and He was love. We won't need to break our backs trying to convince others about Jesus if who we are, before anything else, is love. The reason is simple. Love isn't something we do, like a job. It's someone we become, like Jesus.

How have you been becoming love lately?

GIVE AWAY LOVE LIKE YOU'RE MADE OF IT.

As the Father has loved me, so have I loved you. Now remain in my love.

JOHN 15:9

When my kids were little, I used to hang piñatas from our favorite tree in the backyard as often as possible. Sometimes we did it for their birthdays, but sometimes we did it because it was Saturday, and what better day for a piñata than Saturday? I'd sneak off to the store to get a dinosaur or unicorn or rainbow-colored zebra, fill it full of candy, and two hours later we'd be scrambling through the grass in search of Starbursts.

The more opportunities I've had to blow it as an adult, the more other peoples' responses have reminded me we're a lot like those piñatas from my backyard. When people erupt into fits of rage when they're wronged or surprise us with tenderness when we know they've been hurt, we get to see what's inside of them. We see what they're made of whenever they break.

Hopefully it's not with a baseball bat, but at some point in life something will break you. We can't avoid it, because we're all a little broken and we're bound to get things wrong. Someone will eventually nestle their way into your heart and then let you down. And when they do, you'll either explode in anger or show a steady stream of love. Be love, so love will flow out when people fail you, just like it flowed from Jesus when He took the fall for us.

Give away love like you're made of it. Let it fill you up like candy in a piñata, so when you take a hit, it's what will pour out of you.

What loving thing can you do today for
someone who isn't expecting it?

WHEN JOY IS A HABIT, LOVE IS A REFLEX.

A new command I give you: Love one another. As I have loved you,
so you must love one another. By this everyone will know that you
are my disciples, if you love one another.

JOHN 13:34–35

We've all slept in on a holiday or Saturday and woken up in a frenzy. We were
supposed to be there fifteen minutes ago. We grab the clothes on our floor that
smell the cleanest, splash water on our faces, snag a banana, and rehearse our
excuses as we speed off to an office we were supposed to be at already.

That's the power of habit. Our bodies get into routines that launch us into
motion without our brains taking the time to process what's happening. It's
why we can dial a number on our phones without looking at the numbers. It's
why we know how to spell words without thinking about it. Sure, sometimes
we get it wrong, like when we put milk in the pantry or Froot Loops in the
fridge, but our habits usually get it right.

If our bodies can be trained to act without our conscious awareness, surely
our spirits work the same way: when joy is a habit, love is a reflex. You see it
when a guy falls head over heels for a girl. She can show up two hours late for
a date, and his immediate response isn't anger or irritation—it's pure bliss that
he gets to see her another time.

How do we make joy a habit in our everyday lives so our reflex is always
love for the people around us? I can't think of a better way than gratitude.
When we're intentional about giving thanks for everything we come across,
we can't help but feel joy over the pure gift of another day. And when our joy
has become a habit, our love becomes a way of living.

What new habit of love do you want to start building in your life?

FEBRUARY 6

LOVING PEOPLE THE WAY JESUS
DID IS GREAT THEOLOGY.

If you knew the gift of God and who it is that asks you for a drink,
you would have asked him and he would have given you living
water.

JOHN 4:10

If you've spent much time in church, you've probably met some really smart
people who know a lot about theology. If you're like me, you've been in one
or two Bible studies where it's like people are speaking a foreign language. As
soon as someone starts saying what words mean in Hebrew or Greek, they've
pretty much lost me.

My faith isn't a complicated one. I just know I met Jesus and He changed
my life. He made me kinder and less selfish, and He invited me to do life with
Him. The longer I've followed Him, the more I've realized we don't need all
the answers to all the questions. Instead, loving people the way Jesus did is
great theology.

Jesus gave us some blueprints, and here's one of my favorites: He walked into
a town called Samaria, where Jews weren't supposed to go. Strolling right up to a
woman, which men didn't do, He snagged a seat next to her at a well. He crossed
all the cultural barriers that broke the religious people's rules, and He saw her.
He listened to her. Jesus told her about the living water He could give her. He
didn't say what all this meant in three different languages. He didn't study her
and didn't ask her to study Him. She eventually mentioned her husband, and
He said, "Oh, right, you've had five of them, and the man you're with now isn't
actually your husband." But here's the thing: He didn't judge her.

Jesus didn't walk her through the Romans Road or try to prove some
obscure, hard-to-understand rule of faith. No, He sat, He listened, and He saw.
He went straight to the heart of the matter and saw her heart in the process.
Now, that's great theology.

What simple truth of God's do you need to remember today?

WE GROW WHERE WE'RE LOVED, NOT WHERE WE'RE MERELY INFORMED.

I have been crucified with Christ and I no longer live, but Christ lives in me.

GALATIANS 2:20

When I first met Jesus, I tried to surround myself with people who were on the same path as I was. But over time, there were so many people who looked and acted like me that I lost sight of the way Jesus sought out people outside the fringes. This is what changed everything. I made an effort to become friends with people whose lives looked different than mine. I sought out people with different worldviews. I found people who rolled different than me.

Much to my surprise, there were people who didn't go to church but loved Jesus. For one reason or another, they didn't feel accepted at church or didn't feel like they were truly welcome. They made choices people didn't agree with. They had lifestyles that were unconventional. They had things about their faith they were still working out, and this made some people feel uncomfortable.

These friends reminded me that we grow where we are loved, not where we are merely informed. These new friends were told they had to change in order to belong, so they decided not to belong. They didn't want to stay quiet or hide their struggles, so they stayed away.

What they feared was rejection, so they found people who accepted them just as they were. Some of these friends found different churches, while others just found good friends. They found places where they were loved.

Who is it you have been avoiding? Who is it you disagree with? Who has a lifestyle you disapprove of? What if we showed grace and loved them rather than trying to change them? People grow where they're loved.

Is God inviting you to grow closer to someone who is different from you?

FEBRUARY 8

GIVE AWAY INEXPLICABLE AMOUNTS OF LOVE WITH TREMENDOUS COURAGE.

Two are better than one, because they have a good return for their labor: If either of them falls down, one can help the other up. But pity anyone who falls and has no one to help them up.

ECCLESIASTES 4:9–10

In our busy lives, it can seem like the only way we ever see friends is to make an appointment with them. Whether it's Tuesday night small groups, Thursday morning playdates, or Friday afternoon happy hours, there's a clear script for how and when we connect. These codes can make our interactions feel more formal, and I think it dampens a sense of genuine connection.

In truth, we want to be in homes together, with no end time and no fear of imposing. We want people to stop by unannounced on their evening walk and then stay to join us for leftovers. We don't want to worry about whether the house is clean or the kids finger-painted the walls. We want to be seen by one another in ways that reflect our actual lives.

Who decided friendship needed all these rules? Since most people feel lonely and want to be truly known, why not just change the rules? It takes courage to step outside the norms—to spontaneously show up for people on a Monday night with pizza, or to welcome them into our messes when we want them to imagine we're more like Martha Stewart. But we're not! So why keep forcing each other to act like we've got it all together?

We have the power to change this. People might think we're a little weird, and because of their own fears they might even turn us down. But that's okay. We don't need to settle for typical. We just need to have a little courage.

Who in your life will you let in more to your messy world?

SELFLESS LOVE IS ALWAYS COSTLY. FEAR CAN'T AFFORD IT, PRIDE DOESN'T UNDERSTAND IT, BUT FRIENDS NEVER FORGET IT.

Very rarely will anyone die for a righteous person, though for a good person someone might possibly dare to die. But God demonstrates his own love for us in this: While we were still sinners, Christ died for us.

ROMANS 5:7–8

The person who's taught me the most about love in this life has been my wife and partner in crime, Sweet Maria. I've seen her wake up while it's still dark to bake welcome cookies for friends and stay up late to clean the kitchen after serving friends who showed up unannounced. She has selflessly poured herself out for me and the kids, and she was so patient with us when we didn't appreciate it. At every point, she's shown me grace when I've missed the mark—and that happens pretty often.

I've seen from the sidelines how costly love and grace can be. The mom who always has room for one more kid at the sleepover? She doesn't have more energy than the rest of us, but she gives anyway. The friend who remembers your important meeting and makes it a point to call the moment it's done? The spouse who forgives you for the mistake you made one hundred times? These people have a natural bias toward grace. They forgive when it's costly, not just when it's convenient.

Just as we can't wait for inspiration when we're trying to hit a deadline, we can't wait for all the feelings to catch up to us before we give away extravagant amounts of love. Selfless love is always costly. Fear can't afford it, pride doesn't understand it, but friends never forget it. Make the decision to step out in love today. Even if you don't feel like you can afford to leave work early or say yes to an extra kid around the table, you will never regret that you did it.

Who do you know who has an extra dose of grace in their lives to give away? How can you show appreciation to them this week?

LOVING PEOPLE THE WAY JESUS DID MEANS A LIFE OF BEING CONSTANTLY MISUNDERSTOOD.

He was despised and rejected by mankind, a man of suffering, and familiar with pain. Like one from whom people hide their faces he was despised, and we held him in low esteem.

ISAIAH 53:3

A few years ago, one of my friends announced a change in how he would run his organization. His team helps people all over the world find hope in the midst of poverty. People from all over the world have respected his organization for decades, and the impact his organization has made is immense.

Well, this guy loves Jesus. And because he loves Jesus, he decided he wanted to let more people who love Jesus come work with him. Rather than making sure they checked every box on a religious report card, he chose to hire people based on their love for Jesus and their qualifications for the job. And boy did that blow up! Supporters went crazy when they heard he was widening the circle, and many of them cut off financial support within hours. It seemed like half of earth hated him. A few days later, he reversed his decision, and then the other half of earth appeared to hate him too.

Loving people the way Jesus did means a life of being constantly misunderstood. Some people didn't want to include people who made them uncomfortable. It's totally understandable. We all have people we struggle to include. But we can't be surprised when we step out like Jesus did and people respond the way the religious people did in His time.

The day my friend came under fire, I started sending helium balloons to his office with the hope of filling it. He didn't need another opinion. He needed a friend. We've got to support one another when we get heat for loving people like Jesus did. If you know anyone who's getting flak for the way they love, buy them some cupcakes or send them some balloons. Let's love each other the way Jesus loved us.

**Who do you know who is frequently misunderstood?
How can you encourage that person today?**

IF LOVE ISN'T THE DEFINING CHARACTERISTIC OF OUR FAITH, WE NEED TO FIND OUR WAY BACK TO WHERE WE STARTED.

If the world hates you, keep in mind that it hated me first.

JOHN 15:18

One time Jesus and His disciples wanted to go to a village in Samaria. Here was the problem: the people in the village weren't having it. Apparently, they had an issue with people from Jerusalem. The disciples heard the outcry from the village, and do you know what they said? "Jesus, do you want us to call down fire from heaven to destroy them?" Yikes. It seems a little harsh, yet at the same time not unfamiliar. We're a lot like the disciples sometimes, wanting to tap into nuclear weapons when people say something we don't agree with or rub us the wrong way. At some point, we started to believe that our doctrine is the defining characteristic of our faith. We got it in our heads that knowing the truth and telling others about it was our greater purpose here on earth than simply loving the people God made.

The gospel isn't a set of doctrines we agree with, though. It's actually Jesus. He said He was the way, the truth, and the life. Don't add to it. It's possible to have great doctrine and lousy theology. Loving people the way Jesus did is great theology. The Bible helps us understand how God wants us to live, but never let anything block your view of the fact that He's the one who holds all things together. He's the one who rescued us and who still rescues us when we slip up and need some grace.

There will be times you're not welcomed. There will be times you're misunderstood. There are times you'll be angry about it. We don't need to ask God to rain down fire on the people who have been difficult. Just keep moving forward, eyes fixed on Jesus and off of everyone else.

Is there someone you've written off because of the way they once responded to you?

LOVE'S PLAN IS PRETTY SIMPLE: WE'RE SUPPOSED TO LOVE EVERYBODY, ALWAYS.

While Jesus was having dinner at Matthew's house, many tax collectors and sinners came and ate with him and his disciples. When the Pharisees saw this, they asked his disciples, "Why does your teacher eat with tax collectors and sinners?"

MATTHEW 9:10–11

If you ever went to camp or joined the Scouts as a kid, you knew the insecurity that came with the trips. We were thrown onto smelly buses with lots of new faces, and it was unclear where we'd fit (or whether we'd fit at all). It quickly became clear whether you were in with the cool kids or you were out, and it was a long week if you were out.

We'd like to think we've left those days behind, but our adult lives can look pretty similar. Most of us still try to huddle up with the cool kids and, in a subtle way, blast it on social media. It's no different than those bus rides. The definition of cool has just been tweaked a little bit.

What's crazy is that Jesus spent His whole life engaging the people most of us spend our whole lives avoiding. He found people who thought they were "out" and said they were in. He didn't vet the guy on the cross next to Him. He said, "I'll see you in paradise."

Even wilder, Jesus also showed love to the self-righteous people who excluded those He loved. He called them out but also let them know there was always more room for humble people. When He said to love our neighbors and our enemies, He didn't just mean the easy ones. He meant everyone.

What kind of person do you find it most difficult to love? Jesus says they're in. Don't act like they aren't. Get to know them. I know it'll be difficult, but it will be worth it.

What kinds of people are hard for you to love?

THE BEST WAY TO SHOW PEOPLE GOD IS EVERYTHING WE SAY HE IS, IS FOR US TO BE EVERYTHING HE SAYS WE ARE.

By this everyone will know that you are my disciples, if you love one another.

JOHN 13:35

If you've ever run a business or led a team of people, you know what it's like to send someone in your place. You know they're going to interact with a person who might not know you, and that person will base their opinion about you on the someone you sent. Parents feel this too. We often feel like our kids are little representations of us. If they're kind and respectful, people say we raised them well. If they toilet paper the neighbor's house, we worry others will judge us for our kids' behavior.

God works in much the same way. When people interact with difficult, judgmental people who say they follow Jesus, it's hard to imagine how the God they say they're speaking for is gracious and kind. We can say all the right words, but if we don't model love the way Jesus did, people won't just think we're mean—they'll think God is. I get that.

The best way to give people a glimpse of God is for us to be exactly who He says we are: love. He says people will know we follow Him when they see how we love one another. He put His confidence in us to represent Him because He knows what we're capable of if we'll put down our pride. He wouldn't have put us on the job if He didn't think we were ready.

Remember that you are God's kid, but you're also a tangible expression of Jesus to the world. Don't tell people what Jesus meant; love them the way He did.

How can you more simply express the love of Jesus to others today?

LOVING PEOPLE THE WAY JESUS DID MEANS LIVING A LIFE OF CONSTANT INTERRUPTIONS.

I heard the voice of the Lord saying, "Whom shall I send? And who will go for us?" And I said, "Here am I. Send me!"

ISAIAH 6:8

You might know that I put my personal cell phone number in the back of a couple of books I wrote. When I told my publisher what I wanted to do, they said, "Are you crazy?!" I thought for a minute and said, "Actually, yes and no." I've noticed that the people who have had the most impact in my life were the most available. Granted, I get *a lot* of calls. And guess what? I answer every single one unless I'm on a plane or out of cell range. It's terrific. I can't get a thing done.

Here's the point. It'll be hard to be like Jesus if you don't want to be available to people. It's what He did. Every day. If you don't want to be with people, you're going to hate heaven.

What's more important to God than the people He made? Not much. And if one of those people wants to talk to me, I want to be available. Perhaps this isn't for you. That's fine. Find something else you can do to connect with the people God made in His image. God says people are the purpose. It doesn't matter whether our plans succeed or fail if the people around us don't feel wanted. Loving people the way Jesus did means a life of constant interruptions.

Everything changes when we start to see interruptions as opportunities. We heal people when we show them they matter, when their well-being is our main concern. This isn't hard to do. Sometimes all it takes is picking up the phone and saying hello. Be generous with your time and your presence, and people will feel the love of Jesus.

What can you do today to become more available for loving others?

STOP TRYING TO MAKE SENSE OF GOD'S ECONOMY. HERE'S HOW IT WORKS: THERE'S ALWAYS MORE THAN ENOUGH—FOR EVERYONE.

They all ate and were satisfied, and the disciples picked up twelve basketfuls of broken pieces that were left over.

LUKE 9:17

Jesus always taught for free. There was no honorarium, no speaker's fee, and no long bio reading about His qualifications and achievements before His talk. There were even a couple of times when lunch was included. On those two occasions, thousands of people showed up. Jesus didn't call a caterer. He told the people around them to just bring what they had and let Him make what He wanted out of it.

Jesus' friends came back from the crowd with a few pieces of bread and a handful of fish—not exactly feast material for a few thousand people. Then Jesus' friends started passing out what they had. A fish and some bread for this person, and again for another, and again for the next. The food just kept on coming. I wonder at what point they started elbowing one another, saying, "Did you see that?" After the meal, after thousands of bellies were full, there was loads of food left over. It didn't make any sense. God's economy rarely does.

I don't think God expects us to make sense out of our lives or what we do with them. Maybe He wants to show us how to love extravagantly every chance we get. Even when it doesn't make sense, that's the only way love does things.

The miracle of the story isn't only how Jesus generated all the extra bread and fish. It's that Jesus didn't make just enough—He made what was more than enough for everyone. Jesus' friends were ready to just cancel lunch. Love has a way of multiplying well past what we think is possible. Jesus is providing lunch today. He's not going to provide just enough. He'll provide more than enough. Don't just ask what you're hungry for but what the people around you are hungry for.

What are the people around you hungry for in their lives?

LOVE DOES GREAT THINGS WITHOUT EXPECTING GREAT ATTENTION. BRIGHT LIGHTS DON'T NEED SPOTLIGHTS.

Be careful not to practice your righteousness in front of others to be seen by them. If you do, you will have no reward from your Father in heaven.

MATTHEW 6:1

Meteor showers top the list of my favorite shows in nature. There's nothing more awe-inspiring. You head out with blankets and friends and lie in a field on your back while you wait for heaven's fireworks. If you're like me and you don't know if it's Orion's belt or the Little Dipper you're looking at, you just point with confidence and guess. Who's going to know the difference?

Only a few mishaps—like rainstorms, skunks, and lights from the ground—can ruin these magical moments. Whether it's headlights from approaching cars or city lights in the distance, they steal the attention from the black velvet sky showing off the diamonds.

Man-made lights have a way of getting in the way of God's glory blazing through the sky.

I've noticed we do the same thing sometimes when we try to draw attention to our love. We'll make an extraordinary sacrifice in secret, lighting up a small corner of the world with our love, but then we try to shine a light on it and the glory is gone. Sure, we're supposed to be the light of the world, but spotlights make star lights go missing every time. When we opt to make it about us, it's like the insecure teenager inside of us turned on the truck lights and we couldn't see the beauty in the sky any longer.

The fix is as simple as stargazing. Quit standing up. Lie down. Let your love blaze in the night like a thousand stars. The less extra light we introduce, the better.

What secret loving thing can you do for someone this week?

LIVE YOUR LIFE WITH LOVE THIS WEEK—LIKE YOU'RE EXACTLY WHO JESUS THINKS YOU ARE.

I want you to know, brothers and sisters, that the gospel I preached is not of human origin. I did not receive it from any man, nor was I taught it; rather, I received it by revelation from Jesus Christ.

GALATIANS 1:11–12

There's a story in the Bible about a guy named Saul who had it out for Christians. He devoted his life to targeting them, oppressing them, and hurting them. While he was consumed with anger and hate, Saul met God. You know the story. On his journey to persecute another group of Christians, God struck him blind and told him to go find a man named Ananias in the city of Damascus.

The people traveling with Saul got him to Ananias, who was a Christian and a guy who understood the threat Saul posed to him and the people like him. Ananias went to him anyway and laid his hands on Saul's shoulder: "Brother Saul," he said, "the Lord has sent me to restore your sight and fill you with the Holy Spirit." After everything Saul had done to Christians, can you imagine how Ananias must have felt to have the job of telling Saul he wasn't who he used to be?

Saul got up and immediately began devoting his life to serving God. He carried the message of God's love to people across the ocean, facing ridicule, shipwrecks, beatings, and more than a little jail time along the way. Saul believed God when He told him who he was. He lived the rest of his life with extravagant love. He did it because there was a guy named Ananias who was brave enough to tell him who he was.

What would it look like for you to live your life this week like you're exactly who Jesus thinks you are? God doesn't think you're a mess-up just because you've messed up. He's got a new name and a new job for you. He wants you to be His.

What would it look like for you to live your life this week like you're exactly who Jesus thinks you are?

WE'LL BE KNOWN FOR OUR OPINIONS BUT REMEMBERED FOR OUR LOVE.

Do everything in love.

1 CORINTHIANS 16:14

Conferences have a way of gathering together speakers who fit a specific identifiable set of characteristics. We sometimes call it a person's "brand." Whether it's an academic retreat, a Christian summit, or business development day, we divide people into categories and invite them based on their expertise or area of interest. We've got the justice seeker, the leadership guy, the expert on millennials, the tech-savvy speaker, the innovative woman entrepreneur, or the psychologist. We take a multifaceted, complex, whole human being and give them a tagline. I'm not saying that's all bad—it's just not the whole story.

No one is completely defined by their knowledge or what they've accomplished. At the end of each of our lives, if you ask the people who knew us what they'll miss the most, it'll be the small ways we loved the people around us. It'll be the memories we made and the big mess-ups we walked through together. It will be our kindness, not our qualifications, that outlast us. It will be the time we unsuccessfully tried to wrap a puppy up for Christmas, not the perfect vacation we planned or the raise we got. It will be the fire we started by mistake in the house while trying to make indoor s'mores during a storm. We won't be missed because of the lectures we gave or arguments we won. We'll be missed because someone will want to call us to share a joy from the day and remember we're no longer there to share the celebration.

In short, we'll be known for our opinions, but we'll be remembered for our love. Don't forget what will matter in the end. The love you leave behind will be your legacy.

What's something simple you've done for someone recently because you loved them?

WE DON'T NEED TO CALL IT "MINISTRY," JUST CALL IT TUESDAY. LOVE ALREADY HAS A NAME.

Above all, love each other deeply, because love covers over a multitude of sins.

1 PETER 4:8

I hear a lot of talk about people *going into ministry* or *serving in ministry*. I know it's a term pastors and religious leaders use, but it feels a little weird to hear it thrown around so much. The guy working at the tire store probably won't know what you're talking about.

Most people don't want to feel like someone's stooping down to serve them. They just want someone to empathize with their situation. Whenever I've messed up, the least helpful thing I've ever received was a lecture. The most helpful thing I've ever received was someone's agenda-free presence. They might've been a little older or even a little younger than me, but they never said they were "ministering" to me—they just thought we were friends.

I'm usually doing a good job serving people, right up until I start telling everyone I'm serving people. Because when I do, I make it all about me—and it'll never be about Jesus if we make it about us. We all want to feel like we come together as equals, with each of us bringing something unique and vital to the table. That's how friendship works: we join forces, knowing each of us has something to learn from the other, and both of us benefit from the relationship. You bring the brains, I bring the ice cream, and everyone wins. As soon as someone thinks they're there to "minister," we are no longer equals.

What if we all got together and schemed ways to go make more friends? Whether we make soup for people, or sit down and talk with discouraged kids, or do some tutoring—what if we just did it because it was Saturday or Tuesday and these are great days for new friends? It might make people feel like they're sought after for friendship rather than approached as a project. There's no need to give what we do a new label. Love already has a name.

What's a simple act of love you can do this week to build a stronger friendship with someone?

HOW DO YOU MAKE MORE SPACE IN YOUR LIFE FOR LOVE? QUIT SOMETHING!

I consider my life worth nothing to me; my only aim is to finish the race and complete the task the Lord Jesus has given me—the task of testifying to the good news of God's grace.

ACTS 20:24

You might not know this, but I spent decades working as a lawyer. I know, Jesus had a lot to say about lawyers, and not much of it was good, so it keeps me on my toes. I think I might have been the luckiest lawyer in the world because I partnered with a bunch of people who knew my work at my law firm was just that—it was work. It was a job. It's something I did to provide for my family and then fund all the things I'm passionate about, like building schools for kids in Uganda and Somalia and Afghanistan and rescuing victims of human trafficking in India.

I used to devote way more of my time and energy to being a lawyer, but then two things hit me one day. First, all we'll leave behind is our love, and second, our legacy will be in the people we loved. That's when I realized I had to make a change. My life couldn't revolve around trials and lawsuits. So here's what I did: I quit. I'm not kidding. I got everyone at the law firm together and told them I was out. I took the key to the office door off my key ring and left—and I've never gone back.

I made the necessary changes to free me up to give more time, attention, and emotional energy to people in more desperate circumstances than I was in. I wanted to live a less traditional life. One that fit more closely with the person I had become, rather than the guy I used to be. I asked myself the question that might be worth asking yourself. Are you doing what you're merely capable of or what you're called to?

I've set aside Thursdays now to quit something. It's easy to get so buried under responsibilities that we lose sight of who we've become. So here's the deal.

Quit something! What will it be? What's been holding you back? Taking up too much time? What no longer inspires you? Pick whatever day you want—it doesn't have to be Thursday. Today is a pretty good day to start. Pick today. You don't have to quit your whole job or move overseas, but you can start cutting things out on a regular basis. You'll free yourself up to live a life that will give you a great sense of purpose and feed your passions.

What do you need to quit to make more room for love?

HOW MUCH WE LOVE GOD CAN BE MEASURED BY HOW MUCH WE LOVE PEOPLE.

"Love the Lord your God with all your heart and with all your soul and with all your mind." This is the first and greatest commandment. And the second is like it: "Love your neighbor as yourself." All the Law and the Prophets hang on these two commandments.

MATTHEW 22:37–40

When I first started following Jesus, there were times I was a little confused by what it meant to love God. He's invisible, right? I don't know about you, but I find it hard to love someone you can't see, touch, or hear. I know we can pray (and I've done a lot of it since I had teenagers), but even prayer feels somehow a little different than just loving a God we can't see.

So I looked around at different religious leaders to see what they meant when they said they loved God. It seemed like a lot of them meant they spent a lot of time reading the Bible, or reading books about the Bible, or teaching people how to think about God. I know those are common things people do when they love God, but it still didn't seem like it was the way to love God.

I finally figured it out when I went back to the words Jesus spoke to His friends. Some people asked Him what the greatest commandment could be, and Jesus told them the greatest commandment was to love God with all their heart, soul, and mind. Then He said this: "And the second one is like it." The second commandment is to love our neighbors as ourselves. Loving God started to make more sense when I realized loving a God I couldn't see was a lot like loving the people He made and put all around me.

Everyone is made in the image of God, so every person reflects a part of God's creative expression in this world in one way or another. Think about the people God has put in your life already and the characteristics you see in them that inform your understanding of God.

Who in your life is teaching you about the nature of God's love these days?

FEBRUARY 22

LOVE PICKED US SO GRACE COULD USE US.

Then Peter began to speak: "I now realize how true it is that God does not show favoritism but accepts from every nation the one who fears him and does what is right."

ACTS 10:34–35

Every year when I was in school, we were required to go to "athletics," better known as gym class. I always hated it because there was a possibility we'd play kickball or dodgeball or pretty much anything that required a ball. This meant there would be team captains to pick players. It is a time-honored tradition that picking teams in gym class starts with the best and goes to the worst. I often hoped God would make the bell ring forty-eight minutes early because I knew what was about to happen again. I wouldn't get picked. I was huge. I almost blocked the sun. This was good. But I was clumsy, which was bad.

It was a terrible system, leaving me and all the other uncoordinated guys stranded on the sidelines looking at each other in our gym shorts and T-shirts. It was clear who was cool and got picked and who wasn't. I'm so glad God doesn't chose who will be with Him the way the guys in gym class picked who would be on their team.

If I ever teach a gym class, I'm going to draw a big circle in the middle of the group and say, "Everyone is in." That's how God chose us. The Bible says God loved the whole world, every person in it. Not just the cool ones or the knowledgeable ones or the ones who believed all the right things or made all the right moves. He doesn't want anyone to suffer, and He doesn't want anyone to feel alone. He doesn't want anyone to go through life without Him, and He doesn't want us to spend eternity without Him either.

We don't have to burden ourselves by wondering who's in and who's out, because God already told us: He wants us all. If you're someone who knows about God's extravagant love, you've let grace find you. Once He does, the question is what we'll do next. Love picked us so grace could use us.

Reflect on God's unconditional love for you today. What comes to mind?

MOST OF OUR DECISIONS ARE DRIVEN BY LOVE OR FEAR. FIGURE OUT WHAT'S DRIVING YOU, THEN DECIDE WHAT YOU'LL DO.

Do nothing out of selfish ambition or vain conceit. Rather, in humility value others above yourselves, not looking to your own interests but each of you to the interests of the others.

PHILIPPIANS 2:3–4

Years ago, I was headed out with a friend to see a movie. He zipped around the corner on my street and screeched to a halt in front of my mailbox. Smoke was still swirling around his car as I walked out the front door. *Maybe I shouldn't go,* I thought. But this guy was my friend, and I really wanted to see the movie. As I settled into the bucket seat, I buckled my seat belt and a few of the other seat belts in the car. Then I prayed.

It's kind of a silly example, but there's a truth in it: most of our decisions are driven by either love or fear. *Should I stay or should I go? Should I speak or stay silent? Should I risk it or back away?* In these times, we've got to stop and remind ourselves that fear has many faces. If we're down on ourselves, it's fear saying we won't measure up. If we're worried about what people will think, it's fear saying no one will love us if they see our flaws. If it's a hot rod revving the engine in our driveway, maybe we should just stay home. That's just common sense.

But the truth is, love says we're free to do a lot more than we think. We can love more people, we can trust God more, and we can risk more. If we find ourselves considering others more important than ourselves, serving in secret, or loving without an agenda, then chances are, it's love doing the talking. If we're backing away from opportunities because we're not sure they will work, hedging on our love, and risking little in our relationships, fear might have the microphone. The trick is to figure out who's doing the talking before we decide what to do next.

How is fear getting in the way of your loving others?

WE DON'T NEED TO CHOOSE WHO TO LOVE LIKE WE'LL RUN OUT. GO AHEAD—JUST LOVE EVERYBODY.

I am convinced that neither death nor life, neither angels nor demons, neither the present nor the future, nor any powers, neither height nor depth, nor anything else in all creation, will be able to separate us from the love of God that is in Christ Jesus our Lord.

ROMANS 8:38-39

Sweet Maria is an amazing chef. One of her specialties is making pie. It's one of the ways I know God loves me. And if Sweet Maria is ever making pies, she usually makes several kinds. I haven't decided which of her pies is my favorite because each one is tied for first in my belly. When the pies are out, I usually get a slice of each one—apple, pecan, pumpkin, chocolate. I know, that's a lot of pie, but how can you blame me?

The downside of pie is in the limited number of pieces you can get out of one, even if you cut them into the world's smallest slices. Love doesn't work that way. We can never run out of love, never give or receive too much. Sometimes we start to think it's finite because resources like time and energy can run low. But when we choose to give more love, we get to watch it multiply. People return our love, giving back what we gave away with a little extra. Then the cycle happens all over again, everybody getting a little more than they gave away. Love is one of the few things we don't have to guard. We don't have to be greedy with our love. It multiplies when we give it away.

Don't worry about who to choose when it comes to love. Go ahead and love everyone.

What would you do differently today if you believed that love never ran out?

LOVE SHOWS UP.

Love is patient, love is kind. It does not envy, it does not boast, it is not proud. It does not dishonor others, it is not self-seeking, it is not easily angered, it keeps no record of wrongs. Love does not delight in evil but rejoices with the truth. It always protects, always trusts, always hopes, always perseveres.

1 CORINTHIANS 13:4–7

On one of my trips to Africa, I got malaria. There's not a good version of malaria, but I got a really aggressive kind, and it just about killed me. You learn a lot about love when you end up in the hospital. Love brings your favorite breakfast to spare you the stale pancakes or smuggles a puppy in an oversized purse. Love holds your hand when the doctor finally comes in with the results. Love stays for hours on the faux leather chair next to your hospital bed, maybe overnight if necessary.

Great love leaves little doubt, because great love shows up. Great love doesn't go away, and it never has an eye on the clock to see when it should call it quits. When you're in need, you learn about great love because you see people go all in to ease the burden a bit.

But you don't need an emergency to show great love. We have the opportunity to show up for one another in simpler ways every day. When we drop what we're doing to listen to someone who needs an ear, we show them we're for them. When we honor our neighbors by knowing their names, we tell them they're worth an entire parade.

Great love is about consistently showing up, which is both easier and harder than it seems. It's easier because it's something each of us can do. We don't need to come up with money for extravagant gifts or publish poems in their honor. But it's harder because it demands our time when we're tired, our homes when we're full, or our attention when all we want to do is retreat. What's your next move? Who could you reach out to? Great love makes itself available time and again. It shows up.

Who can you show up for today?

LOVE DOESN'T HAVE A RETURN ON INVESTMENT.

Anyone who has two shirts should share with the one who has none, and anyone who has food should do the same.

LUKE 3:11

I have some friends who are really successful in business. I hear them use this phrase "return on investment" when they talk about their work. It makes sense. What do you put in? What do you get back? Most people are hardwired to want to know their efforts will be effective. This is a business metric that can be used not only in the for-profit world but also in the not-for-profit world. If you donate money to a cause, you want to know how the money will be used and later whether it accomplished the goal. Simple enough. If you send your kids to school, you want to know how much they learned. That's fair. If we're going to spend our time, energy, and resources on something, we want to know it's worth it and that we made a good choice. While that's a good way to look at a lot of things in life, I'm starting to see how we have to ditch that model when it comes to love.

Love was never meant to be transactional. It doesn't give to get. It doesn't create spreadsheets to analyze how well it's working. It doesn't track how much love you put in and measure it against how much love you got back. Yet sadly, that's what we often do. We don't want to admit it, but we're looking for the return on investment. We want to know if our expression of love "worked." Keeping track of your investment is a fine way to gauge progress in the business world, I suppose, but it's a lousy way to measure a relationship because it turns people into projects.

The return on investment with love is love itself. We don't have to know how our love makes a difference for it to be a good idea. We can just give it away like we won the lottery. People aren't projects, and love doesn't need to keep track of the outcomes. Think of a friendship, a relationship, or a venture you're involved in right now where you've been keeping track of how much love you put in and how much you've received in response—and figure out what needs to change.

What would you do differently today if you weren't concerned anymore about getting something in return?

EVERY ACT OF LOVE IS A PROFESSION OF FAITH.

Do not forget to show hospitality to strangers, for by so doing
some people have shown hospitality to angels without knowing it.

HEBREWS 13:2

I used to think we were supposed to do nice things for people so we could get their attention and tell them about our faith. Here's a scenario: Someone needs food, and you meet that need in a tangible way. Then, once you've helped them, you tell them about your faith—and if everything goes the way you were hoping and they are willing, you ask if they want to repeat a prayer after you.

Jesus never healed someone and then asked if they wanted to say a prayer to invite Him into their life. When we look at the life of Jesus, we see Him feed people simply because they were hungry, not because they recognized their desperate need for Him. He healed people because they were sick and celebrated their wellness, not the path to getting there. He turned water into wine because the bride and groom needed more wine to celebrate, not so the celebration would become about Him. Jesus met the needs of people simply because He loved them, no strings attached. We're not always good at that. When we tie a religious experience or expression to our love, we turn our faith into a business deal.

I don't have these things figured out yet, but I've been on the lookout for ways to not make a business deal out of Jesus' deity. We have an organization that builds schools and safe houses and tries to get children out of some really difficult circumstances. When it works, we don't ask people to pray with us once they're free. We just celebrate their new lives. We don't limit the opportunity for a child to get an education to the kids who believe in Jesus. We don't think we lead people to Jesus. We think Jesus leads people to Jesus, and what we have the opportunity to do is to love people without an agenda.

All this doesn't make what we do less worthy or more worthy. It just keeps what we do an expression of our faith, not a transaction. Most people know we love Jesus, and sometimes people ask us about Him. That's terrific. We're always happy to talk about Jesus because He's our source of joy and excitement in life. But there's no undisclosed agenda we have going on behind the scenes. Are there things you're unintentionally doing that feel transactional with your beliefs? Be confident in this. Every act of love is a profession of faith because it whispers His name.

**Who could you love better without
worrying how they'll respond?**

FEBRUARY 28

WHENEVER I THINK I'VE GOT SOMEONE PEGGED, I REMEMBER I'M ONLY SEEING HALF.

Since, then, you have been raised with Christ, set your hearts on things above, where Christ is, seated at the right hand of God. Set your minds on things above, not on earthly things. For you died, and your life is now hidden with Christ in God.

COLOSSIANS 3:1–3

A while back I had a problem with my sight in one eye. It required a couple of surgeries to fix. Afterward, they gave me an eye patch to wear. I was so pumped to finally be a pirate. Wearing it somehow made a lot of sense for a guy who holds meetings on Tom Sawyer Island at Disneyland each week.

You would think an eye patch would limit my sight, and I guess technically it did. But it also enabled me to see in a different way. What my eye patch gave me was a lot of perspective. It helped me realize something I'd missed when both my eyes worked. It's this: the way I usually see things is usually only half the picture.

When I see someone lashing out in anger, I'm only seeing the half they've disclosed in their big show of frustration. What I don't see is the thing underneath the waving arms, the raised voice, and the grimace. In the moment, it's hard to see the other half—the beautiful and loving and terribly insecure person who is the other half buried underneath. When someone is incredibly kind or generous, that's not the whole story either. There's another half to see. Perhaps it's trying to receive validation from someone who withheld love. Maybe there is some deep hurt only they know. It could just as easily be that they had experienced extravagant love and wanted to pass some along. When we're tempted to judge someone for their behavior or think that other person has it easy and all together, put on an eye patch to get some much needed perspective. You're probably only seeing half—and that's rounding up.

When you see faults in others, go a little easier on them. The same applies to you. Don't be so hard on yourself when you blow it, okay? And if you catch yourself overstating the good you've done, do a little bit less of that. Deal? If you're beating yourself up over a mistake or thinking you're the best thing since sliced bread, put on an eye patch and look in the mirror. Your failures and successes are only half the picture. The other half is love, and it'll outlast everything else you'll ever achieve or fail at.

Who are you being a little too hard on these days?

JESUS SPENT HIS WHOLE LIFE ENGAGING THE PEOPLE MOST OF US HAVE SPENT OUR WHOLE LIVES AVOIDING.

A man with leprosy came to him and begged him on his knees, "If you are willing, you can make me clean." Jesus was indignant. He reached out his hand and touched the man. "I am willing," he said. "Be clean!"

MARK 1:40-41

I was at the grocery store one day, hoping to get in and out in a hurry. I was tired and wanted to just grab a couple of things and get home to Sweet Maria. Within moments of entering the store, it happened. It was the classic "I bumped into someone." I saw someone I knew, and I knew they were going through a tough time. I'll be honest—I was tempted to duck behind a pile of grapes or camouflage myself with a pineapple and a few papayas. I'll admit, getting through the check-out line and heading home was more important to me than engaging a friend.

The Bible shares stories of how people in that time avoided the tax collectors and the very ill. I don't know any IRS agents or anyone with leprosy, but I still have the problem Jesus talked to His friends about. He gave examples about people who helped those in need and those who passed by them. These days we avoid people when they are inconvenient or their personalities rub us the wrong way or we strongly disagree with them. We avoid people who make us feel anxious or insecure. We may feign engagement and say something polite, but everyone on the receiving end knows they were just avoided.

The ones we avoid are the ones Jesus engaged. He spent his whole life seeking out the people most of us have spent our whole lives avoiding. When he saw a leper, he saw a person with a dark history and a bright future. When he saw a woman, he saw a leader. When he saw a sinner, he saw someone in need of grace. When we pay attention to the people around us, we find a lot of people who are rejected by others and loved by Jesus. Those are the ones He wants us to move toward, and when we move toward them, we'll learn a lot about the God who moves toward us too.

**Who are you avoiding? What can you do
to put their needs before yours?**

MARCH 2

WHEN WE LOVE PEOPLE WE DISAGREE WITH, IT TURNS OUR FAITH INTO A LIVING BIOGRAPHY.

Everyone who hears these words of mine and puts them into practice is like a wise man who built his house on the rock.

MATTHEW 7:24

In one of Jesus' most popular sermons, He told people how to become love. He told them to be humble. He urged them to turn the other cheek when someone came swinging. He said to give their stuff away, not to store it up here on earth. But the most radical part of the sermon was this: He told people to love their enemies.

Jesus said it's easy to love people who love us back. Anyone can do that. But we're to love those who don't love us back—even those who have it out for us.

I think we water down Jesus' call to love our enemies by thinking of them in broad and extreme categories, like people in countries we're at war with. Terrorists, leaders of drug cartels, criminals who have done great harm. A person walking their dog isn't your enemy, right? A teacher you've never had but have heard stories about how strict they are isn't actually an enemy. How can they be, when you don't know them? Here's the thing: I think our enemies aren't just the extreme examples that come to mind. They are the people who make us crazy. They annoy us with their insincere words or their rash behaviors. They're the bosses who call us into the office on holidays or the parents who gossip about our kids. These are the ones we enjoy the least and disagree with the most.

Whoever it is, Jesus told us they're the ones who will show us how real our faith is. The way we treat people is a report card on how far we've come in turning our beliefs into our biographies. Even when we're sure they're in the wrong, we have an opportunity to remember God's response to us when we were even more wrong: it was total grace. Loving our enemies is a hard test to pass. But when we do it right, we show ourselves to be eager students at the feet of a great and compassionate Teacher.

Who's the most difficult person for you to love these days?
What can you do to draw closer to loving them this week?

WE CAN'T TELL PEOPLE TO COME AS THEY ARE BUT INSIST THEY CHANGE BEFORE THEY ARRIVE. PEOPLE GROW WHERE THEY'RE LOVED.

God does not show favoritism.

ROMANS 2:11

I think there is a universal experience for people who go to church. At some point in the service a baby will start to cry. It's not the baby's fault; it's what babies do. But for everyone else, it starts a multistep process that generally goes like this: feel compassion for the child; realize it's just a child and try not to get annoyed; try to stay focused on the sermon; wonder why the child is still crying; wonder why the parent isn't taking the child away; think about how to make the parent cry; repent from being so annoyed that a baby is disrupting the service. Perhaps we need to chill out a little. After all, it was a baby who brought us together in the first place, two thousand years ago.

We need to give some thought to any number of reactions we have to the distractions. Perhaps it's how someone looks or the way they live their life or express their love that unbalances us. We would never tell a baby to figure out the whole "crying thing" before coming to church. But we tend to have higher expectations for adults. We have a habit of telling people to "come as they are," but seeing how we treat people who are still waiting for their growth spurt, I wonder if we really mean it. We want to include everyone, but we want to include them on our terms. We tell people to come as they are, but we insist they change before they arrive. If this is you, I've got two words for you to take to heart: *stop it*.

That's not who you are, it's not who we are, and it's definitely not who Jesus is. If Jesus were on the stage, He'd probably point us to the baby and encourage us to become more like him. He'd tell us to get that real with our feelings and that safe with Him and each other that we could express what's going on inside of us. Not only do we miss the spirit of Jesus when we insist people change in order to belong, but we miss out on the ride of getting to love people right where they are, with no qualifications. We're meeting people at the starting line, not the finish line. Let them know they're not just invited; they're welcome.

What would change about how you treat others if you accepted more about who they were, messes and all?

MARCH 4

GOD MAKES PEOPLE, AND PEOPLE MAKE ISSUES, BUT PEOPLE AREN'T ISSUES.

Be completely humble and gentle; be patient, bearing with one another in love. Make every effort to keep the unity of the Spirit through the bond of peace.

EPHESIANS 4:2–3

I've traveled to enough churches and conferences to hear plenty of Christian leaders refer to the "issues" their churches are facing. Sometimes they're real issues, like if a church lost their building in a fire and can't host two thousand people on Sundays. Or they don't have enough places to store all the food they want to give away. Those are issues.

But more often than not, issues mean that people who make us uncomfortable are coming to our churches and we don't know what to do about it. They're distracted by who they love or how they live or what they think or what they've done. We start thinking that the people are the issue because they are the ones telling us about the way we should vote or act or which gender gets to take the pulpit. Those aren't issues we're discussing; they're people.

Remember this: God makes people, people make issues, but people aren't issues. The person with an "issue" of [fill in the blank] who wants to lead the church in worship . . . that person isn't an issue. He or she is a person who probably loves Jesus more than I do and wants to use his or her gifts to serve the church. If you want to know more about what these people are thinking, just ask. Will it be uncomfortable? Sure. Will you be misunderstood? Maybe. Do it anyway.

Is there scripture that speaks to the topics you're thinking about? Terrific. Go figure that out for yourself. You're not the sheriff and they're not the enemy. You're two screwed-up people who desperately need Jesus.

These "issues" we talk about are only masquerading as people. Do yourself and the rest of us a favor and separate the two rather than merging the person and the issue into one. Does that mean everyone will agree with each other?

Of course not, but that's the not the point. Don't separate the truth of the scriptures from the issue of the day, but do separate the person from the issue. It'll take some humility and even more guts, but if we do, we'll learn a lot about love, and we'll welcome people who have perhaps felt far away from God.

Who's making you uncomfortable these days? Why?

MARCH 5

WE MAKE LOVING PEOPLE A LOT MORE COMPLICATED THAN JESUS DID.

Dear children, let us not love with words or speech but with actions and in truth.

1 JOHN 3:18

Have you ever had a friend or relative who "loves you so much" they can't have a single conversation without rehashing all the ways they think you're wrong? Or have you been told you're "loved so much" that you can't come around anymore? Or have you been denied something you really wanted and needed because you're "loved so much"? So often someone tells us they're doing it for our good when it feels like it's for their good.

For a lot of people, love looks a lot like telling us we're cut off until we fall in line. Some people call it "tough love," but I don't think Jesus had this phrase in His vocabulary.

We make loving people a lot more complicated than Jesus did. Jesus thought love meant a lot of things. It meant eating meals in people's homes, even when they were the kind of people who had been cut off by religious communities. It was touching the untouchable. It looked like making time for the people others passed by. Jesus wasn't scared away by those who had a reputation for being scandalous or unclean, because He saw through the labels that had been slapped on them and He believed in who they might become.

We'll miss the opportunity to see people grow if we won't meet them with love where they are. Sometimes it appears it's more important for us to be "right" than to be Jesus. No one has ever been argued into a change of heart. No one's ever been coerced into becoming more like Jesus. If you're hoping to spread the love of Jesus to those you think are wrong, try loving people like Jesus.

Next time you feel like you "love someone so much" that you want to give them a piece of your mind, try giving them a glass of strawberry juice instead. Love isn't as complicated as we make it. Just love people. Don't add any qualifiers.

What can you do this week to love someone with actions rather than words?

MARCH 6

WE WON'T BE NEW CREATIONS IF NOTHING EVER CHANGES.

Not that I have already obtained all this, or have already arrived at my goal, but I press on to take hold of that for which Christ Jesus took hold of me.

PHILIPPIANS 3:12

The Bible promises that when we believe in Jesus, He'll start the process of transformation to make us like Him. In a sense, that happens completely in an instant. But as every Jesus follower knows, the change takes a lifetime. This process needs some new space to breathe in your life. Think of it like a scrapbook for your soul. You can't be more like Jesus if you're spending your days staring at all the pictures of who you used to be.

One way to find space comes during a season called Lent, which is the forty days leading up to Easter. The theme of Lent is denying yourself something in order to focus more on Jesus. Maybe it's chocolate or the Xbox, shopping or lattes. Whatever it is, the purpose of Lent is quitting something to make space for Jesus. There might not be a natural connection between giving up chocolate and being transformed, but it's often exactly what happens. The urge to enjoy the thing we gave up reminds us why we gave it up in the first place.

We won't be new creations if we're clutching the things that were yesterday's news. Here's the fix: quit something today. Make some space in your life. I've never met anybody who made space in their life and started knocking off liquor stores. You might not know what will fill its place, but you'll come across beautiful opportunities when you have the space to engage them.

You don't have to wait until Easter to give something up. You don't need a season called "Lent." Just do it because it's Thursday. We all get one of those every week. Quit something today and then wait with expectation for God to show up and surprise you tomorrow.

What are you going to quit today?

WHAT BRINGS US TO TEARS WILL LEAD US TO GRACE. OUR PAIN IS NEVER WASTED.

Weeping may stay for the night, but rejoicing comes in the morning.

PSALM 30:5

Childhood for me was full of BB guns and climbing trees and scraped knees and "be back home in time for dinner." I never thought about utility bills or the mortgage payment or taxes or how much blue jeans cost. When I heard my dad mention he was "changing the oil" in the car, I hoped he was installing something to cause an oil slick behind him like Batman. Parents work hard to shield their kids from the "real world" until they're old enough to understand it. But eventually something happens. It might be a big disappointment that makes you feel like the real world is crashing in or an even bigger responsibility that causes you to play at a much higher level. It's all part of growing up, I suppose. I've never met a single person who's avoided this shift.

The weight of growing up can be immense. Balancing a life, a few relationships, a career, and the uncertainty of it all can feel overwhelming. I've come to understand, though, that what brings us to tears will lead us to grace. God takes the weights of the pressures and disappointments in our lives and turns these into the very things that anchor us in our faith.

We saw this happen in the life of Jesus. He experienced the same sadness we feel, and He endured it so we would know God can sympathize with our sadness. He doesn't judge us or expect us to bounce back from sorrow. He gets down into it with us.

The night before Jesus gave His life for us, He kneeled in a garden and cried as He prayed for the painful night to pass. But He didn't skip over it even though He could have. He knew grace was on the other side of His grief. When we can't see past our sorrows, we can trust God is traveling with us with His love.

What are you sorrowful about today?

MARCH 8

LET LOVE BE LOUDER THAN YOUR OPINIONS.

All the people saw this and began to mutter, "He has gone to be the guest of a sinner."

LUKE 19:7

I've made a habit of reaching out to people when they've stepped into some sort of firestorm on the internet. Maybe they caused it, or maybe people came after them for something they said. However it starts, it's rough to get lambasted by people online regardless of why it happened. I'll see a pastor say something controversial and instead of adding to all the noise already surrounding the comment, I'll send them a cake pop with no return address. It doesn't matter whether I agree with the person or not. I figure they're having a rough time and cake pops make tough days a little more tolerable.

I used to be concerned about being right, but now I just want to be more loving. We'll always disagree with some people, but we'll know we're growing when we're more concerned about the other person than the big disagreement. You'll know you're making progress when your love for people overshadows your opinions about them.

We have a tendency to huddle up with people who look like us and think like us. It makes sense. People who are like us validate our life choices and worldviews. Here's the problem: we miss out on the beautifully diverse ways people see the world when we only associate with "our people." Jesus' tribe was a mix of men, women, fisherman, scholars, and tax collectors. Good guys, bad guys, and undecided. They wouldn't have seen the world the same way, but they all knew love had the last word, and that was enough for them.

Next time someone pushes your buttons, send them a cake pop instead of an angry message. They've probably got enough critics out there, and like most of us, they could probably use a little more love than lecture. Let love be louder than your opinions.

What progress have you made lately in loving others?

LOVE DIFFICULT PEOPLE.

Let your conversation be always full of grace, seasoned with salt,
so that you may know how to answer everyone.

COLOSSIANS 4:6

Because I fly on planes so much, getting through security, boarding, buckling, and getting to where I'm going feels as normal as a morning routine getting ready for work. That's why I get a little rattled when the plane comes to a slow stop and the pilot's voice comes through the speakers: "Ladies and gentleman, all the gates are in use. Please remain seated and we'll update you when we have more information." It's like getting to your car to drive to work and seeing the flat tire. Life has messed with your routine, and you're instantly annoyed and deflated.

I think about those runway stops when I come across difficult people. They usually don't want to be a pain, and, like you and me, they want to be better. But they're stuck on the tarmac for a minute.

Each of us knows how complicated life can be. We know how quickly pressure builds with all the responsibilities that weigh us down. We're well aware of the unique ways those anxieties surface in our lives, especially when they seem to manage us more than we manage them. And we want people to show us grace. We want the benefit of the doubt.

Love difficult people. Give them the grace you want people to offer you when you stall on the tarmac. Give them your pretzels or cookies and remind yourself they've got a little farther to go, just like you.

What makes it difficult for you to love difficult people?

GOD NEVER RUNS OUT OF ROOM WHEN PEOPLE WANT TO BE NEAR HIM. THE MORE PEOPLE WHO COME, THE LARGER THE SPACE GETS.

The commander of the LORD's army replied, "Take off your sandals, for the place where you are standing is holy." And Joshua did so.

JOSHUA 5:15

Every few days there's another flare-up in what people call the "culture wars." Apparently you can load a weapon with an idea, aim it at someone you've never met, and it becomes a war.

What strikes me is how quickly something on the news becomes a flashpoint among people in our faith community. Within hours, pastors and thought leaders often publish articles, weighing in on whether somebody is biblically correct. These critics are usually anything but kind. It gets personal. It feels mean-spirited. I'm not sure if it's obvious to everyone or just a few how incredibly insecure these people are.

These tug-o-wars rarely reflect the kind of love Jesus urged us to embody. When we live in grace and walk in love, we can empathize with people and the circumstances that were the context for the problem. Most often I've thought the most honorable thing to do was to pass on jumping in. Something in us wants to take sides. Joshua had the same experience. He met an angel and asked which side the angel was on. "Neither. Take off your shoes" was the response.

Jesus didn't have to take sides. We don't either. He loved people on every side, and we can too. He didn't see issues; He saw people. He didn't see an article to be written; He saw a bad misstep to be rewritten. He stood with and for whoever was pushed to the edge and was rejected. Their acceptance didn't come at the expense of someone else. There has never been a capacity issue with God. The more who come, the bigger the room gets. Why do we feel so strongly about constructing walls between us to identify who's in and who's out? God sends out an invitation to every single person in the world and checks the mailbox every day to see who RSPV'd. Be one of them.

Next time you feel torn between two sides in a debate, remember God's love isn't as complicated as we make it—nor does it have the divisions we want to enforce.

What side have you taken that you need to let go of?

MARCH 11

GOD DIDN'T GIVE YOU INFLUENCE SO YOU'D LEAD PEOPLE BETTER; HE GAVE IT SO YOU'D LOVE PEOPLE MORE.

You, my brothers and sisters, were called to be free. But do not use your freedom to indulge the flesh; rather, serve one another humbly in love.

GALATIANS 5:13

Have you ever wondered what it would look like if Jesus wrote a book on leadership? The title might be something like *The Greatest Among You Shall Be the Least* or *Don't Worry About It*. Companies would have to invert all their org charts. The CEO would get a mop and bucket, and the janitor would get a corner office and maybe a jet. That's not the message you see in bookstores though. There are books about how to be more influential, make more money, innovate more quickly, manage more effectively. None of this is wrong. In fact, much good can come from organized, focused efforts. Here's the deal though. You can sum up leadership books with one phrase: *Here's how you crush it.* But even though Jesus was the most influential person to ever live, I don't think He would write that book. Here's why: God didn't give you influence so you'd lead people better. He gave it to you so you'd love people more.

Jesus' model for leadership was more interested in our laying our lives down for our friends than increasing the number of people who admire us from afar. Be famous with your family and friends. Leave the building of platforms to painters. Jesus was a carpenter who never cared about them. Any influence we've been given isn't meant to increase the size of our audience. It's so we can welcome even more people into the experience of God's love.

The best leaders don't care whether they're in positions of power. They don't care about their stats on social media or the praise they receive from people who follow them. They love without distraction or distinction and find their reward in the celebration of love rather than by chasing the approval of others. Of course they want to encourage people, because they love big and want that love to spread. But they're in it for others, not for their own egos.

If you find yourself in knots about whether you're leading people in the right direction, just look at whether you're the chief servant. If you're the big cheese, take a breath. Figure out how to become more downwardly mobile. Great leaders don't have time to think about themselves because they're too busy scheming ways to love other people and lift them up. Who can you do this for today? Blow their minds. Give them your office, maybe even your car. It'll sound crazy right up until you do it.

What kind of leader are you?

MARCH 12

WE WON'T BE REMEMBERED FOR WHAT WE SAID BUT FOR HOW AVAILABLE WE WERE.

Jesus said, "Let the little children come to me, and do not hinder them, for the kingdom of heaven belongs to such as these."

MATTHEW 19:14

Thirty years ago, I wrote a letter to a guy I admired a lot. He was one of the early contemporary Christian musicians: Keith Green. Of course, when we write someone who is well known, most of us think we'll never hear back from them. At best, I thought I might get a generic response from someone who worked for him. This isn't what happened. Instead, I got a personal letter back from Keith Green. His letter to me was only three sentences long, but the fact that he took the time to write to me made a lifelong impression.

Most of us undervalue the impact our words and our availability can have on the people around us. We don't get to decide how tall or short or rich or talented we are. I'm never the smartest guy in the room, but I learned a long time ago that I can be the most available one. I also learned from Keith Green the massive impact availability can have in someone's life. More than just incredibly validating, the act of extravagant availability says "I see you," "I hear you," "You matter."

Don't be stingy with your time; fill it with words that matter to someone. Release them into the world like they were hundreds of helium balloons and see what happens in the lives of the people around you. You'll be blown away by what you see.

I receive hundreds of e-mails a day. Anyone who e-mails me gets a response from me. Do you know why? Because thirty years ago, Keith Green got a letter from a young guy he didn't know and instead of ignoring it, or staffing it out, or blowing it off completely, he made himself available to send me three sentences. Honestly, I don't even remember what he wrote—but I remember this: I felt like a boss because he decided to be available to me.

So, what do you think? Is there someone you can be available to? You don't need to do it for a whole year. How about in the next ten minutes you don't make a big deal out of it but write somebody who has reached out to you a note? It only needs to be three sentences long.

Who do you need to be more available to?

WHEN IT'S MORE IMPORTANT TO WIN ARGUMENTS THAN LOVE PEOPLE, WE NEED TO START ALL OVER AGAIN WITH OUR FAITH.

A hot-tempered person stirs up conflict, but the one who is patient calms a quarrel.

PROVERBS 15:18

Whether it was at school with a teacher when we were young or at work after we got our first job, we've all worked with someone who made the fateful decision to go toe-to-toe with the boss in an argument. Bad call. We've cringed when they've launched the initial missile in the form of a confrontational question, declaring war. With raised eyebrows and glares traded with friends, we sit back and wait for the destruction as the two gunslingers square off and pull their jackets back, exposing their six shooters. Even if they're hands-down right, we all know there's a built-in risk when our coworker pokes the dragon. And if the disagreement escalates, we can watch our colleague both win the argument and lose the job in one glorious explosion of bad judgment.

Those moments remind us how foolish it is to try to win an argument instead of preserving a relationship. Don't get me wrong. I've been a lawyer for several decades. I've learned that whether it's with family, friends, or acquaintances online, we lose when we argue without love. Healthy disagreement can help us all grow, but when it's more important to win arguments than love people, we need to start all over again with our faith.

Jesus was right 100 percent of the time, but when people walked away, they felt seen and loved even when they were flat wrong. Jesus looked past disagreements to the question behind their questions. He saw the fears and insecurities that were driving the behaviors. He saw the need behind the façade. And when faced with the choice of winning an argument or loving a friend, He led with humility and let kindness do the talking.

Many of us spend much of our lives trying to win arguments that love won a long time ago. Who has been caught in the crossfire of a disagreement you've had with them? You know what to do next. Get love back in the middle of it, or take a walk around the block and start over again with your faith.

Who do you need to apologize to for arguing
with them? Who do you need to forgive?

EVERY TIME WE SEE PEOPLE AS ORDINARY, WE TURN THE WINE BACK INTO WATER.

What Jesus did here in Cana of Galilee was the first of the signs through which he revealed his glory; and his disciples believed in him.

JOHN 2:11

I've never met a new parent who isn't positive their baby is the cutest on planet earth. Even the so-so ones in their minds could rival George Clooney. The thing is this: parents give their baby the benefit of the doubt. Even the things that drive everyone else nuts they find worthy of celebrating. Parents see an emerging personality when the rest of us hear a scream. They see affection when the rest of us see a toothless child gnawing on a table leg. Every giggle, every curve of the mouth, every grip of the finger. We see squirming behaviors, they see Einstein in a diaper. Parents know something about their babies that some of us forget about ourselves. Parents are certain that their kid is a miracle.

We come across people at all different stages of life, and sometimes we decide that someone is ordinary based on what we observe. All that happened is this: we've missed their quiet moments of courage, their tender moments of inexplicable compassion, the sleepless nights filled with despair. We've caught them in chapter seven of a book with twenty-two chapters, and we evaluate the whole book without knowing how it began and where it will end.

Jesus worked countless miracles while He was here on earth. He brought people to life and brought life to groups of people. Just like the time He turned water into wine when a celebration had jumped the tracks, Jesus was always in the business of restoration. Nothing He touched remained ordinary, and His fingerprints are on every person who shows up on the scene.

Look closely at yourself. Think about some of the people you work with or live with. Look closely at them too. Every time we miss the miracle in ourselves or the people around us, every time we see people as ordinary, we turn the wine back into water.

What miracle is happening in the growth of someone around you that you haven't noticed before?

WHEN WE'RE DESPERATE FOR RIGHT ANSWERS, GOD DOESN'T JUST SEND US INFORMATION. HE SENDS US WISE FRIENDS.

Carry each other's burdens, and in this way you will fulfill the law of Christ.

GALATIANS 6:2

If you haven't hit a time in life when you're crawling beneath rock bottom, you probably know someone who has. It happens when you're married to the love of your life and divorce papers arrive. It happens when the faith that stitched you together begins to unravel. It happens when someone you've loved leaves you or breaks an important promise. Without warning, the lights go out inside of us, we have no candles to light, and we don't know how to walk in the dark.

When our lives fall apart, we don't need trite answers; we need a couple of solid friends. We need presence. We need someone holding our hand for the diagnosis or staying by our side when our big mistake goes public—and viral. We need a friend when we courageously head to rehab to address the problem or to court to receive the verdict. Occasionally we need people to gently ask us the right questions, but more often than not we need friends who will give us a hug and then listen with big ears and seemingly endless amounts of time.

When we're looking for answers, sometimes God sends us wise friends. When He doesn't tell us which way to go, He'll bring people to go with us instead. It's important to know what to look for when we feel like we're falling apart, because God doesn't often send what we think we need. He sends us what He knows we need.

Who's hurting around you? Is it possible God could send you to love them without having you say a word or make a suggestion? Who has been there for you during an uncertain time? Drop them a note. Let them know it mattered. Next time your world is turned upside down, look for friends instead of answers. God's lifeboats usually come in the form of people.

What can you do for someone today whose life is unraveling?

GRACE DRAWS A CIRCLE AROUND EVERYONE AND SAYS WE'RE IN.

Then the master told his servant, "Go out to the roads and country lanes and compel them to come in, so that my house will be full."

LUKE 14:23

You learn a lot about adulthood when you plan a wedding. At first, it's so exciting you wish you could bottle it up in a snow globe. Engagement rings, parties, and toasts. What's not to like? Everything is so blissful. Then you start to plan—photographer, venue, caterer, tuxedos and a wedding dress. It turns out getting married can be quite expensive. The wedding ceremony is just the beginning too. Next, you hear the cost of a plate of food. Corn dogs and fries start to sound pretty good when the reception in your imagination looks more like a room full of price tags instead of friends.

If the engagement survives all of this, you sit down with your sweetheart to make an invitation list. You envision a reunion with your childhood best friends and college buddies, but the other person insists on all the second cousins. You have to make decisions between your fiancé's mother's book club and your brother's girlfriend. There are the people you really want to invite and those you feel obligated to invite. What started out as bonding time turns into a sad ranking of the people in your lives.

God's family works on an entirely different system. He's planning a celebration for the whole world, and He's got an unlimited number of seats. There's no budget and no tab that runs too high. It's already settled: there's enough room and more than enough love for everyone.

We're wrong when we're tempted to think we'll be a guest of honor with God just because we do something nice or sacrificial for someone. The corollary is just as wrong when we think we'll get seated at the table reserved for the troublemakers and ne'er-do-wells just because we've messed up. Because Jesus stood in our place, every seat at God's table is reserved for His family. We just need to decide if we want to come. Don't rule yourself out because you think you've messed up the celebration or the planning. Grace draws a circle around everyone and says we're in.

Who is missing at your family table?

MARCH 17

DON'T BE "RIGHT." BE JESUS.

These people come near to me with their mouth and honor me
with their lips, but their hearts are far from me. Their worship of
me is based on merely human rules they have been taught.

ISAIAH 29:13

We all know what it's like to watch board game night with friends devolve into
civil war. The beginning is always promising: someone brings up Pictionary
or Charades and you split into teams, ready to laugh. Then it all takes a turn
when someone with a competitive streak takes charge. Maybe they were cut
from their middle school basketball team or have an axe to grind because they
lost a board game when they were five. Whatever it is, the competitiveness fills
the air in the room like a thick fog.

Rules emerge that no one knew about. Even the rules have rules. It's no
fun anymore. It quickly becomes obvious to everyone that being right isn't as
important as being together. What happened? It's simple. The purpose of the
game is to enjoy one another, not to win. If someone takes it too seriously, they
ruin it for everyone.

Life works the same way. We can be so consumed with being "right" that
we miss the opportunity to just be together. Humble people stay quiet when
speaking up might cost them a friend. They know life isn't a competition.
There's no winner or loser in God's family because everyone has access to
infinite love and grace. There are no more chips we can collect or play money
to hoard. Don't trade a dozen great relationships for a few unverified rules.

Here's a pro tip: Don't be "right"; be Jesus. Be the one who brings people
together and is self-aware enough to know that the purpose of our lives is to
lift everyone up, not put people down.

**What would change if you cared more about
being loving than being right?**

MARCH 18

IF OUR HEADS ARE FULL AND OUR HEARTS ARE EMPTY, WE'LL JUST TIP OVER.

Come, let us bow down in worship, let us kneel before the LORD our Maker; for he is our God and we are the people of his pasture, the flock under his care.

PSALM 95:6-7

Nothing says relaxation like a slow cruise in a canoe or kayak on a windless summer day. Sometimes Sweet Maria and I sit on our dock in Canada as campers from a Young Life camp next door paddle by. We underhand-throw saltwater taffy to the ones who are close to shore and try to land it in their vessels. For those who are a little farther out, we have slingshots to get the taffy out to them. There's a big difference between being loved on and being shot at. We've all experienced a little of both.

The thing about canoes is this. They're tippy. The same can be true of us. They say when you feel like you might tip over in a canoe, you can avoid it by getting down on your knees and leaning forward. The tip happens when your center of gravity gets too high. The same is true of us. If our heads are full and our hearts are empty, we'll tip over.

The way to avoid a fall in life is pretty similar to the old advice I got from camp leaders in canoes years ago: get on your knees. When we're willing to humble ourselves and get low, we see ourselves and others from another perspective. We listen. We pray. We're able to hear wisdom and receive it instead of getting defensive and taking a dive.

We won't get very far in life on information alone. Eventually we'll realize we were wrong about things we thought we knew, and we'll wish we'd just loved people instead of trying to prove them wrong. Don't lose your center of gravity as you travel through life. Pack light, stay low, keep paddling, and let love lead the way.

**What happens to you when you humble
yourself and get on your knees?**

MARCH 19

IF WE AVOID BEING IDENTIFIED WITH PEOPLE WE DISAGREE WITH, WE'VE TRADED IN GOD'S BRAND OF LOVE FOR POPULARITY.

Jesus replied, "Let us go somewhere else—to the nearby villages— so I can preach there also. That is why I have come."

MARK 1:38

A few of my best friends happen to be creative geniuses. Think Einstein with a paintbrush or a Moleskine making word-pictures. I've learned a lot about the power of well-told stories from them, but even better, I've watched them live beautiful lives. They've taught me we're all constantly telling a story with the things we share online, the people we hang out with, the way we engage or react to the events around us, and the words we use. Brands are what cowboys put on cattle, not what we call our love. The way they engage their lives is more like a watermark. It's something you only really see when you hold it up to the light.

These days, I pay more attention to people's patterns than their statements. Some are like an all-night television show—all theology all the time. Others focus on business and making money. We each have our own metrics for how we define success and contribution to the world.

Have you noticed that someone will say something a certain group thinks is great but another group will tear it to shreds? Or maybe someone will have a bad day, and their tribe will send love and support for all to see, but those who have a different worldview are slow to encourage. They might even be a little combative or give off the impression that they are quietly delighting in the headwinds someone else is facing. It goes beyond these things.

Jesus invited us to walk in a different way. He wasn't concerned with who people saw Him associate with. He was an image bearer, not an image maker. He was seen with religious leaders and loose women at the same events. He didn't care about money or status. He cared about the state of people's hearts. He showed us how to tear down the walls that divide us.

If we avoid being identified with people we disagree with, we join the crowds. We've traded in God's brand of love for popularity. We're just one more voice calling for Barabas. Be like Jesus instead. Stand in silence if you need to, but offer words of hope to all, whether you agree with them or not. Jesus was more concerned with seeing other people than managing how they saw Him.

**What would be different if you cared less about
your image and more about loving others?**

LOVE HAS THE KIND OF POWER THAT CRITICISM ONLY WISHES IT HAD.

Better a patient person than a warrior, one with self-control than one who takes a city.

PROVERBS 16:32

My sons, Richard and Adam, used to be wild boys. Nothing's really changed, and today they're wild men. Now that they're grown, their love of adventure makes them a great team. But when they were little, they did what all siblings do—they fought with each other. We hid all the sharp objects in the house, knowing they might be used. It usually started over toys or who was going to take the lowest branch first in a race to climb the tree. Fighting can be cute when it involves plastic trucks or barricades made of pillows. Our boys eventually grew out of it. Some people don't.

When our boys couldn't resolve an issue on their own, I would swoop in to pick them up, one in each arm. As their dad, I would try to approach the moment with tenderness and strength to bring a sense of peace, order, and calm in the midst of the meltdown.

I often remember those days when I see people leaning toward criticism. Like little boys pulling hair and yanking toys, unfettered criticism doesn't show strength; it's evidence of weakness and insecurity. It masks itself as strength because it wants to establish dominance at the expense of relationship. It comes out swinging and yelling but is as transparent as it is ineffectual. Real strength builds up; it doesn't tear down.

Love has the kind of power that criticism only wishes it had. Where criticism attacks, love mends.

Sometimes love shows us our blind spots. Young and old alike have something to learn. But love is always humble and always kind. It always wants the best for other people, and it's never defensive. Love sees who people are becoming even if they're not there yet.

Next time you're tempted to lash out, go in for the hug instead. Even if your feelings have you all wound up, gestures of love toward others can bring down your blood pressure too.

What kind gesture can you give to someone you've been harsh with today?

MARCH 21

LOVE PEOPLE LIKE THE RULES WE'VE
MADE UP DON'T APPLY.

Be devoted to one another in love. Honor one another above
yourselves.

ROMANS 12:10

Birthdays are the only time we celebrate people just because they exist. They don't have to do anything special that day—no book launch or graduation or job promotion or space shot. We celebrate them because they were born.

I love birthdays so much that I've started doing away with the birthday system where we only get to celebrate people one time a year. Think about it: Jesus performed thirty-seven miracles, depending on how you count them. Our friends are the thirty-eighth miracle. Now, that's something to celebrate. Those closest to us are a gift every day—fall, winter, summer, and spring. They make bad days more bearable with their comfort and attention. They make sweet moments all-out celebrations because their presence amplifies our joy. Whose idea was it to only set aside one day a year to bake them cakes and shower them with gifts?

That's why I make it a point to send friends balloons on random Tuesdays or flowers at the end of a mundane workday or a package full of surprises, just because. Sometimes I throw a dinner party with Secret Santa gifts in July. I'll get on the grill and Sweet Maria will bake a cake and we'll shower a friend with affection because they were born and they bring us such joy. It's not to cheer them up or affirm their achievements; it's just to tell them they're a gift to the world.

Break the rules that say you have to contain your love to specific days. Pick a person and celebrate them today. We don't need to wait for permission to throw a party.

Who can you celebrate today? What will you do?

MARCH 22

WE DON'T NEED TO TRY TO CONTROL THE WORK GOD IS DOING IN OTHER PEOPLE'S LIVES.

We are God's handiwork, created in Christ Jesus to do good works, which God prepared in advance for us to do.

EPHESIANS 2:10

One of my best friends from college turned out to be an amazing artist. We gave him a hard time in school, telling him he'd always have a place to stay on our couch or in our basements. Then he surprised us all and made it as an artist! People pay top dollar for his paintings, and his work shows up these days in museums all over the country.

When I look at his paintings, I think about where on the canvas he started and whether the picture resembles the one he imagined. I marvel over the way he could capture a moment in his imagination and then move his hands and brush and put it on display for the whole world to see. I don't think I will ever understand how he does it.

I often think about what he'd say if I walked up midway through the process and told him he was going about it all wrong—that he needed more purple instead of red or swirlies instead of dabs with the brush. It would be ludicrous because I'm not the one who imagined the painting. I know very little about how to make the strokes that move an image from his mind to a canvas. The truth is, I make a better observer than artist.

It must look a little like me telling my friend how to hold the paintbrush when we try to control the work God is doing in other people's lives. He created them, and He knows who they're becoming. He's got a plan in place to turn them into a masterpiece, and He's got the brushes He needs to make it happen. God sees the whole picture when He looks at His creation, and He knows exactly what we need when we need it.

Have you been reaching for the brushes in someone else's life? Are you racing God to finish the canvas He's painting in your life? Take a breath. God's going to do what only He can do both in our lives and in the lives of the people around us. He doesn't need another artist to finish His work. His hope is that we'll delight in watching Him as He completes what He's started.

What is God doing in your life or in others that will end up being beautiful and good?

DON'T SEPARATE INTO GROUPS WHAT GOD SAID WAS A FAMILY.

After this I looked, and there before me was a great multitude that no one could count, from every nation, tribe, people and language, standing before the throne and before the Lamb.

REVELATION 7:9

My friend, Ben, is an amazing musician. He writes songs and travels around the country playing the piano and jumping on stages with his guitar. Maria and I go to his shows every chance we get; we sing the words to his songs we've memorized, which is all of them, and we elbow each other at the first note of our favorites.

I've noticed concerts bring people together like few things do these days. You'll see guys in tailored suits squished between women wearing bandanas and cutoff jeans. You could be next to someone you've always had a hard time with and still smile and sing without even thinking about it.

I think shows like my friend Ben's give us a little glimpse of heaven. God never intended for us to separate into groups; He calls us a family. He doesn't want a bunch of people going it alone either. Think symphony, not soloist. He said we were brothers and sisters, that we belong to one another and we don't need to settle for just tolerating one another. Sure, family members don't always see eye to eye and there are times we might not even choose one another; but still, try. Is it going to be tough at times? Of course it will. Is it possible you'll take a hit? You will. Do it anyway.

It's okay to surround yourself with people who are loving and supportive and easy to be with, but huddles are best when they're open for more people to join. The next time you have a tough run-in with a family member or an old friend from high school on the internet, go to a concert with them, tap your feet, sing the words you know, and don't worry about the ones you don't. Don't let the difficulties you've had with someone keep you from singing along together.

Who are you drawn to even though they're so different from you? What can you do to get closer to them?

WHEN YOU LOVE JESUS, YOU'LL DISCOVER YOU LOVE BEING LAST IN LINE.

So the last will be first, and the first will be last.

MATTHEW 20:16

Could you imagine what people would think if we had a couple of shouting matches on the fringes of the church parking lot? We should have plenty of arguments at church; let's just argue about the right stuff.

Maybe folks would be more interested in filling spots inside if we arm wrestled for the worst parking spots on the outside. We're all creatures of habit. These routines and patterns can free us up from making many of the distracting decisions we would otherwise need to be tracking. This can be good, but there's also a back side to that wave. We get comfortable. We become grafted into our routine. We're on autopilot. We park in the same spot, occupy the same pew, go to the same restaurant afterward for lunch. When any of that gets disrupted, we act like it's an assault on our rights. If we're not careful, our preferences will become the most important thing to us, and it will show. Here's the problem: when we want everyone to defer to us on Sundays, we abandon altogether the whole revolution Jesus started. "Whoever wants to become great among you must be your servant, and whoever wants to be first must be your slave," He said.

There's no middle ground with Jesus on this one. Like He said time and time again, to truly follow Him is to get familiar with taking cuts to the back of the line, to coming in last. We ought to be fighting to get the worst parking spots at our churches, not the best ones. And not let it end there. That's what people are hoping to see when we talk about the kind of love Jesus came to give—selfless, irrational, sacrificial love.

How can you get extravagant with your love today? It starts with mixing up some of the routines we've become used to. Every day, we get another chance to shake up the status quo and extend love's border in our lives. Here's how you win in Jesus' reverse economy: Don't settle for the best spots. Fight for the worst parking spots.

How can you get extravagant with your love today?

HUMBLE VOICES ALWAYS CARRY THE FARTHEST.

Humble yourselves before the Lord, and he will lift you up.

JAMES 4:10

Some of my sweetest memories include friends playing music on the dock at our lodge in Canada. It's still light at 10:00 p.m. during the late summer evenings. With the sun and the moon hanging together, we huddle around when our friends begin to sing. They'll close their eyes and sing from their hearts as tears stream down all our faces.

What makes these times even more magical is the way the soft voices carry for miles, bouncing off the mountains and echoing into the night. Who knew nature had its own surround-sound system?

Those intimate moments always remind me that humble voices carry the farthest in the world. It's never the person making a statement on a soapbox that sticks with us. They might get our attention in the moment or capture the news cycle for a day, but their moments are brief and their influence quickly fades to silence.

Humble people speak love whenever they see an open heart, whether it's on a stage or by a hospital bed. They speak their words quietly, whether they are in the limelight or in a dark night. They don't need a megaphone because their actions amplify their words and people are drawn to their message, which can be heard from afar even when it's whispered. Because they're faithful in small ways, their influence reaches farther than a viral video ever could.

God has a way of making humble voices travel far. No matter where we are, God amplifies true and kind voices who confidently speak the language of love into the world. Don't be loud; be humble. Why? If you want to reach the whole world with your message, humble voices always carry the farthest.

In what ways is God inviting you to step more fully into humility today?

MARCH 26

EVERY UNSELFISH ACT OF LOVE
WHISPERS GOD'S NAME.

Truly I tell you, this poor widow has put more into the treasury
than all the others. They all gave out of their wealth; but she, out of
her poverty, put in everything—all she had to live on.

MARK 12:43–44

Have you ever been to a fancy fundraiser where they put the names of donors
on the big screen as the money comes in? If you send a text with your credit-
card number, your name and the amount you gave will be announced—and if
there's not applause, you can be sure the whole crowd knows. I get why we do
this, and I'm sure the live reports generate excitement around giving, but Jesus
told His friends a story about a different way.

He was at the temple when a bunch of rich people paraded to the front to
give large gifts. Everyone saw what they had done. Trailing behind them came
a poor widow who humbly placed two copper coins in the treasury. No one
even noticed—except Jesus. "This widow has given more than all the others,"
Jesus said. "They gave out of their wealth, but out of her poverty, she's given
everything she had to live on."

Jesus knew that in God's economy a small, humble gift given in secret goes
further than a big check written with the hope of being seen. The size of the
gift doesn't matter as much as the heart behind it, because God doesn't need
our stuff—He just wants our hearts.

God delights in our secret sacrifices. He created us with the hope that we'd
join Him in restoring all that's gone wrong with the world, wherever we find
ourselves. He uses the big, grand things everyone knows about, but He also
uses the barely seen. Don't worry about the size of your gifts or whether people
will know you did it for Jesus. Every unselfish act of love whispers God's name.

What small, humble gift can you give to someone today?

LABELS ARE HELPFUL FOR GROCERIES, NOT PEOPLE.

Here is my servant whom I have chosen, the one I love, in whom I delight.

MATTHEW 12:18

When a trial lawyer is picking a jury, there's not a lot of information to go on. How people dress, the inflection of their voices, the look on their faces, how they sit in a chair. It's not much, but that's what they use to figure people out.

We all do the same. Have you ever taken a sip of a drink expecting it to be one flavor but it turns out to be something else? If you're a die-hard Coca-Cola fan, you know what I'm talking about.

Sometimes it's good to know what's inside the bottle before you drink it, and that's where labels come in. Labels give us a trustworthy starting point and help us batch the little details of our lives in useful ways. They help adjust our expectations and find what we're looking for within the brackets of our desires.

Pizza = cheesy, delicious, guilty pleasure. Kale = cardboard, disgusting, not food. Ice cream = breakfast food, right?

It's all well and good scrounging through the fridge. The trouble starts, though, when we do the same with people. Our minds want to kick into human label makers. Without realizing what we're doing, we can find ourselves running around putting stickers on all the people we know (and some we don't know!).

Lazy, nerdy, avoidable; charming, the funny guy, full of themselves; pretty, popular, will say no to promposal.

Labels can be helpful, but when we let other people decide who we are, that's when we need some adjustments. We can't be poured into convenient identity containers. We're people after all—each one of us expertly crafted to uniquely display aspects of an immeasurable love.

We can't stop other people from making judgments about us based on very little information, but we can pump the brakes when it comes to doing it ourselves. Let's stop giving control to other people to figure us out. Leave sizing people up to lawyers and undertakers. Don't let other people decide who you are. Perhaps one of the best ways to start is to rip off the stickers we've placed on other people.

Whose voice is loudest when it comes to telling you who you are? What's different between their voice and God's?

NO ONE'S GOING TO BELIEVE ANY OF OUR ANSWERS IF WE DON'T LET THEM KNOW WE HAVE QUESTIONS TOO.

When Jesus saw her weeping, and the Jews who had come along
with her also weeping, he was deeply moved in spirit and troubled.

JOHN 11:33

Most people of faith go through times of questioning when the foundation cracks and we brace ourselves, waiting to see if the whole structure will crumble. Maybe a college student gets challenged by a respected professor. Or perhaps you see the behavior of someone who has been saying their faith is important to them and are so disappointed you might just walk away. You don't always hear people voicing their uncertainties, because the people up front who appear to have it together also seem to have all the answers. But doubt finds each of us at different times and in different ways.

Most of us are constantly surrounded by unanswered questions. We wonder whether our kids will make it through their battle with addiction or what we'll find on the other side of stage-four cancer. We don't want someone else's answers, and we don't need someone's opinion, because more opinions just create more anxiety. What we really want to know is that we're not alone. We need to know someone else has endured nights of barely breathing and they kept waking up to new mornings.

Over the years, I've learned the most compassionate response we can give someone who's not okay is, "That must be really difficult." That, plus a hug. It doesn't resolve their question or relieve their fear, but it reminds them we're in this together. It removes the sense of shame we feel when we struggle in secret and removes the façade of needing to pretend we have the simple answer to really complex issues. Just enter into the ambiguity with the hurting people around you. Admit that you don't know what they are feeling, but you do know you're with them. They're not looking for a quick answer; they need a good friend. No one's going to believe any of our answers if we don't let them know we have a couple questions too.

**Who around you needs a hug and a
reminder that you're with them?**

THE WORLD WILL KNOW WHAT WE REALLY BELIEVE BY SEEING WHO WE AUTHENTICALLY LOVE.

As Jesus walked beside the Sea of Galilee, he saw Simon and his brother Andrew casting a net into the lake, for they were fishermen. "Come, follow me," Jesus said, "and I will send you out to fish for people." At once they left their nets and followed him.

MARK 1:16-18

Did you know there are churches in cities across the country that meet outside, in parks and under bridges? It's true. These people know church walls can sometimes keep people out, so they take Jesus' message to the streets. If you show up on a Sunday morning, you'll see homeless people leading worship and kids eating hotdogs during the sermon. Some are sitting and others are standing. There's no separate room for the babies who cry or the deeply wounded souls who forgot how to. No one tells the people who come to be quiet because it's more like a celebration than a study hall.

Jesus said following Him meant going where He went, and He went to people who couldn't make it to Him. People with criminal records were welcomed with compassion. Desperate men and loose women were accepted. Those with disabilities weren't shunned because they were different. Groups of people who were typically excluded from community found a safe place to be themselves in Jesus.

If we look around our lives and only find a crowd of people like us, it's time to make some changes. Sure, we could love people by creating a special group for them that meets on Tuesday nights when the church is otherwise empty, but why not grab your knees, do a cannonball, and join them? Imagine what would happen if we changed the comfortable rhythms of our lives to include some new friends, peers, and people we've merely been polite to while staying distant from.

The world will know what we really believe when they see who we authentically love. If it's our buildings that keep people out, let's get rid of the buildings.

If it's membership that is creating a divide, lose it and let everyone in. God always seems to show us the most from the most unlikely of teachers. Who can teach you more about something you're sure you already understand? Which new friend would show others what you believe? Go find those people.

What would be different in your life if you truly loved people who others assumed were far off from God?

TELL PEOPLE WHO THEY ARE, NOT WHAT THEY WANT. WE DO THE LOVING; GOD DOES THE GUIDING.

The virgin will conceive and give birth to a son, and they will call him Immanuel (which means "God with us").

MATTHEW 1:23

When I turned seventeen, I decided to drop out of high school and head to Yosemite for a life in the mountains. I didn't have a job or a particular plan in mind, but I had a 1971 Volkswagon bug and a tank full of gas. On my way out of town, I stopped by my friend Randy's house to say goodbye. He'd been a Young Life leader, and I wanted to thank him for looking out for me through the years.

Much to my surprise, Randy asked if he could go with me to Yosemite. On the road, Randy didn't say anything about sticking it out until I finished high school. He didn't tell me what a bad idea it was to drop out or tell me I would need a stable income to make rent and that finishing high school would probably help with that. He just kept saying he was "with me" no matter what I did. When God sent Jesus to be with us, He said to name Him Immanuel—which means, "God with us."

I had gone to every store and pancake house in Yosemite Valley at least twice looking for a job, and no one was hiring. After a few nights camping, I had run out of money. What I thought was going to be the rest of my life turned into a three-day camping trip. With a lot of disappointment, I told Randy I might as well head back to finish high school. Do you know what he told me? Simply this: "I'm with you."

Randy figured out something a lot of us are still trying to get a handle on. Throughout our entire trip to Yosemite, Randy told me who I was instead of telling me what I should want. He told me I was his friend and he was "with me." These days when I'm trying to figure out how to help someone in need, I think of Randy's example. He was content to be with me, rather than busying himself trying to educate me or change me.

Who is someone you can just be "with" today?

QUIT SETTLING FOR A REASONABLE FAITH.

He said: "Truly I tell you, unless you change and become like little children, you will never enter the kingdom of heaven."

MATTHEW 18:3

There's this moment plenty of people face when they get to be around forty years old. They stop and ask themselves, "Is this it?" The routines of life and all that they've worked toward start to feel a little empty. At least it's not living up to the hype and their expectations. Facing a future filled with several decades of monotony is paralyzing. It's not what we imagined when we were kids.

Some people buy motorcycles or get new tattoos when the boredom settles in. Some get into trouble and ruin the few beautiful things they had going for them. What I did was this: I traded in my office in a downtown Seattle high-rise for a spot at Tom Sawyer Island.

We don't feel the dull ache of boredom because we don't have options. We feel the ache because we've forgotten the magic in everyday moments. Here's the good news. We're all just one good decision and a trip to Tom Sawyer Island away from the life we can still remember and really want.

God put us on a playground with billions of people to hang out with. He told us we could be a part of His plan to make every person feel seen and celebrated. He gave us cotton candy and Ferris wheels, pianos and people who make music. He gave us imaginations so we could dream things no one's ever done and a sense of humor so we'd find delight in everything.

Sure, quitting my own law firm and moving to Tom Sawyer Island was a bad economic move, but it was a great "new-creation" decision. Don't miss the chance to make yours today. Take the shot. If your faith feels boring, it's probably because you lost your sense of wonder a while back. Quit settling for a reasonable faith. Trade it in for something far better: faith like a child's.

What could innocent, childlike faith do to change your perspective today?

APRIL 1

LOVE COSTS EVERYTHING. WE DON'T NEED TO HAGGLE OVER THE PRICE.

"Truly I tell you," Jesus said to them, "no one who has left home or wife or brothers or sisters or parents or children for the sake of the kingdom of God will fail to receive many times as much in this age, and in the age to come eternal life."

LUKE 18:29–30

When you find the perfect house and you're ready to close the deal, you know there are two different prices on the home: the one that's listed and the one they'll accept. If you have a good Realtor, you can play hardball and walk away with enough money left over to put a treehouse in the backyard. We all know this is how it works: people aim for the high price and predictably settle for less.

But when it comes to love, Jesus settled the question. He was approached by a guy who wanted to know what it looked like to follow Him. The guy wanted to become love. Jesus told Him to follow all the commandments. This guy said he had, so Jesus said if he really wanted to go all in with love, he had to sell everything he had and give the money to the poor. Well the guy, who had never broken a law, thought about how much he had and walked away sad because he couldn't give it all.

Going all in on love isn't like buying a house. We can't make a deal and get away with giving less. Love's asking price is everything, and there's no negotiation. I don't know if Jesus meant we have to go sell our stuff and give it away today, because He also told us to cook meals for people in our homes, which means we can hold on to our houses. But the heart of His message is clear: love costs everything. We don't get to haggle over the price.

What has God asked you to surrender
that you keep holding on to?

JESUS DIDN'T WANT US TO JUST BE BELIEVERS. HE WANTED US TO BE PARTICIPANTS.

Whatever you do, work at it with all your heart, as working for the Lord, not for human masters.

COLOSSIANS 3:23

When my kids were young, they loved to read *Choose Your Own Adventure* books. They would speed read up to the points where they were faced with a choice that would alter the direction of the story based on what they decided. They would make a choice, turn to the page where their new storyline took off, and then they'd speed read again to get to their next big choice.

I got into the books, too, because you get to feel like you're participating in the story. We all like that feeling where we're not just passive readers waiting to see what happens; we're characters, we're protagonists, we're heroes. We all like to shape the story while we're living it.

These books mirror the story God is writing through us. We might not encounter obstacles on exotic islands like the kids in the stories, but we face choices every day that move the narrative in one direction or another. We're active participants in the story God's writing. We're not just observers. We've been invited to be active participants.

None of us will know all the outcomes until the end. It's a good bet we'll find out God has made right some of the wrong choices we made along the way. Some of the choices we thought were right will no doubt turn out to be wrong. Here's the thing: Jesus didn't want us to just be believers; He wanted us to be participants. God set His story in motion with us in mind, inviting us to join with Him as He moves to bring restoration to everything around us.

Don't settle for being a passive observer in the story God is writing around you. Jump in the action right where you are and take note of what happens.

In what ways is God inviting you to be more of an active participant in what He's doing?

APRIL 3

LOVING PEOPLE THE WAY JESUS DID WILL TAKE LEAPS, NOT STEPS.

You still lack one thing. Sell everything you have and give to the poor, and you will have treasure in heaven. Then come, follow me.

LUKE 18:22

Confession: I'm a little ambivalent about personality tests. I don't mean the kind that tell you if you're a Griffyndor or a Slytherin or what your rapper name would be. At the time I was writing this devotional, one test called the Enneagram was all the rage. People can't tell if it's a cult or something. People are always asking me what "my number" is or they're telling me what my number is, *they're just sure of it.* While I'm not against a little self-understanding, knowing more about yourself should never head-fake you into thinking you've become more like Jesus.

A test might help you take steps toward a healthier and more well-balanced life. But loving people the way Jesus did will take leaps, not steps.

Jesus said to take all our time, our energy, our dreams, and our things and to handle them like gifts for others to unwrap. He invited us into a selfless way of life that changes where we live, how we live, and who we love. Loving like Jesus means having a spirit of welcome for everyone—even the people who talk too loud and drink straight from the carton in our fridge. It means our first response is yes when we're asked to help someone move on a Saturday morning.

I think if Jesus came up with a personality test, it would ask all about how we love sacrificially. And if we're looking for something to improve or a way to grow, Jesus' life is the only test we need.

What feels uncomfortable inside you as you ponder going all in with Jesus?

APRIL 4

I'D RATHER HAVE AN IMPROBABLE FAITH THAN A PREDICTABLE LIFE.

I know that you can do all things; no purpose of yours can be thwarted.

JOB 42:2

When my kids were in grade school, they came up with the idea to write to all the presidents, prime ministers, and dictators in the world to ask if they could come and see them. They wanted to take what Jesus said about being peacemakers literally, and they thought there would be more peace in the world if they could get leaders who didn't get along to connect. They decided to ask these leaders what they were hoping for, so they could share those hopes with other leaders to clear up any misunderstandings.

Wanting to encourage their ambition, I said, "That's a great idea!" So our kids sent letters to every world leader. It turns out the kids wrote to hundreds of them.

We never thought any of the world leaders would respond, but sure enough, invitations started arriving. We got the cheapest airplane tickets we could find and our family sat down for meals and meetings with presidents and princes. We all learned so much. But I learned the most about faith from my kids. I learned anything can happen if you can dream it. We need to do more than dream it up, though. We need to lick the stamp, pick up the phone, or get on the airplane. Even when your hopes seem unlikely, I learned it's better to have an improbable faith than a predictable life.

It's easy to fall into the boredom of a routine life, where your thoughts revolve around your waistline, your job title, or the number on your bank statement. But kids remind us the only thing standing between our current life and the adventure we want is faith. Big faith risks making big requests.

Don't settle for a life that is just like your neighbor's; risk believing Jesus meant what He said about our doing greater things than Him.

If you're willing to take a risk, buckle up because you're about to see some things start happening in your life.

What call are you going to make today?
Who are you going to write to?

GOD GIVES US THREE POWERFUL WORDS: *BE. NOT. AFRAID.*

Suddenly Jesus met them. "Greetings," he said. They came to him, clasped his feet and worshiped him. Then Jesus said to them, "Do not be afraid. Go and tell my brothers to go to Galilee; there they will see me."

MATTHEW 28:9–10

The disciples were dejected in the days after Jesus died. I can understand why. They had gone all in banking on Him to be the Savior who would rescue them. But after beautiful miracles came a betrayal and a violent crucifixion. They were all out of hope. Sure, they knew He said it was all part of the plan: He would be torn down and built up again three days later. But the gap between the grief and the miracle was long enough for them to lose sight of hope, and they rewrote the story in the dark. This happens to all of us at one time or another.

They were huddled in the second story of a house with the doors locked when Jesus appeared. Wait, what? He understood their sadness and sense of loss, but He told them two powerful words: *"fear not."* Even after the lights had gone out, He told them not to be afraid.

Few times are as loaded with negative energy as the space between bad news and good. It doesn't matter what the doctor says after he's told you something's wrong; you just want hopeful test results. No kind words bring reassurance after you're let go at work unless it's someone else saying you've been hired. Even if you know there's light on the other side of the storm, it's lonely to travel in the dark.

When the lights have gone out and you can't find your way, remember the end of the story has already been written. What difficulty are you facing? Have you been hoping for something and were let down? Be not afraid. Even if you don't feel like hope is here right now, it's waiting for you just up the road.

What are you afraid of today?

A BODY THAT HONORS EVERY PART REFLECTS HOW GOD LOVES US.

Now you are the body of Christ, and each one of you is a part of it.

1 CORINTHIANS 12:27

Isn't it weird how you barely remember you have a pinky finger until you sprain it? After years of taking it for granted, suddenly your pinky makes itself known every time you pull out a credit card or reach for a fork. It reminds you every part of your body matters. What about a stubbed toe? Isn't it amazing how a one-inch toe can bring a six-foot man to his knees?

God says we're His body here on earth. It sounds strange to think that we'd be standing in for an infinite God, but it all makes sense when you think about how He set things up. He uses small things just like they were big things. Fingers, toes, you, me. Jesus had to go for a while, so He told us He would leave His Spirit with us and we would do the things He did. He said we were going to be His body here on earth.

If we are God's body on earth, every part has a role to play. Whether it's the eye, the mouth, the heart, the pinky, or the toe, we've all been assigned an important and irreplaceable part. Just like we can't overlook the smallest of parts, we can't overlook any of the people God made because He's given each of us a gift; everyone reflects a different part of Him. And when we work together, allowing each person to live the role God designed just for them, people will know and feel the love of Jesus.

God knew we would be weak on our own and stronger together. The way we love each other is the best evidence that Jesus is still alive. Whether you are big or small, tall or short, wide or narrow, your Christlike love for other people is how we move forward as God's body on the earth. What's your part? What's your role in the body, and how can you work with the people who have a different role? Can you do it without any expectation of reciprocation?

What role do you play in the body of Christ?

EVIL ALWAYS LOOKS LIKE IT'S GOING TO WIN—RIGHT BEFORE IT DOESN'T.

We know that in all things God works for the good of those who love him, who have been called according to his purpose.

ROMANS 8:28

I have a bit of a bias for predictable movies. I want the hero to win and the bad guy to get his just desserts. I want the complicated love story with the uncomplicated ending. I want the asteroid destroyed before Earth gets obliterated.

But even with these kinds of films, there's always an unpredictable turn. The hero is caught in the inescapable chamber. The couple falling in love hurt each other in ways that can't be mended. The bomb designed to save Earth malfunctions during the countdown.

I love these kinds of movies because I think they're an accurate reflection of life. We all know life is unpredictable. The unexpected diagnosis, the lost job, the lost love. Things rarely, if ever, turn out the way we think they will or should. For various reasons, in unexpected ways, life messes up our plans, and that can make us feel unhinged and directionless. What we were counting on evaporates before our eyes, and we're left empty-handed and empty-hearted.

I think God is the best screenwriter and knows exactly how to land your story, how you'll move through the tension and the challenge toward the truth in your life. Just like in the movies, we already know God rescues all of us in the end. Even when it looks like evil is about to win, we know Jesus rose from the grave, kicked death in the teeth, and gave grace the last word.

Don't give into fear just because life took an unpredictable turn. We already know how the story in each of our lives is going to end.

What's unpredictable in your life right now?
How are you responding to it?

APRIL 8

GOD HAS A WIDE-ANGLE VIEW OF YOUR LIFE. DON'T LET YOUR FOCUS GET SO NARROW THAT YOU MISS THE BEAUTIFUL PICTURE HE SEES.

Trust in the LORD with all your heart and lean not on your own understanding; in all your ways submit to him, and he will make your paths straight.

PROVERBS 3:5-6

When I was in college, I packed up my car and drove across California to win back my high school sweetheart. She had written me a letter outlining all the ways this frat boy she had met was a better fit for her, and I was devastated. I knew she was *the one* even if she had temporarily forgotten. So I hopped in my VW bug and headed south, rehearsing my speech for eight hundred miles.

The day didn't go as I had planned. She was kind enough to let me in when I showed up unannounced, but her kindness felt more like pity than rekindled affection. As I returned to my car to face my new life as a single guy, I knew my heart would forever beat a little slower.

I've often looked back on that lonely drive home with such gratitude. It reminds me that sometimes the best gift God can give is keeping us from getting what we want. We latch on to a vision of what we think will make for the "perfect life," but it turns out our vision is a little shortsighted. God has a much wider angle for your life and mine on His lens. If I had won back my high school sweetheart, I would've missed out on Sweet Maria, and my old girlfriend would have been stuck with me. I never would've known what God had waiting for me if I had only aimed at what I already had.

God is always better than the plans we imagine for our lives. It's okay to dream big, but let's hold our plans loosely in case God wants to give us something different and better. Remember that whatever you're aiming for, God's better.

What situation in your life right now do you need to trust in God's outcomes, not yours?

APRIL 9

GOD ISN'T WOWED BY FANCY WORDS.
HE DELIGHTS IN HUMBLE HEARTS.

Let us draw near to God with a sincere heart and with the full assurance that faith brings, having our hearts sprinkled to cleanse us from a guilty conscience and having our bodies washed with pure water.

HEBREWS 10:22

I wasn't raised in the church. After putting my hope in Jesus, I went to Bible study. I wasn't really sure what that was, but I remember we would always pray at the end, each person following the next around a circle. There was one guy who always *knew* how to pray. Know what I mean? His words would come out eloquently like he'd been reading Shakespeare all day or had a speechwriter on staff. A couple of times I opened my eyes just a little bit to see if he was reading from a teleprompter. "Lord, God, Father, Almighty One, we beseech You" led every sentence in the keynote address. I remember thinking I would be a little weirded out if someone beseeched me after calling me "Mr. Goff, Robert, Bob, Hey you."

I'd get all tongue-tied and didn't have anything to reach for except really simple words and phrases. I felt like a kindergartner in front of these learned and well-versed believers who might as well have been reciting *Hamlet*. I didn't have the Bible memorized. I didn't have a big vocabulary. My prayers felt more like my conversations with imaginary friends when I was little, with a few more requests and apologies.

I'm not knocking people who are good with words—it's a true gift and one I appreciate. But you can imagine my relief learning God isn't wowed by fancy words. He delights in humble hearts. He knows what we want already, and He sees through our words, big and small, to the heart behind them. He's not looking for code words; He's just glad to hear from us.

God's more interested in a conversation with us than a rehearsed speech.

He values the relationship, and relationships happen with real people who use whatever words they can to communicate what's inside. We don't need to worry about impressing God when we come to Him. We've already won His heart.

What would be different about your interaction with God if you approached Him more informally?

LET GRACE BLOW YOUR HAIR BACK LIKE YOUR HEAD'S OUT THE WINDOW.

In his hand are the depths of the earth, and the mountain peaks belong to him. The sea is his, for he made it, and his hands formed the dry land.

PSALM 95:4–5

I love it when I'm driving down the road and see a big, shaggy dog with its head out the window, tongue flapping in the wind. It seems so free to me, so unconcerned and pure. Maybe I love it so much because I used to do it as a kid. I would stick my head out the window as far as my seat belt would let me and squint my eyes as the wind roared past, pretending I was flying like Superman or sprinting like the Flash.

Looking back, what I loved most about it was the pure feeling of being completely enveloped by the world around me. I think God created the world with so much beauty to remind us about Himself. And He gave us the senses to take it all in. We'll never be able to wrap our minds around His extravagant love, so He gave us mountains and oceans and told us to go swim and jump and climb and, yes, put our heads out the window a couple of times. We'll never understand how grace holds us, so He gave us the wind and said to let it brush against our faces.

God is everywhere if we have the eyes to see Him. We feel His Spirit when we listen to a symphony and sense His kindness in the eyes of a newborn baby. Whenever the words we use to talk about God start to get jumbled, it's time to step outside the words and into His world. Let grace blow your hair back like your head's out the window.

As you look around your surroundings, what signs do you see of God's presence?

GOD DELIGHTS IN OUR IMPOSSIBLE PRAYERS.

Surely the arm of the LORD is not too short to save, nor his ear too dull to hear.

ISAIAH 59:1

Most of us have whispered impossible prayers at some point. We pray for an A on the exam after we blew study days at the beach or for the police officer to forgive us for going twenty over the speed limit. Some of us have prayed more serious impossible prayers when we heard our parents fighting, when our teenagers are out way past curfew, or when we hear about atrocities in our country or around the world.

No matter if your prayers seem impossible or even downright ridiculous, God delights in them. He created us for relationship, with Him and other people, and communication is the heartbeat of a strong relationship. God loves it when we go to Him with our anxieties, big and small. When we could easily escape our feelings altogether, it fills Him with joy when we choose to turn to Him instead.

One of my favorite verses in the Bible says God's arm is not too short to save us. I love the image: we can never fall too far out of His reach. At any point, no matter how unlikely it seems, God can reach into our impossible circumstances and rescue us. Sometimes God will use what seems like an impossible circumstance to remind us of our desperate need for Him.

Next time a voice tells you not to pray for something because it's so small, pray anyway. Next time you feel like God doesn't care about the details of your life, pray anyway. And when you feel like the problem is too huge to be turned around, even by the hand of the Creator Himself, pray anyway. God delights in hearing our impossible prayers because it reminds us of our absolute need.

For what impossible situation in your life is God inviting you to have greater faith in Him?

GRACE ISN'T JUST WAITING FOR US. IT'S REACHING FOR US.

He reached down from on high and took hold of me; he drew me out of deep waters.

PSALM 18:16

When Sweet Maria and I go to the lodge in Canada, one of our favorite things is hosting a small group. Our invitation is as simple as Jesus' invitation to His friends: "Come aside and rest awhile." It's a little bit like adult summer camp with lots of free time. We jump off cliffs, walk through waterfalls, and generally get into some really fun mischief. At the end of our time together, we have a tradition where we each take a bit of nylon cord, wrap it around one wrist, and melt the ends together. The only way to take it off is to cut it. More than merely a cute tradition, we learned this from modern-day sailors. Have you ever tried to pull someone back in the boat when they've gone overboard? Because their hands are so wet and slippery it can be nearly impossible to get a good grip. Sailors use those cords so they have something to hold when someone goes overboard. It's the kind of knot a deckhand, not a captain, would wear.

We wear those cords to remind ourselves that we are there for each other, to pull one another up when we go overboard. We're just the deckhands, not the captains of the ship.

Plenty of our friends have gone for an accidental swim. Yours have too. But instead of shaming them or walking away, we lean over the rail of the boat like deckhands and start fishing for something to grab on to.

That's what God does; that's what grace does. God never asks us to get ourselves back in the boat as if we don't need His loving grip. He isn't waiting for us to prove ourselves. Our biggest successes don't qualify us, and our even bigger mistakes don't eliminate us. He comes to us before we even know we need Him, He reaches out toward us, and He lifts us up if we're willing.

In what ways can you see God reaching out to you?

GOD CAN'T ADD BEAUTIFUL THINGS TO OUR HEARTS IF THERE'S NO ROOM IN OUR LIVES.

Forget the former things; do not dwell on the past. See, I am doing a new thing! Now it springs up; do you not perceive it?

ISAIAH 43:18–19

It's a little alarming to do an inventory of all your stuff when it comes time to move. We think it's going to be a breeze and then open a closet to find stacks of high school yearbooks piled on top of boxes with twenty-year-old bank statements. Then we rediscover attic storage we had forgotten about packed tight with broken lamps, old tennis shoes, picture frames, and pool cues for a pool table we don't even own. How do we acquire so much stuff without our awareness?

To push back against my hoarder tendencies, every time I move, I give away as much as I can and vow to keep space open for more beautiful things to be added. If we want to make room for beautiful things to be added to our lives, we have to get rid of some of the old stuff. This doesn't just apply to the physical things. It applies to the hurts and memories we collect over time.

Just like our closets fill up, our schedules slowly fill up with every yes we give. It's all good stuff. It's hard to say no. It's like drowning in chocolate. Even when our time is packed with great people and opportunities, we have got to learn how to pump the brakes and make some room.

The sweetest moments in life happen unannounced. They're long drives down country roads in autumn or hikes that leave room for exploration. They're quiet evenings with people you love, when you can sit together in silence and still feel heard. God can't add beautiful things to our hearts if there's no room in our lives. What will you quit so you can get some rest? You'll never regret making space for the treasures you've been too busy to cherish.

What do you need to let go of so you can make more space for what's truly good and beautiful?

APRIL 14

GO PALMS UP AND YOU'LL GET CLOSER TO BEING LIKE JESUS.

Be still before the LORD and wait patiently for him.

PSALM 37:7

I love Palm Sunday. It's the one time of year we get to bring trees into church and wave them around like lightsabers. You don't have to meet a certain standard to participate. There are no bad palm wavers. Every year when Palm Sunday rolls around, I get my branch and get ready to go palms up as we recite the story of when Jesus rode into Jerusalem to launch what we now call Holy Week.

And every year as I wave my branch, it gets me thinking about what it would look like to go palms up the rest of the year. I don't mean we should carry trees around with us wherever we go; I mean we could be palms up with our hands. Here's what I mean.

Did you know it's almost impossible to be defensive when we sit with our palms facing upward? Try it! Right now. Sit with your feet flat on the floor and your hands resting on your legs with your palms up. The position of our bodies and the position of our hearts are connected, so it's hard to be angry while sitting in a posture of welcome.

What if you went palms up every day of the year? Instead of arguing with people or getting defensive, what if you made a habit of keeping a posture of welcome? It'll change you.

What changes inside you as you go palms up?

QUIT AIMING FOR WHAT YOU'RE ABLE TO DO. PICK A COUPLE OF THINGS ONLY GOD COULD DO.

Truly I tell you, if you have faith as small as a mustard seed, you can say to this mountain, "Move from here to there," and it will move. Nothing will be impossible for you.

MATTHEW 17:20

When our organization, Love Does, decided to help people all over the world, we knew there was no way we could do it. We didn't know what people in Uganda needed; we just fell in love with some Ugandan friends and wanted to help make life better for them. We didn't know what we could do in India or Nepal either. Somalia didn't have a government and Afghanistan's leaders were under attack.

We prayed for God to show us how we could be helpful, and then we asked friends in each of the countries what they needed most. Our friends in each of the countries said they needed better schools and safe houses, so we did what it took to get started. And guess what? It worked. Not at first, but eventually. One schoolhouse became two, then three, then five. Eventually the one-room schoolhouses became a boarding school for more than one thousand students.

In the early days of Love Does, we decided not to aim for things we could do, because the truth was, we couldn't do much. We had bigger plans in mind than we could afford, so we asked God to do what only God could do. He connected us with local leaders who had way better ideas than we did. He continued to bring money to fund the work, money we never could've come up with on our own. At every point, God showed up and surprised us with the way He's taken our small hopes and turned them into futures for kids He adores.

What is it you've been dreaming of? What seems impossible? Quit aiming for what you're able to do. Pick a couple of things only God could do. You won't see miracles if you only set out to do things you already know you can accomplish.

What's a dream you have that would be impossible to consider unless God does something miraculous?

APRIL 16

HEAVEN TOOK A DEEP BREATH AND HELD IT BECAUSE EVERYTHING WAS ABOUT TO CHANGE.

I am with you and will watch over you wherever you go, and I will bring you back to this land. I will not leave you until I have done what I have promised you.

GENESIS 28:15

Every time my parents drove through a tunnel when I was a kid, I used to hold my breath and make a wish, sure it would come true if I could hold it to the end of the tunnel. Anticipation built as my face turned red. I would stretch in my seat to catch a glimpse of the crack of light announcing the end was near. It was the nervous excitement of knowing there was life on the other side, if only I could make it.

I think that's what heaven felt in the days between Jesus' death and resurrection. God watched as sadness swept through His people. They had lost their only hope, and they didn't know if there would be life on the other side of it. They saw no crack of light in the darkness. So heaven took a deep breath and held it because everything was about to change.

God knew it was coming. The angels took a breath in anticipation. They knew in just a few days Jesus would kick death in the teeth, burst out of the tomb, and call His loved ones by their names. God sees things we can't see from our tiny corners of the universe, so when He tells us not to be afraid, we can believe Him. He sees the light at the end of the stretch we're anxious about, so He tells us not to worry. He knows life is waiting for us when we step out in trust. Grab His hand today. You don't need to close your eyes or hold your breath. Just take a step.

**God is doing something unseen in your life.
What trusting next step can you take?**

ONE OF THE BEST SWAPS IS WHEN WE REPLACE WHO WE THOUGHT WE'D BE WITH WHO GOD THOUGHT WE'D BE.

The last will be first, and the first will be last.

MATTHEW 20:16

If you knew kids who were in theater or choir when you were in school, you knew the anticipation of auditions. Maybe you've tried out for a school play or a talent show and hoped you were destined for stardom.

You can get knocked down a few notches when you learn your assessment of your talents doesn't match up with everyone else's. Very few people aspire to the role of the donkey in the stable to witness Jesus' birth or set their sights on playing tambourine behind the band or becoming vice president someday.

Even more difficult to accept than the role of Tree #4 is the supporting role we often play in real life. We might not admit it, but most of us imagined ourselves growing up to take the lead. If it's business, we imagine ourselves as the boss. If it's ministry, we envision ourselves as lead pastors. Aspiring writers dream of bestselling books, and musicians dream of hit singles.

But God's kingdom doesn't work like the world. Jesus said the real heroes are the servants, the ones who take cuts to the back of the line. He said our impact isn't measured by our accolades but by the sacrifices we make.

We'll know we're growing when we let God replace who we thought we'd be with who He thought we'd be. Your face might not be on the cover and your song might not be on the charts, but you'll be more humble. It won't be our successes that point people toward Jesus; it will be our kindness.

What can you do today to step into God's invitation to love others like He does?

APRIL 18

WANT MORE FAITH? DO MORE STUFF.

The world and its desires pass away, but whoever does the will of God lives forever.

1 JOHN 2:17

I joined a bunch of Bible studies when I first started following Jesus. Everyone around me was in at least one, so I thought there must be some rule or eleventh commandment and I had just missed it. We sat in circles, and I assumed we'd either start making friendship bracelets or start talking about Jesus. We ate chips and cookies, and I heard lots of opinions about every social topic, about whether it's okay to watch rated R movies, and about what words meant in Greek and Hebrew. It wasn't long before I started to feel bored with the whole thing.

That's when some friends and I started a "Bible Doing" group. We read what Jesus said and then schemed ways to actually go do those things. It might sound strange, but think about it: Jesus never said, "Study Me." He said, "Follow Me."

Jesus invited us to find people who don't have food and to get them something to eat. He said to hang out with people in prison. He said if you know someone who doesn't have a place to stay, help them find one. He was all about doing things for widows and orphans, not becoming informed about them.

Following Jesus is way more exciting than studying Him. Do we need to know the Scriptures? You bet. But don't stop there. Our faith can start to get confusing and boring when we exercise it by debating about it. I'm not really sure what happens when we get to heaven. We'll find out when we get there. What we do know is this: Jesus invited us to be a part of the redemptive movement He started when He was here. It's a pretty extraordinary invitation, and it's easy to understand. You want more faith? Do more stuff.

What message of Jesus do you need to obey today?

DARKNESS FELL, HIS FRIENDS SCATTERED, HOPE SEEMED LOST—BUT HEAVEN JUST STARTED COUNTING TO THREE.

See, darkness covers the earth and thick darkness is over the peoples, but the LORD rises upon you and his glory appears over you.

ISAIAH 60:2

It was a dark and lonely Friday. One of Jesus' close confidants handed Him over to those who wanted to kill Him. The rest of His friends scattered when it looked like their lives might be on the line too. He was taunted until He ran out of breath. When He died, thunder crashed, and the lights went out on earth. Perhaps in the whole universe.

Much like stars unseen until the darkness falls, hope flickered out among Jesus' friends. Only then did we get a glimpse into the heavens with the women at the cross. His mother and His precious friend, Mary, sat weeping and praying, holding each other as they mourned. These women awoke before dawn Sunday morning so they could take incense to the tomb where Jesus lay. These women were still searching for the Savior.

The hope they showed with their consistent presence whispers the side of the story so many miss: the time in between miracles. This is where most of our lives are lived. The last miracle almost forgotten and the next one merely hoped for. These women were counting on Jesus to surprise them, even if they didn't know when or where or how. They knew it wasn't the end of hope. They lived in anticipation in those moments of despair. They knew they were in the middle of a story, and they were the first to see Jesus at the tomb on Sunday morning.

When heaven started a countdown to the resurrection, Mary Magdalene and the mother of Jesus were counting on Jesus to show. Hope doesn't go to sleep just because it's dark outside; it lights a candle and stays up waiting for the rest of the story. Are you living in anticipation of God surprising you? This is the place where God meets us with the power of the resurrection. It's in the dark places. He finds us in the places between the miracles.

In what ways is God surprising you in your life right now?

NO TOMB COULD CONTAIN WHAT
LOVE WAS ABOUT TO RELEASE.

He said to them, "The Son of Man is going to be delivered into the hands of men. They will kill him, and after three days he will rise."

MARK 9:31

I'm a lawyer and keep secrets for a living. But there's one big exception. I'll confess, I'm not great at keeping secrets when it's a surprise for someone I love. When I was a kid, I'd spill the beans the moment I heard about a Christmas gift someone was going to get. I just couldn't contain my excitement. Surprise parties? Forget about it. My grins and leading questions gave it away faster than a viral video. I've grown a little in this area, but only because I've told friends to limit the details they share with me. I'm just too big of a gamble.

It's easy to get excited when we know something good is about to happen. We do this when we know what's coming will change someone's life for the better. Their future joy is our joy right now, and we can't keep quiet.

I think that's how the angels must have felt when they knew Jesus was going to burst out of the tomb. They had to stand guard and keep watch as Jesus' friends mourned and accepted the death of a revolution. The angels knew better. I bet they were thinking, *The disciples' minds are about to be blown.* Just like us, the disciples had lost sight of what Jesus had told them about what would happen next. They returned to life with no imagination for the miracle about to come three days later.

There was no way to ruin the plans God had made since the beginning of time. The Roman soldiers stationed guards at the tomb to try to control the outcome. The reason was simple. They wanted to get ahead of the narrative so they could stomp out any sign of a miracle. But Jesus busted through anyway. No tomb could contain what love was about to release.

What is Jesus releasing in your life today?

APRIL 21

WHEN JESUS ROSE FROM THE DEAD, HE SHOWED THAT OUR LIVES ARE THE BEST SERMON WE'VE GOT. PILE ON LOVE INSTEAD OF PILING UP WORDS.

Jesus said to them, "Come and have breakfast." None of the disciples dared ask him, "Who are you?" They knew it was the Lord.

JOHN 21:12

Shortly after Jesus rose from the dead, His friends were embarrassed and confused. So they went back to what they knew best: fishing. I don't blame them. It's comforting to do things you know you're good at when you feel bewildered or ashamed or insecure.

Jesus' friends pushed back out into the water and started fishing. A voice came from the shore and said something that must have sounded familiar. The voice told them to throw their nets on the other side of the boat. This had happened before. It was life bookended with the same statement. You know how the story ends—these men ended up with so many fish, they almost broke their nets. That's when the nickel dropped. Peter knew it was Jesus. He immediately jumped in the water and swam to the shore. Sans swimsuit.

When Peter got to shore, he saw a fire burning with fish on top and some bread set aside for them. Jesus didn't say the biggest "I told you so" of all time. He didn't chastise His friends for deserting Him in His greatest moment of need. He didn't take advantage of a "teachable moment" to tell them what to do the next time they were tempted to say they didn't even know Him and desert a friend. What He did was simply this: He made them breakfast. He let His presence on the shore with them do all the talking.

If we commit to becoming the kinds of people God created us to be, our lives will tell better stories than our words ever will. They will be the testimony people need to see and feel before they hear a word we're saying. Who is it you think you need to teach a good lesson to? Don't make a lot of noise in their lives; make them a stack of pancakes.

Who will you make a stack of pancakes for? When?

THE WAY WE LOVE EVERYBODY AFTER EASTER MORNING IS THE BEST WAY TO EXPLAIN WHAT THE CELEBRATION WAS ALL ABOUT.

Praise be to the God and Father of our Lord Jesus Christ! In his great mercy he has given us new birth into a living hope through the resurrection of Jesus Christ from the dead.

1 PETER 1:3

It's easy to be in love on your wedding day. Your best friends pack out the chapel. The flower girl runs out of petals halfway down the aisle. The bride practically levitates as her dad walks her to the groom. The vows fly out just like the getaway car waiting outside will do the moment the doors close behind the newly minted couple.

Not too much later, the first fight comes. Maybe it's during the honeymoon because you forgot to bring fancy clothes, and you're stuck with a flannel shirt and jeans for the fine dining restaurant. Some couples fight about how to load the dishwasher or who left the lid up. Before the wedding, your spouse-to-be thought it was cute when you messed up. Those days have passed. The wedding is over, and it's time to be married.

The way you love people on any Tuesday will say a lot about what the wedding was about. The wedding was just a celebration of the love that would come; it was the proclamation of vows that were yet to be tested. It's a lot like Easter Sunday. The marriage is what happens next.

Easter morning is the time to get up and put on our Sunday best to celebrate the greatest act of love the world has ever seen. We sing and proclaim the truth of God's grace on Easter Sunday, but the truth of that love is the story we tell with our lives in the days that follow. The way we love everyone around us is the best way to explain what Easter is all about.

What part of you is God bringing to new life?

THE WAY WE LOVE DIFFICULT PEOPLE IS THE BEST PROOF THE TOMB IS EMPTY.

Hatred stirs up conflict, but love covers over all wrongs.

PROVERBS 10:12

Every group of people has a few who clearly didn't get enough hugs when they were kids. You know the ones. They're usually easy to spot because they never like the food they order at a restaurant and they don't laugh at any of your jokes. There's a familiar phrase: "When you're a hammer, everything looks like a nail." Well, they're some of those hammer people, and you've been nailed a couple of times. It's tempting to want to tag out and call it quits with people like that. Life is so much easier when you don't have to deal with difficult people, isn't it?

But the way we love difficult people is the best evidence we have that the tomb is as empty as we've said it is. We spend a lot of time talking about exactly how it happened—how Jesus defeated death and made grace the currency we would spend for the rest of history. We have beautiful ambitions for everyone around us. We want people to know they're forgiven. We want them to know evil won't have the last word. We want them to know Jesus isn't a philosophy or a worldview or just a historical figure.

The best way for us to convince people love won over death and is still alive is to live like His love is still alive in us. We won't convince people with our arguments or Bible verses; we'll move them with the kind of sacrificial love that precludes every other explanation.

It's easy to love people who love us back, but the empty tomb has far more depth to it than that. The resurrection says God loves the good people and the difficult ones too. Don't downplay the story and miss the message by only loving the easy ones. Go a little deeper with your love. Engage the people you've avoided. Delight in how different they are. Will they still be hard to love? You bet. Do it anyway.

Who's the difficult person in your circle? What can you do to change your perspective about them?

APRIL 24

"I AM." WHEN YOU HAVE ALL THE POWER, YOU DON'T NEED ALL THE WORDS.

God said to Moses, "I AM WHO I AM. This is what you are to say to the Israelites: 'I AM has sent me to you.'"

EXODUS 3:14

Parents know their words have power. When they say their kid's name, it's game over. When you broke the expensive vase or thought you won the war with the vegetables on your plate, you heard your name. A fit in the toy store came to a screeching halt when you heard your name. When parents say the *middle* name, kids know they're in some troubled territory.

Our parents didn't have to elaborate. Because of their position of authority in our lives, and because we knew we were dependent on them for snacks, they didn't have to give a speech. Just saying our name would do.

God knows this about names. He had a meeting with Moses in the desert and told him he would go back to Israel to lead his people out of slavery. God told him to march into the dictator's house and inform him all the workers would be leaving. Moses understandably wanted some information to take with him. He thought maybe if he knew God's name, maybe a little backstory, it would help his case.

But God has all the power, and when you have all the power, you don't need all the words. God simply responded, "Tell them 'I AM.'"

God created the universe, and He created beauty; He battled death and won. We know He has all the power and He uses it for good. God's not towering over you with His hands on His hips when you mess up. He knows your name, and get this—He calls you His beloved child. Wear that name today like it's yours, because it is.

What "I am" do you need to trust in today?

APRIL 25

HOPE IS BETTER THAN ANYTHING UNCERTAINTY PUTS IN FRONT OF US.

In his great mercy he has given us new birth into a living hope through the resurrection of Jesus Christ from the dead, and into an inheritance that can never perish, spoil or fade.

1 PETER 1:3-4

I've been with plenty of friends when they received a devastating diagnosis. I've learned there's nothing you can say to someone who just learned they have one year to live. There is no pep talk for someone who's just been told they'll likely never get out of the wheelchair. Sometimes the only appropriate response is to grab a hand and cry.

I've also lived long enough to watch these friends stare into the face of uncertainty and choose hope. They've chosen to say, "Sure, the odds are against me, but God is not." They've chosen to hope for an extra decade with their families or to imagine one more walk by the ocean. Why? Because choosing the way of hope is far better than anything uncertainty puts in front of us.

We might not have faced anything as devastating as these things, but we've all faced the choice between hope and fear. Whether it's questions about what exactly will happen when we pass away or uncertainty about whether we'll find love in our lives down the road, we've had to face the unknown. But when we stand at this intersection, fear tries to shrivel our hearts and shrink us down. Hope is the opposite, though—it swells our hearts and makes us expand. Hope restores the life fear tries to steal. Yesterday already happened and tomorrow isn't here yet. We only have today. We've got people to encourage and another huge invitation to a life of whimsy. We can either wring our hands about what we don't know, allowing fear to take over the moment, or we can choose hope and let love reign. The path is yours and mine to choose every day.

What will it be for you today?

APRIL 26

WHEN JESUS ROSE FROM THE DEAD, HE DIDN'T MAKE A BIG SPEECH. HE ATE A MEAL WITH HIS FRIENDS.

On the evening of that first day of the week, when the disciples were together, with the doors locked for fear of the Jewish leaders, Jesus came and stood among them and said, "Peace be with you!" After he said this, he showed them his hands and side. The disciples were overjoyed when they saw the Lord.

JOHN 20:19-20

Speeches can be a great show, but most of the time not much comes of them. Speeches are great for inciting passion or bringing about awareness. But after a while, the words pile up—and piles of words will never magically become action.

Jesus was aware of what a mountain of words would stack up to, and that's why He let his actions do the talking. When He rose from the dead, Jesus didn't make a speech to the world or chastise his closest friends who scattered. Instead, He made breakfast for them. This action was a reminder from Jesus that His friends belonged, that they weren't disqualified because they'd made a mistake, and that the dream of God's love was still alive—for them and everyone else.

We create space for change in our lives when we put down the megaphones, stop shouting at everybody else, and show up for our own faith. No heart can be transformed by a bunch of words. Change comes from belonging, and belonging is borne out of being with others. But it can't stop there. Belonging without doing feels like a clique. It feels empty. Whether we're invited onto the stage or posting on a Facebook account, we're tempted to think that our words equate to real change. That's just a first step. Let your lives spring into action, and let what comes of that do the talking.

Instead of telling someone what we think or believe—or telling them what they should think or believe—what if we just ate a meal with them? It sounds insignificant at first, but it's not. Love in action has the kind of power many of us haven't tapped in to. Maybe you're bummed to hear this, but a casserole or a bag of In-n-Out Burgers say more than any five sermons on how Jesus loved us.

**Who do you need to change your approach
with and just sit down for a meal?**

GOD USES UNCERTAINTY IN OUR LIVES TO REMODEL OUR HEARTS.

You will keep in perfect peace those whose minds are steadfast, because they trust in you.

ISAIAH 26:3

One of the worst feelings in the world is going on a hike and realizing you've strayed *waaaay* off trail. *But it looked like a trail,* you think, as you're standing all alone in the middle of the forest. Then it occurs to you that bears travel the same paths, and you might be on the menu. It isn't long before you're negotiating with God, promising not to cuss anymore or to become a full-time missionary or to stop cheating on your taxes if He'll just lead you back to a safe place so you can get to your car and drive to a Starbucks.

Life can be a real bear too. The future we imagined for years is suddenly threatened by a career change we didn't anticipate. The family we've always wanted feels just beyond our reach when the doctor tells us our odds for kids are slim. The uncertainty of our lives reminds us we're not in control. We can't Google our way to a solution or change our circumstances by simply trying harder. All we can do is trust God is still good, and He'll use the circumstances in our lives to bring about beauty somehow, at some time.

Those are the times when childlike trust has the opportunity to transform us. God is bigger than the mountain where you're lost, and He exists off the trail and off the map. It's an adventure He's invited us on, not a business trip. He's not out to destroy our dreams; He only wants to make us more like Him. God uses uncertainty to remodel our hearts. Don't waste your time looking for a way out of the difficulty you're in; look for Him in the midst of it. He's not the destination we're aiming for. He's the guide along the path.

What situation do you need to trust God's guidance for?

GOD DOESN'T WANT ANYTHING FROM YOU BECAUSE EVERYTHING YOU HAVE IS ALREADY HIS. BE GRATEFUL.

He is before all things, and in him all things hold together.

COLOSSIANS 1:17

Parents save their kids' lives at least once a week until they're teenagers. They keep them from running into streets after the basketball that got away from them. They pull their hands away from the hot stove top. They invest in floaties and driver's education classes and bicycle helmets.

I think God has been like our parents in the ways He's sustained us. It hasn't always been obvious to us because He's done it so consistently for so long we just assume that's how the world works. We can live our lives believing we've provided for ourselves through hard work and personal sacrifices. But this is only because we haven't seen the ways He's guided us toward life when we went bounding toward danger. We didn't see Him behind the person who stepped in to take our hand when we were on the verge of giving up altogether. It's easy to forget He breathed life into us in the first place, and He holds us together when we would have otherwise fallen apart.

At every point, whether we've known it or not, God has protected us and sustained us. Our good behavior didn't earn it, and our failures haven't ruined it. When we get puffed up with pride about what we've accomplished, let's stop for a moment and give credit where it's due. If you are financially secure, that's God's provision. If you're fit as a fiddle, that's God's mercy. If your marriage is thriving, that's God's love. We wake up to new days, we take our next breath, we dream some dreams because of God's grace. We did nothing to earn any of this.

God doesn't want anything from you, because everything you have is already His. If you want to dazzle Him, give Him thanks by sharing what you've been given. Freely, with gratitude. No strings attached.

**Looking back on the last week,
how has God been sustaining you?**

GOD WON'T TRADE HIS LOVE FOR OUR GOOD CONDUCT. WE'RE THE ONLY ONES WHO ARE TRYING TO MAKE IT A NEGOTIATION.

Truly he is my rock and my salvation; he is my fortress, I will not be shaken.

PSALM 62:6

It's hard to believe the religious leaders were the ones lobbying to crucify Jesus. Of all the scandalous people Jesus hung out with—the prostitutes, tax collectors, and drunks—the self-proclaimed "righteous" people were the ones who took Him down. Stop and sit with that for a moment. It's worth wondering why Jesus was so offensive to them. Why did they think He posed such a threat?

I think it was because Jesus didn't come to impress them. He didn't come to cower before them either. He passed right by the people who thought they were already good enough for God's favor. They were looking for a pat on the back, but He wasn't impressed by well-behaved people. He saw through their deeds to their hearts. He didn't applaud their accomplishments or sort the world into columns, putting the capable on one side and the rest of us on the other. He knew there were no good or bad people but a bunch of well-intentioned, confused people who easily lost their way, some more noticeably than others.

Here's the thing: Jesus is offensive to people who don't like dependence on someone else or who find their worth in feeling morally superior to everybody else. Just when we think we might have earned our way into God's good graces, we find out God won't trade His love for good conduct. We're the ones trying to make it a negotiation. He's not.

The simple message of the gospel is that our best isn't good enough and our worst doesn't disqualify us. Jesus gave His life so we wouldn't have to prove ourselves anymore. Yesterday's successes aren't enough to get us in, and today's failures aren't enough to keep us out. We're in because Jesus says we are.

What parts of your life do you need to
trust God in more fully today?

FEAR ONLY HAS THE POWER WE GIVE IT. HOPE WORKS THE SAME WAY.

Do not fear, for I have redeemed you; I have summoned you by name; you are mine.

ISAIAH 43:1

I love the movie *Monsters, Inc.* Ever seen it? In the story there's a world full of the monsters who scare kids at night. They go into kids' closets through special doors, scare the bejeezus out of them, and those screams are harnessed as the natural resource that powers the monsters' lives. Think electricity, but the outlet is a screaming five-year-old. Scaring and screaming seem normal to the monsters until one of them encounters a precocious little girl who doesn't seem afraid at all. She thinks the monster is a pet, and she just laughs. It's a great movie—you should see it. When I watch that movie, here's what it shows me: monsters only have the power we give them.

Fear works the same way. We lose sleep dreading scenarios, we toss and turn thinking of all the horrible outcomes, and then we wake up to another new morning. We could've skipped over the sleepless nights if we had only given in to hope instead of fear. We might not be able to laugh like the little girl in the movie, but perhaps we could muster a grin knowing the outcomes are God's to decide, not ours. Fear is usually a story we tell ourselves. We tell ourselves people wouldn't love us if they really knew us. We tell ourselves trying means failure and failure means worthlessness.

We don't need to be stuck looking up at the ceiling worrying. We can choose to tell ourselves a story of hope instead. One that says we'll be even more loved when we're seen as we are. That the monsters really aren't that scary and probably aren't even real. Hope reminds us there's always grace when we fail. Hope reminds us we just might succeed too.

Take all the power you're giving to fear and hand it over to hope instead.

What power are you giving to fear today?
What will you do to give God that fear?

THE MORE WE STAND IN AWE OF GOD, THE LESS WE'LL STAND IN JUDGMENT OF EACH OTHER.

Love your enemies, do good to them, and lend to them without expecting to get anything back. Then your reward will be great, and you will be children of the Most High, because he is kind to the ungrateful and wicked. Be merciful, just as your Father is merciful.

LUKE 6:35-36

For the longest time, I only put things on my calendar for nine months and one day. You see, it's been my life's ambition to be a grandparent. This isn't something new. I've wanted to be a grandparent since junior high school. Some people want to be math teachers because they had a great math teacher in school. Others want to be professional athletes because they had a great coach. I wanted to be a grandparent because mine were great at it.

My grandfather was a fireman on the docks in the San Francisco Bay for forty years. He worked the graveyard shift, and in the entire time he was there, he never put out a fire. I don't even know if he knew how to. My grandmother never learned how to drive a car and worked as a telephone operator in the San Francisco stock exchange. These are hardly the kinds of jobs people write books about. Do you know what they did best? They lived without expressing any judgment of the people around them, no matter what. It was just beautiful.

I think the reason they felt so free to not live in judgment of the people around them is that they lived in awe of the life around them. It was a simple awe, not a complex or expensive one. They had the same car, which had been given to them, for as long as I remembered. I don't think they ever rode on an airplane or went on a vacation. Yet they saw more sunsets for free than anyone I knew. They were in awe of the world, and of me, and they let me know it—every day.

They were completely unencumbered by the petty offenses others seemed to cling to for so long. In their simplicity dwelled their power. They lived simple, humble, grateful lives. This is my ambition. This is my goal. To be this type of grandparent. What it's going to take is so simple it escapes many of us. I want to live so much in awe of what is going on around me, there will be no time to live in judgment of the people around me.

What kind of grandparent do you want to be?

GOD IS NEVER AS NERVOUS ABOUT OUR FUTURE, OR AS CONCERNED ABOUT OUR PAST, AS WE ARE.

Do not let your hearts be troubled. You believe in God; believe also in me.

JOHN 14:1

I have some good friends who make movies. They write, direct, and produce them, and I love celebrating with them when the movie opens on the big screen. I don't know much about movies, but I know a thing or two about good stories, and there's always a plot twist or two just to keep you engaged.

You know how it works. Midway through the first scene, something is terribly wrong. You don't know if the couple's love will be strong enough to endure or whether they will receive the approval they're looking for. You're anxious someone won't survive when the plane makes an emergency landing or when the ship flips upside down. You don't know which soldiers will make it out of the battle alive and which one will prove to be the unlikely hero. Regardless of the plot, this is the kind of stuff that keeps us coming back. The reason is simple. We want to see how it all turns out.

The only person who isn't worried about how it all turns out is the director. He or she sees each scene in light of the whole story and knows how it will all resolve. The director is familiar with every detail of every character's life. What the director wants is for the character to simply play their part and not be distracted by the rest.

When God looks at our lives, it's like He's sitting in the director's seat. He's never as nervous about our future or as concerned about our past as we are, because He knows how the story will end. We get to a twist and feel like all is lost, but He knows the twist is only going to heighten the triumph. Although it might feel like the worst part, it's actually setting up the best part.

Stay calm when things don't make sense. Play your part. Keep your head in the game. Remain focused when you don't know where the story is going. God does, and He's a terrific storyteller. Let your life continue to unfold.

What are you allowing to unfold today?

HOPE MAKES OUR LIVES PAGE-TURNERS.

Being confident of this, that he who began a good work in you will carry it on to completion until the day of Christ Jesus.

PHILIPPIANS 1:6

Sometimes when I've got a few minutes to spare in an airport, I head to the bookstore to flip through some of the new releases. While people rush around me to buy their almonds and newspapers, I flip to the middle and read a page here and there to get a sense of the story being told.

I get a glimpse of the book when I start in the middle, whether the writer is serious or funny or uses big vocabulary words. I know I miss most of the picture by doing this. It would be crazy to think I could flip to chapter twelve and pick up on the ending to come or why the characters are worth rooting for, right? If I flipped to the middle of a biography, I might think it was a story about a guy trying to get girls to date him in college rather than a story of a beautiful marriage. I might think a pastor's story was a memoir about life in jail because I hadn't gotten to the part where the pastor came to faith in jail.

No book is a chapter, and no chapter tells the whole story. The same is true in our lives: no mistake defines who we are. God sees our mistakes in light of the grace that will turn them into stories of redemption. We're not in the first chapter, and most of us aren't in the last one. We're somewhere in the middle.

Hope makes our lives page-turners. Every good story has some unexpected twists, and even the best hero might lose her way for a few chapters. Don't worry about it. God is writing more chapters. He has the power to turn the story around with us. Don't let one bad chapter (or five) convince you that you know your whole story. You're in one of those middle chapters. There are more to come.

What chapter are you in right now?

MAY 4

JESUS WON'T ELIMINATE THE CHAOS IN OUR LIVES, BUT HE WILL GIVE IT MEANING.

In this world you will have trouble. But take heart! I have overcome the world.

JOHN 16:33

If you open the Bible to almost any chapter, you'll find stories of people just like you and me. The same people who cast out demons and defeated giants also made mistakes that would send the rest of us to jail. Seriously—consider what these guys did. They'd get life with no parole these days. Those who left everything to follow Jesus didn't get better jobs or more stable lives; they just got Jesus. They got a gulp of living water.

Sometimes you hear Christians say following Jesus will make you more successful. Just watch some of them on TV on a Sunday morning and you'll hear it. They say God wants to bless you, and by "bless" they mean make you rich. Sometimes it sounds like God is a short-order cook and will make us whatever we ask Him for. But Jesus never said anything like that. He said He didn't come to make life easier for us—He came to rescue us and make our lives more purposeful by making us more like Him.

Jesus never promised to eliminate all the chaos from our lives; He said He'd bring meaning to them. He invited us into a story of grace and redemption, probably because these are the stories the disciples got wrong, time and again. If you wonder why you still face some of the same struggles you brought into your relationship with God, you're in good company. He doesn't magically erase them like a product from an infomercial; He promises to be with us while we reach toward Him to find more meaning in our circumstances. That's the real blessing.

What trouble are you facing right now?

GOD KNOWS WE'LL GET IT WRONG SOMETIMES. LOVE FORGIVES AND THEN LOOKS AHEAD.

As far as the east is from the west, so far has he removed our transgressions from us.

PSALM 103:12

I have a friend who has this condition she calls the "Angel Complex." She feels so driven to perfection that any slip is like a deadly sin. In about five seconds she'll forget the thankless way she helped or did a random act of kindness. But it will take her five years to forget the little mistake that caught her boss's attention or caused disappointment with her spouse. She's stuck in the past and can't move on. Her mistakes have become like links in a chain that bind her heart. It makes me so sad, and I try to remind her about all the good she's done and how wonderful she is. But she simply can't hear the words.

Then it occurred to me God knows the feeling I get when I tried to encourage her—because I'm just as hard to reach sometimes too. He knew we would get it wrong before He came to be with us, but He came anyway because that's what love does. Love forgives and then looks ahead. Love leaves old failures in the past. God doesn't keep score, and we don't need to either.

God said our sins are as far from Him as the east is from the west. You don't need a tape measure to figure out that's a long way. They're erased from our history as far as He's concerned. But shame keeps bringing them back up. It says we're disqualified. We're unworthy. Shame tries to shackle us to who we *were* to keep us from becoming who we *are*.

Don't take the bait and waste your energy rehashing things God said you can forget. You lost a little time when you made the mistakes; don't lose more by dwelling on them now. What do you need to let go of? What's in your past that you keep dragging into the present? Let it go.

What past mistake are you still allowing yourself to hold on to?

MAY 6

FEAR CALLS OUT OUR DOUBTS;
GOD CALLS OUT OUR NAMES.

"'Lord, if it's you," Peter replied, "tell me to come to you on the water."
"Come," he said.

MATTHEW 14:28–29

A quick boat ride away from our lodge in Canada, there's a hidden cove with a magnificent waterfall. Hardly anyone knows about it, so when I go, it feels like it's all mine—like God made a water park just for me.

My friend Don and I made a trip to the cove years ago. Don and I waded over to the waterfall, and he stepped through the fall and stood next to the rocks while I stayed on the outside. Don was yelling my name. "Bob! Come through! You'll make it! I'm just on the other side! Come on, Bob!" I could barely hear him as the water crashed between us. But his voice was an invitation that demanded a response. It wasn't mere agreement he was looking for; it was actually me taking a step forward.

Despite my fear, I shuffled forward as the freezing water forced down on me. It felt like a long way, but it really wasn't. After a few steps, I joined Don on the other side. It was the best version of a baptism you can imagine! Looking out toward the cove from behind the waterfall, I understood a little better about the time Jesus walked on water and invited Peter to join Him. Jesus wasn't looking for agreement or affirmation that this would be a great idea for someone else to do. Jesus wanted Peter to take a step.

Sometimes God asks us to step out (or through). We don't know what we'll see until we go through the deluge. It's scary to step into the unknown, but it's also where we find Jesus; and wherever we find Jesus, we find life. Fear calls out our doubts; God calls out our names. When you hear Jesus calling your name, there's only one way to respond. Take a step.

What's your next step? What's been holding you back?

MAY 7

THE WORDS WE SAY HAVE TREMENDOUS POWER. BE PICKY ABOUT THE ONES YOU CHOOSE.

The voice of the LORD is powerful; the voice of the LORD is majestic.

PSALM 29:4

It's funny the memories that stick with you from the time when you were a kid. Maybe you can imagine in vivid detail the Christmas morning when you got your first bike—the room, the tree, the texture of the carpet, and the fact you were out of bed at 3:00 a.m. Maybe you can remember a teacher who called out what was great about you, a compliment you can still hear like she's whispering it in your ear. These memories connect end to end and become who we are, and the words that stick on our hearts shape us the most.

Just like some heckling kept us off the field because of how we threw or ran like a giraffe in roller skates, the right words from the right people put us on track to become nurses, public servants, or human rights advocates when they told us our talents could change the world. Powerful words gave us the gentle push we needed, the courage to push past. If we were to trace our steps back along the path that led us here, we would likely find it all started with a few well-placed words from someone we trusted.

It's no surprise when you think about it: God set the universe in motion with words. He called for light, and the stars burst onto the backdrop of the night sky. He wanted kangaroos and koala bears, so He spoke them into existence. God's words have the power to create life. He gave our words the power to shape lives.

Here's what we need to do: be picky about the words we say. They have the power to shape our lives and the lives of the people around us. Equally important, be careful about the words you cling to. Don't read the junk mail. Check out the return address first. If it didn't come from Jesus, it's not worth listening to.

What words have you been listening to lately, other than God's?

MAY 8

DON'T PUT DOWN SOD WHERE GOD IS PLANTING SEED. HE WANTS US TO GROW, NOT LOOK FINISHED.

Brothers and sisters, each person, as responsible to God, should remain in the situation they were in when God called them.

1 CORINTHIANS 7:24

When spring rolls around, I always admire my neighbors' lawns. I only have to walk by a few before I start to wonder why mine doesn't look as good as theirs.

You can imagine how excited I was the year I found out I could plant sod instead of seed and have a manicured lawn in an instant. For a little extra money, I could take a shortcut and have a pristine yard in no time. I learned in the process, though, that sod delivers a pretty lawn faster, but faster isn't always better. After a few months, some sections were patchy and parched. It's because the grass is grown on different soil. Good looks aren't always a reflection of good health.

When we let His grace take root in our hearts, we don't just act like Jesus on the outside, we become more like Jesus on the inside. We become more patient with people who need a lot of grace. We're less interested in our image and more interested in people who are rejected by everyone else. God has you planted right where He wants you. Don't envy your neighbor's lawn or wish you were growing at a different rate. We might be able to look the part faster if we fake it, but our shortcuts will fade and become like a patchy lawn.

Don't plant sod where God wants you to put seeds. Trust His process in your life. He's more interested in making us grow than having us look finished.

Where are your feet planted? What would it look like for you to bloom there?

MOST OF THE THINGS I'VE WORRIED ABOUT DIDN'T HAPPEN. MOST OF THE THINGS I'VE HOPED FOR DID. KEEP DREAMING.

I tell you, do not worry about your life, what you will eat or drink; or about your body, what you will wear. Is not life more than food, and the body more than clothes?

MATTHEW 6:25

We usually feel alone in our anxiety, but did you know most of us worry about the same kinds of things? We worry about whether our kids are safe. We worry we're not very attractive. We worry we sounded bad when we spoke up in a meeting or that we won't make ends meet financially. The root of our anxiety may look a little different for each of us, but our hand-wringing looks the same. Worry and distraction always travel together. We're worried, so we're distracted—and people who are distracted can't be present. How do we get back to being where our feet are?

Most of the things we worry about don't actually happen. That's why Jesus told us not to worry about the future. He said to look at the flowers, how they're clothed with outfits kings couldn't recreate if they tried. He pointed to birds in the sky and reminded His followers the birds don't earn money or save things in barns, yet God always provides them with something to eat. Jesus said to look at things that actually exist, not all the things that don't.

God hasn't brought you this far only to forget your name. Jesus said we won't add anything to our lives by worrying; we'll just miss seeing Him at work. Rather than live our lives distracted, we're better off trusting that God will come through once again. Instead of hiding under the table, He wants us to grab a front-row seat so we won't miss the action.

If we're going to spend time thinking about the future, we might as well spend it hoping instead of worrying. Most of the things we worry about don't happen, but most of the things we hope for do. What are you worrying about? What has you wrapped around the axle and distracted? What are you hoping for? How come? Keep dreaming, and don't be surprised when you find out God has been dreaming with you all along.

What do you find yourself worrying about?

STAND FIRM. GOD DIDN'T BRING US THIS FAR AND THEN FORGET OUR NAMES.

This is what the Sovereign LORD says: "I myself will search for my sheep and look after them."

EZEKIEL 34:11

Did you ever get lost as a kid? Like, wandered too far in the woods behind your house, took a few too many turns on your bike, or hid in the department store clothes rack for too long? You look up and realize you have *no idea* where you are or that *no one* you remotely recognize is anywhere to be seen. Then the anxiety floods in.

Do you remember what a relief it was to see your parents' car rolling down the road, hear their faint voice in the woods, or your name come through the speakers? Right when you felt the despair wash over you, your name was called and you knew people were coming to find you.

We never outgrow the anxiety of feeling lost. As grownups, we usually feel it when we suddenly realize we don't recognize the face in the mirror. We feel it when we lose track of the person we set out to become or the principles we sought to live by. It's like who we've become went wandering a bit too far and can't find its way back.

God didn't bring us this far only to forget our names now. You might not hear it as clearly as the voice booming through the department store speakers, but God calls your name every day. He's cheering us on, always ready to grab us by the hand when we ask Him to lead the way.

Whether you feel like life has dropped you off in a strange place or feel like you've lost your way, know God's already there, and He's got you.

How do you notice God pursuing you right now?

MAY 11

DON'T LET YOUR FAILURES TALK
YOU OUT OF GOD'S GRACE.

"Come now, let us settle the matter," says the LORD. "Though your
sins are like scarlet, they shall be as white as snow; though they are
red as crimson, they shall be like wool."

ISAIAH 1:18

Have you ever seen the house of a hoarder? I haven't, but I caught one on TV
once and it gave me the creeps. Little pathways between mountains of stuff lead
to other rooms filled with magazines and dolls and dollar-store deals. While the
majority of us don't live this way in our homes, plenty of us do in our hearts,
clogging them with memories of our past failures. We stack our errors like old,
outdated newspapers, and then we pick them up and read them.

Past failures lie to us about who we are. The acclaimed author Brené Brown
coined the idea that mistakes are something you *do,* but shame is something
you *are.* A hoarding heart full of past failures can eventually convince you that
you didn't just fail—but that you *are* a failure. Here's a load of truth for you.
You're not. Why? Because God says so.

If mess-ups were push-ups, I'd be totally ripped. Aren't you glad God's
response to our failure is always grace? Jesus said forgiveness from Him is an
unlimited resource—it never runs out. We might make the same mistake we've
made dozens of times before, and God will keep drawing us close. Is it fair? Of
course not. Don't worry about it. God still delights in us.

Don't let your failures talk you out of God's grace. Grace moves us toward
God and other people. When our failures try to keep us isolated, grace says
it's safe to show up and be seen once again. Yank open the curtains and clear
out the clutter. Grace is like the sunrise: it's there for us every day whether we
choose to enjoy it or not. God already took care of the cost of grace. Why not
receive it with joy? Bring your clutter to God with confidence He has the power
to replace our memories with His Son.

What's holding you back? What's your biggest mess-up?

ON THE OTHER SIDE OF OUR FAILURE IS AN OCEAN FULL OF LOVE AND ACCEPTANCE.

Let us not become weary in doing good, for at the proper time we will reap a harvest if we do not give up.

GALATIANS 6:9

When my kids were little, every once in a while they'd ask to go roller-skating. Sweet Maria and I loved to say yes. But because I was a little older and didn't roller-skate very often, the next morning I was made aware of muscles I didn't even know existed. Who knew you could be so sore from going in circles on tiny wheels? Hiking up a mountain can be the same way. The next day that uphill trudge becomes a lesson in Muscles 101, and you feel like you're failing the class.

But there are three things I've learned about climbing a mountain. First, there's almost always a point when you want to give up. Second, you don't get the breathtaking views until you push to the summit. And third, the summit is almost always just after the point when you want to quit.

Life seems to work the same way: on the other side of our failures is an expansive horizon of love and acceptance. God already told us there's nothing we can do to change the way He feels about us. He wants us to keep pushing forward, to keep climbing, because He already knows the mind-blowing view He's got waiting for us. If we need to rest for a while, that's okay. He's not disappointed. He'll just wait with us while we're catching our breath. Don't give up. I know it's hard. Keep going. When you feel like giving up, remember something breathtaking is only a few steps ahead.

What's your next step? What's your next move?

WE'RE REFLECTIONS OF THE PEOPLE WHO HAVE LOVED US SELFLESSLY.

Since, then, you have been raised with Christ, set your hearts on things above, where Christ is, seated at the right hand of God. Set your minds on things above, not on earthly things.

COLOSSIANS 3:1–2

Our house in Canada is right on the ocean, but there are no beaches. Cedar-covered mountains slope right into the water. Because it snows a lot during the winter, spaces between these mountains that don't drain into the ocean collect the most perfect, crystal-clear water you can imagine. It reflects the sky and surrounding mountainsides like an exact upside-down replica.

One day our family decided to have a picnic next to these natural reflecting pools, and it got me thinking about what we reflect in our lives. I started listening to my kids talk as they were using phrases and gestures that Sweet Maria and I use. Then I realized I was saying and doing things that some of my best friends and most trusted confidants do. The more evidence I saw of our reflections in each other, I concluded we become reflections of the people who have loved us most selflessly. The ones who have been the most available, the most forgiving, the most like Jesus in our lives.

I also realized that you really can't escape this dynamic, for good or for bad. Have you ever heard someone say, "I'm becoming just like my mother!"? That could be the best compliment or a cause for serious dismay.

Just remember that whoever you surround yourself with, their reflection will work its way into you, and vice versa. Reflect selfless love to others and you will have a lasting impact in their lives. They'll always be seeking your waters.

Who are you surrounding yourself with, and how are they rubbing off on you?

IT'S IMPOSSIBLE TO OVER-HOPE.

In this hope we were saved. But hope that is seen is no hope at all.
Who hopes for what they already have? But if we hope for what
we do not yet have, we wait for it patiently.

ROMANS 8:24-25

There's a reason Jesus pointed to kids when He talked about faith and the kingdom of God. Kids, by nature, are trusting and earnest. They're willing to go on the adventure without getting all the details. They're just happy they were invited. They're fine with being dependent on others too. Put another way, they don't have all the layers that adults accumulate over the years.

As we get older, pain and rejection start to shift us away from the beautiful naivety of our youth. These voices tell us it's too risky to hope for our passion to come to life because there's a chance our dream will be squelched. Rejection chimes in and says it's better to keep your distance because if you let people in, you become vulnerable to being let down. The pain of our past tells us to play it safe by protecting ourselves. Don't take the bait. We were wired for hope.

Jesus had a lot to say about hope. He said hope is the fuel that keeps the fire in our hearts burning. It's the oxygen we breathe. Hope is the foundation of our faith because it reminds us we haven't arrived yet; we're still on our way home.

Jesus said all the pain in the world will one day come to an end, and we'll all celebrate with a giant banquet. The apostle Paul said faith was confidence in what we're hoping for and assurance in what we haven't yet seen. While we're waiting for the party to begin, keep hoping. Are you facing difficulties? Keep hoping. Are you confused? Keep hoping. Get the idea?

Don't let fear keep you from going all in on hope. It's the only safe bet there is because God is hope and He's already won the game.

What are you hoping for today?

WE SPEND A LOT OF TIME REMEMBERING FAILURES GOD SPENT A LOT OF LOVE SAYING WE COULD FORGET.

You are a chosen people, a royal priesthood, a holy nation, God's special possession, that you may declare the praises of him who called you out of darkness into his wonderful light.

1 PETER 2:9

Memorizing is easy for me. Any lawyer worth his salt has to earn a black belt in remembering stuff just to pass the bar. Too bad it doesn't seem to work for remembering names. If remembering names is hard, why is remembering failures so easy?

My bar-passing regimen consisted of crafting crazy amounts of flashcards. I cycled through the stacks until recalling them was a reflex.

Over. And over. And over. And over again. We handle our failures like that.

We spend a lot of time remembering failures God spent a lot of love saying we could forget. The Bible talks about God separating our failures from us as far as the east is from the west. If we start thinking of failure like God does, we'll find ourselves saying no when it tries to catch us.

We live like God's keeping score, like He's watering a garden of our wrongs to make us eat later when the time is ripe.

God is very familiar with failures; nothing about them intimidates or baffles Him. He's seen it all before, and His policy isn't to feed them to us until we choke. Instead, God wants to bury our failures so He can grow new ways of thinking.

The next time we find ourselves rehashing our failures over and over, studying them like flashcards, let's create a new set—cards that remind us we're met every morning with love and grace and the names *son*, *daughter*, and *beloved*.

God wants us to memorize those.

So let's lose the old ones. We don't need them anymore.

What does God say about who you are to Him?

SOMETIMES GOD LETS US LOSE HOPE FOR A MOMENT SO WE'LL RETRACE OUR STEPS AND FIND HIM ALL OVER AGAIN.

The Lord is not slow in keeping his promise, as some understand slowness. Instead he is patient with you, not wanting anyone to perish, but everyone to come to repentance.

2 PETER 3:9

If I ever pick up a memoir, it's usually by someone who is almost done with their race in life. Why? As they walk us through their story, they recount years of wandering down paths that didn't seem to make sense. Maybe they left their job as a pastor and spent the next five years working as a real estate agent before deciding to go back to school to become a nurse. Sometimes they took detours that led to dead ends. A couple of things worked for a while, and even more didn't.

Reading these stories is encouraging because we all feel lost so often in our lives, and it's comforting to see people who looked lost for a while when they were actually in the process of finding their way. I'm reminded to stay calm when I can't see how one chapter fits in with the larger story because the path looks more like a single wave than a straight line.

Sometimes God lets us lose hope for a moment so we'll retrace our steps and find Him all over again. God gave us agency so we're free to choose Him the way we're free to choose one another. It's one of the qualities of relationships that makes love so sweet. The people who love us weren't forced to—they chose us because they wanted us. God wants us to want Him enough to find Him.

God is looking for the same kind of relationship with us. He won't force us to love Him, so sometimes He lets us wander in our circumstances until love compels us to make our way back to Him. Don't panic when a chapter of your story doesn't make sense. God writes really great stories, and He'll write His next one in your life if you'll find your way back to Him.

What about your life right now is causing confusion in you?

FAILURE ISN'T PART OF LIFE; IT'S MUCH OF LIFE. THE REST IS JUST LEARNING HOW TO GROW FROM IT.

My flesh and my heart may fail, but God is the strength of my heart and my portion forever.

PSALM 73:26

I'm the only person I know who failed kindergarten. I'm not kidding! After the first week they politely asked me to pack my things and try again next year. How does someone flunk out of a class where you haven't learned anything yet?

My parents were both educators and were really embarrassed when this news hit the papers. I eventually got back in kindergarten and made it through grade school, but I failed more classes than I'm proud to admit. It's not easy to pay attention to math lessons when you've got more important things to do, like make friends and take care of the lizard you brought to school in your pocket.

If I could just get through high school, I thought to myself, I wouldn't have to deal with these kind of failures anymore. And you know what? I was right. I found new things to fail at.

Somewhere along the way I realized failure isn't a part of life; it's actually much of life. We fail to be patient with people we love. We fail to find the right words to give to someone in their moment of need. Sometimes we fail at fulfilling commitments to people we love, in big ways and small.

Failure isn't a one-time event we have to endure; it's an ongoing reality that will make us better if we'll let it. Jesus showed kindness to people in the midst of their failures, and He always made a way for them to grow through them. There was always more grace then, and there still is now.

Next time you fail something or someone, listen to the lessons it can teach you. It'll make you wiser and more gracious if you let it. What has been your biggest failure? Bring it to Jesus. Let Him show you how you'll grow from it.

How could you grow from your biggest failure?

QUIT THINKING THE BATTLE FOR YOUR HEART WILL BE A FAIR FIGHT.

The Philistine said, "This day I defy the armies of Israel! Give me a man and let us fight each other." On hearing the Philistine's words, Saul and all the Israelites were dismayed and terrified.

1 SAMUEL 17:10–11

Don't you just love the story of David and Goliath? David is the superhero of the little guys. He was a young boy with seven older brothers, and he looked after the family's sheep. He protected them from wild predators with a *slingshot*. (As a kid, I always thought that was boss. Still do, actually.)

David's people were at war with the Philistines, and the Philistines were led by a warrior named Goliath. I know you've heard of this guy. He was built like Dwayne "The Rock" Johnson, was as tall as your house, and had the latest battle gear. Every day for more than forty days, Goliath taunted the Israelites, asking if anyone had the courage to fight him. One day, when David came to deliver food to his brothers, David heard the challenge. You know how the story goes.

The battle for our hearts can feel a lot like David versus Goliath. It seems like evil stacks the odds against us. Here's why: evil never plays by the rules. *Do I have what it takes?* we wonder. But God is with us. *Am I strong enough?* Remember, we rely on God's strength, not ours. God has already won. Take a breath. There's nothing left to win.

Deep down you probably have some sense of who God made you to be: an artist, a politician, a pastor, a coach, a CEO, a mom, or whatever. Evil's great scheme is that it wants to squash who you were made to be, like Goliath thought he'd squash David. Don't give in and don't give up. Just reach into your pocket. I bet you'll find God has slipped in a few stones for you.

What giant is facing you right now?

MAY 19

GOD USES OUR FAILURES TO DISARM OUR PRIDE.

Whoever conceals their sins does not prosper, but the one who confesses and renounces them finds mercy.

PROVERBS 28:13

You're never as good as your greatest success, and you're never as bad as your worst failure. That's something I tell students on their first day at the law school where I've been teaching for almost a decade. When everything is going your way, it's easy to strut. When everything is crumbling, it's easy to think you're a loser. What I'm getting at is this: our identity is not anchored to our best or our worst moments. We live between them.

A big theme that immediately develops when we follow Jesus is the need to start living by a different set of rules. The world says the more money you have, the more important or powerful you are. God says the more money you have, the harder it is to be like Jesus. Why? Because money gives you options and independence. And God is inviting you to become more dependent on Him and have less confidence in what you own. The world says the more followers or fans you have, the more popular you are. But God says if you want to be popular with Him, you'll stay close to the lowly in heart where He is.

Jesus was drawn to the people who couldn't seem to get it together. He's crazy about the ones who are killing it, too, but often they just don't feel as desperate for Him. For most of us, there will be a time when this all changes. Something will happen that makes what we put our faith in, other than God, fall like a house of cards. Each of us will experience a defining moment that will shape our faith if we'll let it.

I think God uses our failures to disarm our pride. He meets us in the wreckage, and He makes us more humble. If you're riding high on a run of fortunate events, keep your eyes fixed on Jesus. If you're getting battered by a run of unfortunate events, remember that you're in good company.

**What past failure has taught you about
humility and dependence?**

GOD ISN'T AN EDITOR, HE'S A CREATOR. HE'S NOT LOOKING FOR TYPOS IN OUR LIVES. HE'S LOOKING FOR THE BEAUTY IN THEM.

I will forgive their wickedness and will remember their sins no more.

HEBREWS 8:12

I didn't set out to be an author. I wanted to build a school in Africa for child soldiers. If I wanted to bake cupcakes to sell, people would die. I'll stick with schools and words. A friend of mine encouraged me to write a book, so I did. I figured if there were a couple of typos—no big deal. We sold way over a million of them and gave all the money away, so I wrote another book. I learned I'm much better at living stories than making sure all the punctuation is correct, so I have a few people in my life who love that sort of thing, and they helped me out. One of them is Jon, who is married to my daughter, Lindsey. Jon is an engineer, but that also means he's really good with details, and he really likes grammar. (I still don't understand why, but I'm thankful nonetheless.) Jon would read my words and graciously fix all the errors I made. He didn't point out each one and shake his head in disapproval. He just took what I wrote and made it better.

I used to think God was like an editor trying to find all the typos in my life, standing over my shoulder like a schoolmarm ready to whack me on the knuckles with a yardstick. But I've learned that God isn't an editor; He's a creator. He's not giving us the hairy eyeball when we make mistakes. He's pointing toward the horizon with a gleam in His eye and asking us to lift our eyes up toward a better story. He wants to tell a story of redemption. Of everyone He could use to tell it, He's made you one of the main characters. He wants you to keep your eyes on Him.

If there's a typo or two on a couple of pages of your life, don't obsess over it. Keep writing. God's got this. He'll help you make the changes you need to make, but His purpose for your life is much bigger than giving you a failing grade.

What typo have you been obsessing over?

MAY 21

QUIT LETTING FEAR CALL THE SHOTS. GET BACK TO BUILDING THE ROCKETSHIP THAT WAS SUPPOSED TO BE YOUR LIFE.

The Spirit God gave us does not make us timid, but gives us power, love and self-discipline.

2 TIMOTHY 1:7

Because I'm a lawyer, one day I decided I would put my fears on trial. You can interrogate fear and give it a legitimate trial. You get to be the prosecutor and the defense. Is the fear valid, or is it trying to head-fake you into paralysis?

God gave us fear for a reason. It keeps us from going down that dark alley where a bunch of hoodlums are standing around. It compels us to leave the hurtful relationship. When fear works correctly, it keeps us safe. Nothing's wrong with that.

The problems come when fear misfires. If you let it go unchecked, fear will push you into a corner and lie to you about your worth. It'll steal your lunch money while you're distracted. Fear tells you hope is your imagination talking and pitches cynicism as courage. Fear will tell you that the big dream you have will never work and everyone is going to think you're crazy. Give fear too much power and it will rob you of your life. In a word, don't let fear punk you.

God gave us a spirit of wisdom so we would know when to listen to fear and when to shut it down. We get to be the gatekeepers who determine how much of it we'll let into our lives and in what circumstances. So next time you're racked with fear, put it on trial and judge whether the fear is warranted.

If it's not, which is usually the case, quit letting fear call the shots in your life. Get back to building the rocketship that was supposed to be your life.

Name the fear that you need to bring to Jesus.

THERE'S A LOT TO BE CONCERNED ABOUT.
THERE'S MORE TO BE HOPEFUL FOR.

Jesus said, "My kingdom is not of this world. If it were, my servants would fight to prevent my arrest by the Jewish leaders. But now my kingdom is from another place."

JOHN 18:36

I don't watch a lot of TV. I think the real world is *way* more interesting. But because I have several friends who work for the US government, and I serve as the Honorary Consul for the Republic of Uganda to the US, I need to stay up on things. I'll be honest, though—watching the news can be a real grind. It can make a person think everything is doom and gloom and that nothing good happens *ever*. I guess that's good for ratings. But the sad truth is, throughout the world, every day something devastating is happening. A country overrun by war, a community crushed by a mass shooting, a person targeted for a hate crime. Still, I believe God is at work to put an end to this suffering.

Sure, there's a lot to be concerned about, but we have even more reasons to be hopeful. Here's why: Jesus said His kingdom wasn't of this world. He said evil would win for a while, but that His kingdom of love would have the last word. And He said those of us who follow Him will be the ones who are laying the groundwork for His return. We'll be the runners who sprint ahead with the good news of what's coming.

Don't believe the people who tell you there's no hope. It's everywhere. It's like the smell in the air right before the rains come. We have hope because we trust in the God who sits above every conflict. We bring hope when we choose to fix our eyes on Jesus rather than on all the distractions around us.

Next time you hear bad news, ask yourself how you can be hope in the midst of it.

What are you feeling hopeless about?
How will you bring that to God?

MAY 23

GOD'S LOVE ISN'T AS COMPLICATED AS ALL OUR DISCUSSIONS ABOUT IT. KEEP IT SIMPLE: LOVE EVERYBODY, ALWAYS.

The teachers of religious law and the Pharisees sit in Moses' seat.
So you must be careful to do everything they tell you. But do not
do what they do, for they do not practice what they preach.

MATTHEW 23:2-3

God is love. He said so. It's easy to get confused when you stroll through the Old Testament and find harrowing tales of wars between people with names ending in -*ites*. Where is the God supposedly synonymous with love in those stories? Or what about when the Bible reads like a phone book and lists off generations of people with hard-to-pronounce names? (We're talking about you, Gomer and Uz.)

If God is love, we should spend our effort learning love, not dwelling on parts of the Old Testament God said He came to fulfill. It may feel good to correct someone's pronunciation of an obscure place in the Middle East or walk them through a maze of theological steps in the Minor Prophets. Some people delight in masking their own insecurity by making others feel small. They make faith complicated. Jesus had some stern words for them then and no doubt will in the future.

There is no end to the learning the Bible can provide. But if we're learning to be "right" instead of learning to love people the way Jesus did, we've missed the lesson.

There's nothing for us to gain from practicing love—no base pay, no guaranteed tenure, no arm patch or leg up in spiritual discussions. Instead, we'll find ourselves succeeding in introducing people to the real Jesus, not the one often argued about. We'll have hearts ready to learn what love is all about and hands ready to help whoever love is chasing. And spoiler alert, it's every person you ever have met or will meet.

God's love isn't as complicated as our discussions about it are. Keep it simple: love everybody, always.

What simple act of love can you do for someone right now?

MAY 24

ANXIETY NEVER LEAVES A RANSOM NOTE WHEN IT STEALS OUR LIVES.

The righteous cry out, and the LORD hears them; he delivers them from all their troubles.

PSALM 34:17

I have a friend who started an organization to help people struggling with depression and thoughts of suicide. He's a compassionate guy and sees the hurt and need underneath the surface of people pretending they have it together. He's a great example to me. And he reminds me that there's this myth going around that if you believe in Jesus, feeling joy should be your default position. But the Bible talks a lot about sadness too—it doesn't try to minimize it or sweep it away with saccharine phrases. The book of Psalms should come with Kleenex.

What I'm getting at is that you don't have to feel bad for feeling sad if you're a Christian. Even Jesus was racked with sadness at times in the Bible. But God also says His mercies are new every morning—even the ones when you don't want to get out of bed. With every sunrise, God gives us another blank sheet of paper and invites us to fill it up with things that make us come alive.

All of us experience negative emotions from time to time, and some of us were born with an extra dose of them because of our genes. Don't perpetuate the stigmas hovering around people already. Let people be sad if they need to be. Go ahead and be sad yourself if you need to. Then find your way back to hope. If you've lost your way, find someone who is safe and who you can trust. Find someone who will reach out to you the way God reaches out to all of us—fiercely and without stopping until He's got us wrapped in a hug.

If you know someone trapped by their hurts, go to them. Don't make a list; make a call. And if you're the one hurting, be sad, but don't get stuck. Find someone to travel the path with you. You'll know you've found the right person if they don't try to fix you—they'll just want to be with you the way Jesus was with us.

Who do you know who is grieving something right now? How can you bring God's message of love and hope to them?

SOMETIMES WE ASK FOR HELP AND GOD GIVES US HOPE, NOT BECAUSE IT'S DIFFERENT BUT BECAUSE IT'S THE SAME.

You are the light of the world. A town built on a hill cannot be hidden. Neither do people light a lamp and put it under a bowl. Instead they put it on its stand, and it gives light to everyone in the house. In the same way, let your light shine before others, that they may see your good deeds and glorify your Father in heaven.

MATTHEW 5:14–16

My friend Doug and I volunteered as summer camp counselors for Young Life when we were in college. Young Life introduces youth to Jesus by loving them like He loved us—with no agenda. The young people who come don't have to know Bible verses or Christian songs or take positions on the social issues of the day to feel like they belong. We know, just like Jesus did, that we meet each other at the starting line, not the finish line.

Spending every day outside with kids for weeks was a lot of fun, but it had us begging for a day off. Really, anything would do—even a twenty-four-hour virus. God answered those prayers by letting us catch something else instead: a renewed vision for what He was up to with the kids. Right after I'd pray for an illness-induced rest, one of the kids would open up to me about his lifelong desire to feel like his dad actually liked him or tell me his time at camp was the first time he had felt truly seen and loved. Just when Doug was ready to escape camp by canoe in the night, a kid would tell him he didn't want to use drugs anymore because he was starting to believe his life mattered.

These experiences taught me that sometimes when we ask for help, God gives us hope instead. When we want help getting through another day, God gives us hope in what He's doing in and through us.

The next time you find yourself looking for a way out, look for evidence of God on the move in someone's life around you. They've probably been asking God to give them a little hope, and what God is giving them is you.

What evidence do you see of God using your life for good?

THE STORIES WE TELL OURSELVES SHAPE US. LISTEN TO THE ONE BEING NARRATED BY HOPE.

Jesus spoke all these things to the crowd in parables; he did not say anything to them without using a parable.

MATTHEW 13:34

My worst subject in school was always . . . school. I couldn't focus in class and would fidget until the bell rang at the end of the day. I had an excuse for everything. Being late, not turning in homework, not coming to school at all. I was terribly bored, so I became incredibly detached.

There was one teacher, though, who wasn't so focused on having his students just memorize information so we could pass the test. Instead, he tried to get us excited by telling us the backstories hidden within history. He told us about the less likely things, the surprising turns and feelings behind the failures. He wove together a true-to-life picture of real people in real danger, not just facts about battles won or lost.

When cold facts were taught with threats of failure if we didn't memorize the data, I usually failed. Most of us don't learn because we're threatened or cajoled or shamed into it. But when stories were told about kind or compassionate or courageous people, setting an example for who we might become, I leaned in and my mind opened up. We're all wired this way.

Jesus rarely spoke to anyone without telling them a story. The reason is simple. We accept the stories told to us with our faith, our life experience, and our hearts. Because well-told stories are so powerful in our lives, it's not surprising when we realize the stories we tell ourselves have tremendous power to shape us. If you tell yourself you're a bad student, you'll probably become one. If you convince yourself you don't have enough time to help in the soup kitchen, you probably won't. If you say to yourself you're not fun to be around for long enough, you probably won't be.

Listen to who God says you are and what He believes is possible in your life. Breathe in hope and breathe out your life. Be picky about listening to the stories you or others have been telling over your life that just aren't true. You'll know if it's God telling the story because it will always be one filled with hope and possibility.

What story is God telling through your life this year?

HOPE FOR OTHERS WHAT YOU HOPE FOR YOURSELF.

Therefore we do not lose heart. Though outwardly we are wasting away, yet inwardly we are being renewed day by day.

2 CORINTHIANS 4:16

As Sweet Maria will tell you, I haven't always been the most patient person. I think fast food takes too long. The best part about sushi is you don't have to wait to cook the fish. My default setting is all gas, no brake. Sometimes I have a hard time slowing down long enough to have the deep conversations I'd otherwise like to have or be asked the hard questions. But I'm trying to do better. Have you ever said that to yourself with an issue or trait you just can't seem to get some distance from? *I'm trying to do better.* While the people around us are hoping we'll try a little harder, you know you're giving it everything you've got—even if it doesn't look like a lot.

We can give ourselves the benefit of the doubt because we know God is always changing us and transforming us into people who look a little more like Jesus. He's taking the long view with us. Thank goodness for that.

Have you ever noticed how easy it is to give yourself some grace, but it's a lot harder to give it to someone else who we don't think is changing fast enough? What if we gave others the benefit of the doubt we're quick to extend to ourselves? When someone snubs us or makes us feel inferior, what if we remembered they're still in the process of becoming? They're probably just as insecure as we are and just made the kind of mistake we make all the time. Just like we're growing out of the impatient or unkind or dogmatic or pretentious people we used to be, other people may be changing too. Give them a little grace while it happens.

So when someone slips up, celebrate how far they've come—don't think about how long it took them to get there.

Think of someone close to you who's been going through a difficult time. What kind of growth have you seen in their lives lately? Share that with them today.

HUMBLE PEOPLE DAZZLE GOD.

Do nothing out of selfish ambition or vain conceit. Rather, in humility value others above yourselves.

PHILIPPIANS 2:3

When I was in college, I started paying attention to the people who lived like Jesus. I wanted to figure out what made them different and set them apart from everyone else. It quickly became clear that one of the qualities they all shared was this: they were humble. They didn't seem too concerned about what other people thought of them. They were too busy thinking about other people.

We often think humility means being down on ourselves. You know, the people who brush off compliments with self-effacing barbs. We think humility is the opposite of the guy at the gym who stares at his flexed muscles in the mirror. We know humility doesn't brag or name-drop, but we mistake being humble for becoming wallflowers. Humility doesn't insist we hide or make ourselves look small. Humble people aren't concerned with seeming less important. They just don't think about themselves much at all.

God said humble people consider others more significant than themselves. Considering others means thinking about them, praying for them, doing the unlikely acts of love with no expectation of reciprocation. Considering others means taking all the time we obsess about how much people like us (or how much we wish they did) and thinking instead about who in our lives might need another friend just like us.

God delights in humble people because they continue the work Jesus started in the world. Humble people pray for God to open their eyes to the pain of people around them. They give in secret without a second thought. They don't keep track of all of the good they've done. It's these kinds of humble people who dazzle God.

What have you done out of humility in the past week?

GRACE MEANS TOMORROW'S ALWAYS A FRIEND AND YESTERDAY ISN'T AN ENEMY ANYMORE.

Forget the former things; do not dwell on the past.

ISAIAH 43:18

Peter Pan has a unique shadow. You might recall the scene from the Disney movie when Peter and his shadow chase each other around the kids' room until Peter wrestles his shadow down so it can be sewn back on his shoes. Sometimes our past gets stuck to us like our shadows. As much as we try to shake it off or outrun it, we turn around and there it is. I suppose you could eliminate your shadow by living in total darkness, but that's no life either, is it? Sometimes I wish I could just detach my past from myself permanently. There'd be no chase on my part. I'd let it run out the door and wave as it headed down the street.

We can't escape our shadows like Peter Pan did, if only for a while. In some ways our past is stuck to us no matter what we do. We don't need to let who we used to be decide who we're going to be. When we treat the shadows of our past like they're living, breathing versions of ourselves today, we give our past too much power. Here's a truth that's worth believing: the stuff that happened yesterday that's hounding you is irrelevant to the tomorrow waiting to greet you. We can move forward in grace, knowing the fight with yesterday is over. Grace won, even if we don't realize it yet.

Tomorrow is our Neverland, where our tries never run out of time. You can't escape your shadow, of course, but you also don't have to give it as much airtime. Grace means this: tomorrow's always a friend. It isn't that yesterday didn't happen. It just doesn't matter anymore.

What from your past do you need to let go of today?

MAY 30

FEAR AND HOPE ONLY HAVE THE POWER
WE GIVE THEM IN OUR LIVES.

Do not be afraid; do not be discouraged, for the LORD your God will
be with you wherever you go.

JOSHUA 1:9

Someone once said, "Attitude is the difference between an adventure and an ordeal." So change your attitude and have a better life, right? If you're like me, you're thinking, *Right. Easier said than done.* Consider this: we can control our attitudes by choosing where we put our hope. If you're the kind of person who sees everything as an ordeal instead of an adventure, what you need is a big dose of hope.

Hope and trust always travel together. Hoping without trust is just a wish. When my son Adam was learning to fly our plane and I'd give him the controls in the copilot seat, you can bet that I was wondering if this would end up being an ordeal or an adventure. I knew he was a trustworthy guy and an great pilot, so instead of just hoping, I had my parachute handy. I leaned over, then said to Adam, "You got this."

When you're standing between an ordeal or an adventure, find someone you trust to go with you, and choose hope along the way. Hope can turn a crisis into a chance to grow. It can change a heated argument into an opportunity for deep connection. When we approach our days with hope, we loosen our white-knuckled grip and see something beautiful on the other side. We can turn an ordeal into an adventure. With someone we can trust and hope as our perspective, we'll find adventures where we used to see crises. God sent His Son into the world with a message for us. Jesus was someone we could put our trust in. He was someone who could help us when we needed more hope than we could muster ourselves.

When things go sideways on you, find your way back to Jesus. If you listen closely enough in the chaos, I wouldn't be surprised if you hear the words "You got this" whispered over you.

What are you facing right now where God might
be whispering to you, "You got this"?

ACQUAINTANCES WILL KNOW US FOR WHAT WE'VE DONE. FRIENDS WILL REMEMBER US FOR HOW WE LOVED.

A friend loves at all times, and a brother is born for a time of adversity.

PROVERBS 17:17

It's always a little strange to hear someone introduce a person by reading a long biography at an event. Bios like this are usually lists of the most impressive things they've done, credentials they have, and recognition they've received. The idea is to tell people why the speaker is qualified, why they deserve our attention for the next twenty or thirty minutes, and why they are an authority we should trust on a subject. But I always wish the bios sounded more like something a friend would write. I wish they sounded more like a wedding toast.

When friends describe us, they share stories of how we dropped everything to be with them when they lost someone they couldn't imagine life without. They usually slip in an embarrassing story of a mistake we made during a time in our lives we're still trying to forget, and they always talk about how well we loved the people around us. You don't hear many highlights from their résumé and their education or degrees or title. You just hear about love and friendship.

Acquaintances will know us for what we did. They'll know about the nonprofit we started or the award we received. They might even know about our reputation for being kind and gracious. None of this is bad, of course. These are stories *about* our lives. They just don't have the same weight as stories *from* our lives. Friends will remember us for how we loved. They'll be impressed by our accomplishments only because they know the heart behind our actions.

Keep in mind, we'll be known for our opinions, but we'll be remembered for our love. I can think of no better introduction, no better bio, than for people to say our greatest expression of love in the world was that we were a faithful friend.

What expression of friendship have you received this week?

JUNE

JUNE 1

PRIDE IS ALWAYS SIZING UP OTHER PEOPLE; HUMILITY IS ALWAYS SHOWING PEOPLE HOW MUCH THEY CAN GROW.

The LORD God said, "It is not good for the man to be alone. I will make a helper suitable for him."

GENESIS 2:18

It's easy to spot someone who thinks a little more highly of themselves than the rest of us. Take a sports team for instance. There's often a player with extraordinary talent, but he's not necessarily the most valuable player because he hasn't figured out how to bring out the best in his teammates yet. He's the guy who doesn't pass the ball. Who knows where this comes from? Maybe it's the kid from school who got too much attention for his or her looks and not enough for their character.

It's much easier to be talented than it is to be humble, but it's hard to be successful without humility. When we aim for fame instead of sound character, pride slips in the back door every time. It lies to us not only about our value but about everyone else's. It says either we're not good enough or they aren't. Pride loves to compare itself with the next person in hopes that they don't quite measure up. Humility says there's room for all of us to flourish side by side, doing our best. Pride says success means beating the competition, and everyone is the competition. Kindness passes the ball and lets everyone take a shot.

The hidden cost of pride is isolation. We create distance between us and people who are difficult to be around. Sometimes we create it instantly, and other times it takes awhile, but the result is usually the same. Since pride feeds on being better than other people, we rob ourselves of the opportunity to lift others up when we're consumed with proving we're better than them. Pride springs from insecurity that tells us there's not enough love, attention, recognition, and success to go around, so it grabs as much as it can. Humility sees rivers of opportunities and delights in seeing others have their time in the spotlight.

Isolation is costly. It will cost you your friends, your beautiful opportunities, and your reputation. None of us can afford it.

In what ways have you been isolating yourself? Or, do you know someone who is isolating themselves?

JUNE 2

PEOPLE WHO SPEND ALL THEIR TIME TRYING TO MAKE MONEY SPEND ALL THEIR MONEY TRYING TO MAKE TIME. BE WEALTHY IN FRIENDSHIPS.

Do not think of yourself more highly than you ought, but rather think of yourself with sober judgment, in accordance with the faith God has distributed to each of you.

ROMANS 12:3

According to researchers, we're bombarded with upward of five thousand advertisements a day. That's a big number. These ads tell us we'll be more likable if we buy the right car or soap or get in better shape. Without really knowing why, other than the desire we all have for love and acceptance, we get the car or soap or buy the new gym membership, some trendy workout clothes, and cutting-edge supplements. The ads tell us we'll be more at peace if we remodel our home, so we set our hearts on marble countertops and a new deck outside, imagining the dinner parties we'll have and the compliments we'll get.

Advertisers know that what we long for more than anything else is connection. We want to be accepted unconditionally and have deeper relationships where we're more fully known. But they make us think we need more stuff to make it happen, so we spend our time trying to make the money we hope will lead to more intimacy. They know they have us when we believe that we need to spruce ourselves up to get what is already incredibly available to us.

Don't take the bait. We don't need to present a different version of ourselves to make new friends; we need to be more authentic with the ones we already have. I've enjoyed dinners on friends' decks before, but I've never left thinking about the deck. I left thinking about the laughter, about the deep conversation, about the beauty of talking about real life. We don't need to renovate our kitchens to invite people over for dinner parties. We just need to make sure the local pizza place delivers.

Money will make you happy from time to time. Living into the simplest version of who God made you to be will always make you rich in friendships. These friends don't care what you have. They love who you really are.

Who do you feel most comfortable being yourself with?

JUNE 3

LOVE DOESN'T NEED TO KEEP TRACK OF THE OUTCOMES. PEOPLE AREN'T PROJECTS.

And over all these virtues put on love, which binds them all together in perfect unity.

COLOSSIANS 3:14

When my kids were young, we designated a spot on the wall in our kitchen to keep track of how fast they grew. Each of our kids had a section, and we marked their height in pencil every few months. It was fun to see how quickly they sprang up, and it let Sweet Maria and I know where all the food was going. Sadly for the kids, they knew this also meant we'd stand our ground about eating broccoli. That wall became a measure of progress—both for their growing bodies and for our effectiveness as parents.

We all want some metrics to look at so we can see if we're making progress. That wall reminds me of the tendency we all have to know that our efforts are making a difference. We're hoping for a raise at the end of the year. A more important job title. During a fund-raiser, we want to see the thermometer get filled in with a marker until we hit the goal. If you're a college student, you tally each class, credit, and semester to the ultimate goal of a degree. It's normal to want quantifiable results from our efforts. It helps us make our choices.

Love, on the other hand, resists all our attempts to measure how well it's working. Whether it's a close friend, a family member, or a young person we've taken under our wing, we love them simply because they're worthy of love. When love has an agenda, it isn't love anymore. It's just another program. We choose to give away love for no other reason than our recognition that people are worth it.

People aren't projects; people are people. For us that means that love doesn't need to keep track of how much it costs us or try to control the outcomes.

Who can you show today that you see them as a person not a project?

JUNE 4

TELL PEOPLE WHO THEY'RE BECOMING,
NOT WHO THEY WERE.

Encourage one another and build each other up, just as in fact you are doing.

1 THESSALONIANS 5:11

One of my favorite things about Jesus was His knack for seeing who people were becoming and helping them move in that direction. When He walked by Matthew, He didn't see a tax collector who was likely ripping people off. He saw a friend who would stick with Him like a brother—one who would eventually write a book about His life. When a woman was pulled from a scandalous love affair and thrown at His feet to be scorned, He didn't see an adulteress. He saw a person who was about to begin living a better story. He knew what the power of redemption was when it was let off the leash. He knew love had the power to transform anyone, and He lived like everyone He met was in the process of turning into love.

It's easy to look past our own shortcomings because we know the person we're becoming. We know the lessons we've learned, the efforts we've made, the sleepless nights we've endured, the promises we've made to ourselves. We know our own good intentions, and we're able to believe there's hope for personal growth, even if we have a few setbacks along the way.

Grant that same grace to others. Don't go for the low-hanging fruit. Start with a few of the people who may have hurt you. Maybe you thought you were moving in the same direction, and they changed. Maybe you were betrayed and haven't quite healed. Jesus endured the ultimate hurt when He was nailed to a cross, and even then He proclaimed a better future for the ones who were responsible and for the thieves by his side. Jesus set the example for us: tell people who they're becoming, not who they used to be.

Who will you encourage today with words of affirmation?

JUNE 5

SOMETIMES WHEN WE'RE LOOKING FOR AN ANSWER, GOD SENDS US A FRIEND.

Listen to advice and accept discipline, and at the end you will be counted among the wise.

PROVERBS 19:20

When I was younger I owned a yellow truck that you'd be generous to call a clunker. I was pretty neglectful of the maintenance needs, especially changing the oil. It actually became a kind of game to see how badly I could treat that bucket of bolts and see how long it ran. I was kind of hoping the engine would burst into flames while I drove down the highway. How cool would that be? Because I was always driving with the strong possibility I'd soon be hitch-hiking, there's a special place in my heart when I see a driver stranded on the side of the road, smoke billowing around them while they look at the engine, probably for the first time in their life.

While they're guessing which thing is the engine and which one is the radiator, a wave of relief washes over them when the friend they called twenty minutes ago slows to a stop behind them, yellow lights blinking. Instead of pulling out the oil stick or banging something with a wrench, all they needed was someone with more knowledge to help.

The same is true for many other problems we face in life. We think we need to become an expert on a given topic to figure out how to solve a problem when all we really need is someone else to come alongside us. It's true when we need to fix a car, and it's true when we want to understand grace. Sometimes when we're looking for an answer, God sends us a friend.

What problem are you facing that you need help with?

JUNE 6

THE PEOPLE WITH THE GREATEST LOVE, NOT THE MOST INFORMATION, WILL INFLUENCE US TO CHANGE.

The heart of the discerning acquires knowledge, for the ears of the wise seek it out.

PROVERBS 18:15

In the early seventeenth century, Galileo fell in love with the telescope and made some big discoveries. When he looked through the lens to observe all the other planets, he realized the sun didn't actually revolve around the earth. It was the other way around.

It seems obvious to us now because it's been common knowledge in our lifetime, but it was a groundbreaking discovery then. It also contradicted the teaching of his church. Their beliefs about the Bible's description of the earth and the sun made them hold fast to a doctrine that the earth was the center of the universe, and Galileo's discovery threatened to unravel their framework for understanding the world. They actually charged him with heresy and threw him in jail.

Sometimes we think we have all the information, and we cling to it for our security. We think we have the truth, and we're sure we're right about really complicated things. Then we find out the information was wrong. Things aren't quite as certain as they seemed. It goes against what we thought was absolutely true.

When that happens, we can only hope we're the kind of people who put our trust in God rather than our knowledge. We'll want to be the kind of people who went all in on love so if our understanding of the truth changes, we're still good.

It will be the people with the greatest love, not the most information, who influence change. Knowledge is important, but our ideas change—and God's already given us His greatest idea. Love.

What belief are you holding on to that isn't leading you to become more loving?

THE PRICE OF ACCEPTANCE IS TOO HIGH IF IT COSTS WHO YOU ARE.

Fear of man will prove to be a snare, but whoever trusts in the LORD is kept safe.

PROVERBS 29:25

A friend of mine invited me to a NASCAR race one time, and I love this friend, so I thought, *Sure, why not?* I'd never been to a car race before, so I wasn't quite sure what to wear. Most of the people I know who love NASCAR wear racing jackets and hats with a bunch of logos on them. Right around the time I was Googling drivers to try to figure out which driver's jersey I would wear, I remembered I don't know any drivers and I don't know anything about NASCAR. Here's the thing: it didn't matter what I wore. We don't need to dress like the rest of the crowd just to enjoy an afternoon with a friend. We just need to show up the way we are.

We spend a lot more time than we realize thinking about what others might think. We worry about whether we'll wear the right clothes, or say the right words, or be accepted by whichever group we're around. The truth is, it gets in the way of us just being who God made us to be.

We don't need to conform in order to belong. You'll rob people of the opportunity to see the world through your eyes if you try to act like everyone else—or even worse, somebody else. The price of acceptance is too high if it costs who you are.

Do you want to do something awesome for God? Go be you. The more yourself you are, the better chance we have to see a little bit more of Jesus uniquely expressed through you.

In what ways are you focusing too much on what others think about you?

JUNE 8

THE TEACHERS I'VE LEARNED THE MOST FROM DIDN'T THINK THEY WERE TEACHING ME; THEY JUST THOUGHT WE WERE FRIENDS.

Come, see a man who told me everything I ever did. Could this be the Messiah?

JOHN 4:29

In certain circles, "witnessing" means approaching total strangers and asking them very personal questions about what they thought would happen when they died. Maybe you've been approached by someone doing this, and it threw you on your heels for a second. Even if you follow Jesus, it can feel a little strange to be accosted by a stranger with an agenda no matter what they're selling, even if it's eternal life.

Once I became a lawyer, I found out what witnesses actually do. Witnesses are called to the stand to tell people what they *saw and heard and experienced*. They give details about how they experienced what was being testified to. They don't take the stand to say what it all means. This is left to the experts. I started to wonder if that's what Jesus meant when He told us to bear witness of Him by simply telling people what we've seen and heard.

Bearing witness to the story of Jesus can happen in any form and in any place, but it seems to happen best when we have relationships of trust with people. We don't have to gain a bunch of knowledge and figure out all the answers before we share our thoughts about our faith. God invites us to let people know what we've seen and heard and experienced. We're all amateurs, not experts, when it comes to faith.

The teachers I've learned the most from didn't think they were teaching me, and they didn't claim to be experts; they just thought we were friends. They didn't come at me with a step-by-step plan to move me in a certain direction or talk me into faith. They just told me what they had seen and heard and experienced firsthand.

If you have to choose between being a teacher or being a friend, be a friend. We bear witness to an immense God by being the most authentic version of ourselves.

**Who in your life needs you to bear witness
to God's love by being a true friend?**

THE WORLD DOESN'T NEED A COPY OF SOMEONE ELSE, IT NEEDS YOU.

You created my inmost being; you knit me together in my mother's womb.

PSALM 139:13

When I was little, I had a friend with a pet parrot. I used to love going over to his house after school. I had seen a lot of birds by then, but this was the only one I had seen that could talk. My friend taught his parrot some words he probably shouldn't have, and I remember standing there with my mouth open when the parrot gave me an earful.

My fascination with the parrot got me thinking about what it would say if it didn't just have to repeat what other people said. Think about it. If a parrot is smart enough to mimic the sounds of English, maybe it's smart enough to express some original ideas. I'd love to get inside a parrot's head.

We'll never know what life looks like from the parrot's perspective, but my curiosity about the parrot's ideas made me curious about what other people think. Each person has a unique perspective they bring to the world. They have different characteristics that show us some small part of who God is, and they open our eyes to new ways of seeing when they let us in on their experience.

A lot of us end up acting like parrots, though—just repeating things we hear from other people. We miss the opportunity to tell people about our unique perspective because we're too concerned with sounding like everyone else. The world doesn't need another copy of someone else; the world needs you.

In what ways can you be more authentically yourself today?

FRIENDS ARE PEOPLE WHO HOPE FOR THINGS IN OUR LIVES WE HAVEN'T EVEN THOUGHT OF YET.

May he give you the desire of your heart and make all your plans succeed.

PSALM 20:4

I love being around someone who's chasing an audacious dream. Everything they do and how they see the world is all about moving toward it. It's infectious. I've been hosting gatherings we call Dream Big where we get people of all ages together and ask them about their big ambitions. Then we work together as a group to put some wheels on their dreams. Some of the people who come to Dream Big already know what they're chasing. Others come because they feel stuck and their lives need a rocket boost.

By the end of our time together, this group of strangers becomes lifelong friends, which is so beautiful. Sharing our dreams has this affect on us. It involves vulnerability, creates community, and with this comes intimacy and relationships. My favorite part is when we break into groups so everyone can get some outside perspective from their fellow dreamers. What happens is that these dreamers think of totally new things for themselves when they hear about each other's ambitions. They come up with ideas that unlock a problem or broaden a horizon for someone else. Everyone ends up imagining a new possibility they had never even considered before.

That's what friends do. They hope for things in our lives we may not have been able to hope for ourselves yet. They see pathways of possibility that had looked like dead ends to us. They have clarity that comes from objectivity, and they see what's possible for us, not all the obstacles that could hold us back.

Find some good friends and bring your biggest ambitions. Spread them out on the table and talk about them. Why is it that you want what you want? What are the setbacks you've experienced? What needs to happen to land the plane with your idea? You'll know you've found the right friends to share your ideas with if their hopes for you outdistance even your own hopes for yourself.

What big ambition are you holding in your heart?

WE WON'T BE REMEMBERED FOR WHAT WE SAID BUT FOR HOW AVAILABLE WE WERE.

"What do you want me to do for you?" Jesus asked him.

MARK 10:51

For the most part, I don't set meetings. I just ask people to call me whenever they want to talk. To some of my friends, this sounds a little weird at first. Some of them have careers where setting up and attending meetings takes up much of each day. Here's what I've found: most of us spend more time setting up a meeting and then moving it a couple of times than we do meeting.

The tension here is that we want our days to be predictable and measured. We want to be efficient because our lives are already crammed with competing activities. But this efficiency comes at a price. If we're not careful, we can turn our friendships into appointments. We'll trade a life of engagement for a bunch of engagements. But when I look at Jesus, I see a person who was willing to be constantly interrupted. When a little child or a person in need came to Him, He didn't ask one of His disciples to find a slot later in the day when He wasn't booked. He stopped what He was doing to find a woman who had touched Him. He had lunch with a guy who was hanging out in a sycamore tree.

One time He and His disciples were traveling together with a large crowd around them. A blind man named Bartimaeus cried out to Jesus, begging Him to have mercy, and the crowd kept hushing him. But Jesus thought Bartimaeus was more important, so He asked them to bring Bartimaeus so He could restore his sight. Jesus saw Bartimaeus as a person, not a problem. Jesus never saw people as interruptions. He saw them as opportunities.

Don't carve out time for people in your life. Make your whole calendar an opportunity to be more like Jesus. We might be known for how much we knew or what we said, but we'll be remembered for how available we were.

Who can you be more available to today?

THE HIDDEN COST OF OUR FAITH IS THAT EVERYTHING DOESN'T GET TO BE ABOUT US ANYMORE.

Seek first his kingdom and his righteousness, and all these things will be given to you as well.

MATTHEW 6:33

We live in a world pretty obsessed with celebrity. We have celebrity chefs, celebrity pastors, celebrity gymnasts, and celebrity athletes. You can be a celebrity if you eat the most hot dogs or bake the biggest cookie. It seems most of the world around us says the pinnacle of existence is to become a celebrity at something. The same dynamic plays out on social media platforms. They become a measure of our popularity and influence—the more followers the better. We've engineered our world to amp up ourselves.

But Jesus had a way of making life about everyone else. Think about your birthday. It's a day you get to revel in the attention. For Jesus, His birthday is an annual reminder that He came to give Himself to others. He gave up the heavens to come be with us in the mess we had made. There was no day in His life when Jesus was all about Himself; His concern was always the lonely and forgotten. He did incredible, new, worthy things in people's lives, and He usually whispered to them, "Tell no one." This was His plan for self-promotion.

The hidden cost of our faith is that everything doesn't get to be about us anymore. Being like Jesus means giving up our comfort and security so we can widen the circle to include more people. Not just the "cool kids." Following Jesus means we don't get the last word anymore; we defer to others instead.

The great thing about following Jesus is that we don't have to worry about self-preservation or popularity, because our purpose shifts from promoting ourselves to helping other people. To whatever degree people look to you, you don't need to deflect attention. Instead, reflect your faith by skipping the curtain call and getting back in the crowd to lift up more people. If we make everything about us, it'll never be about Jesus.

What would shift inside you if you focused more energy and perspective on pursuing God's kingdom today?

JUNE 13

WE'LL KNOW WE'RE GROWING IN OUR FAITH WHEN OUR LOVE FOR PEOPLE DWARFS OUR OPINIONS ABOUT THEM.

Follow God's example, therefore, as dearly loved children and walk in the way of love, just as Christ loved us and gave himself up for us as a fragrant offering and sacrifice to God.

EPHESIANS 5:1-2

I'm not a big fan of routines. They tend to make life a bit too predictable for me. There are a few I keep though, mainly to make sure I get out of bed and don't leave the house with one pant leg tucked into a sock. Routines, or beautiful habits, can be clarifying for us. They can be great reminders of what's important to us and guide us back to those important truths. The problem arises when we apply our habits and routines to the people around us. What I mean is, we tend to box people into our assumptions and expectations about how others should spend their time. You'll know this is a problem for you if you develop an impression of someone because of what you've experienced them doing and, without really meaning to, stop seeing the possibility that they could change or surprise you with some new, beautiful aspect of who they are.

Here's a routine I've started: I've stopped letting my opinion become a filter that interprets someone's every move or every word. When someone does something I don't understand yet or reacts differently to a situation than I would, I assume that God's up to something beautifully different in their life than He is in mine.

What if our default setting toward others wasn't a pile of opinions? What if it was a load of assumptions that they have wonderful motives tempered by the same insecurities and failures at execution we experience?

If we're going to do this, we'll need to reprogram the way we see each other. Changing this routine isn't an overnight exercise. It'll take practice and diligence. It is rooted in believing we ourselves are loved and being self-aware enough to realize we all have a few rough edges we're working to smooth out. It's allowing others the same grace we want for ourselves. Next time you engage with someone and assume they'll be the same version of themselves, pause for a moment. Find a new routine. Carve a new groove in your brain. God created each of us, and much of the work He's doing in people is happening in their hearts where we can't see it yet.

Make love your routine, even when (especially when) someone reinforces the opinion that they're difficult. We'll know we're growing when our love for people dwarfs our opinions about them.

What new routine could you create that would enable you to be more consistently full of love?

WE GROW WHERE WE'RE LOVED.

The righteous choose their friends carefully, but the way of the wicked leads them astray.

PROVERBS 12:26

A buddy of mine was telling me the other day how proud he was of his daughter. She's smart as a whip and was being pursued by a lot of top universities because of her test scores and top-of-class GPA. What surprised me, though, was when he told me she wasn't choosing college based on the pedigree of the institution but by the caliber and quality of students who go there. When I asked why, he said that she wants to surround herself with the kind of people she wants to grow into. While she could have a framed degree from a world-famous university, she'd rather have a heart that reflects the values she cherishes.

It made me wonder: What if our personal growth depends less on what organizations and social issues we identify with and more on who we're surrounded by? When I look at Jesus, He seemed less concerned about the place and more concerned about the people in it. He wasn't interested in recognition by the biggest instituitions or most powerful people. He seemed more drawn to those in need and less mesmerized by people who had little influence as society may measure it.

If you're on the cusp of a major transition in life or just feel a little stuck in the life you have, take a look around at the people. Are they people who are pouring love into your life? Are you putting a big load of your love into them? Are they interacting with the world by leading with their opinions, or do they see the world through the lens of love?

You can trade all the accolades from strangers and a dozen degrees from pedigreed institutions for a couple of good friends. We only really grow where we're loved. Don't trade one for the other.

Who are you surrounding yourself with these days? What influence are they having on who you're becoming?

GOD MAKES MOUNTAINS TO DAZZLE US AND FRIENDS TO LOVE US.

Ask the animals, and they will teach you, or the birds in the sky, and they will tell you; or speak to the earth, and it will teach you, or let the fish in the sea inform you. Which of all these does not know that the hand of the LORD has done this?

JOB 12:7–9

It's amusing to watch little kids hard at work with a box of crayons. Their tongues stick out a little while they concentrate on staying inside the lines or make a messy explosion of colors and swirls. Regardless of the style, it seems every little kid runs up to mom or dad when they're done, waving the picture in front of them. They want to know if they did a good job. Their work feels like an extension of them, and they want to be praised for it.

When God created Mount Everest and the beach in my backyard, He was showing us a little part of Himself. Out of the overflow of all the joy and life within Him, He threw stars in the sky and told the sun to rise every morning. He made hippos and mice and giraffes and kangaroos with pouches for more kangaroos. I think He wanted to instill in us a sense of awe and wonder when we see these things. God wasn't looking for our approval when He did these things. He was hoping maybe we'd look to the One responsible for the beauty and see how He delights in creation and in us.

Since God isn't here with us in physical form, sometimes it's easy to feel like He's distant. It can be hard to know how He feels about us or what His character is really like. I think that's why God painted parts of Himself into creation. He said He made human beings in His image, each of us reflecting a little part of who He is.

If you don't feel like you can see God very clearly today, look up and look around: He hid parts of Himself in everything He made. You hold part of His essence. Your friends do too. So do the mountains and lakes and trees. Breathe it in. Take it in today. Give thanks to God for the countless ways He chose to dazzle us with His creative expressions in the world.

What attributes of God do you see as you orient yourself to nature and God's creation?

JUNE 16

WISE PEOPLE KNOW THE RIGHT
ARGUMENTS TO LOSE.

Why do you look at the speck of sawdust in your brother's eye and
pay no attention to the plank in your own eye?

MATTHEW 7:3

I grew up in a family where my sister and I didn't get along very well. God's idea of putting us in families wasn't a mistake. It was a terrific idea. It's great having people bring us soup when we're sick and help to rake the leaves. When we're kids, a sibling becomes a built-in playmate to find mischief together. One of the biggest ways families are a gift is how they teach us to disagree with one another. Here's why.

Our family shows us that our feelings matter and people are meant to have different perspectives and opinions. We find out early on that sometimes we're right and sometimes we're wrong. We also have the opportunity to learn that, most times, being "right" isn't as important as staying in our relationships. We also learn to say we're sorry and make amends when we've hurt someone's feelings.

All this is a good warm-up for the rest of our lives. We will encounter people we disagree with every day, and Jesus calls us to love those people, not just tolerate them. Jesus never told us to be "right." He told us to be gracious. He told us to love people who disagree with us and to even love our enemies. There are ways to disagree poorly and well, but love knows how to do it right and do it often.

Wise people know the right arguments to lose. The fact is, it's most of them. If it's more important for you to be "right" than to be like Jesus, then it's time to get back to the basics of your faith and your relationships. Good relationships can last a lifetime. Don't let an argument spoil even a few moments.

What plank do you have in your own eye?

GOD DESIGNED US TO NEED EACH OTHER. THINK BUS, NOT UNICYCLE.

Dear friends, let us love one another, for love comes from God. Everyone who loves has been born of God and knows God.

1 JOHN 4:7

Sometimes it can be tempting to go it alone. When the time it takes to teach someone the job exceeds the time it would take us to do it, we think, *I'll just do this by myself.* When you've had an argument with a friend or spouse, it's tempting to want to tag out. Don't do it. We need a community around us because we need each other.

God designed us to do life together, and He teaches us love's greatest lessons in community. Why? I'm not really sure. Here's what I do know: if you have a solid community of people and fail big time, they'll still be there when the smoke clears. If you ace the test or get the big promotion, your friends celebrate with you, but they're not fooled. They know you're more than your accomplishments. At its best, a community shows us how God feels about us and is a living demonstration that He's not going anywhere either.

When I think about the relationships that matter the most to me, they are the people who run toward me when I mess up, not away. They lean in when I'm trying to understand a big dream, and they help me get there without telling me what to do. They show up when I'm stuck in bed with the flu or take the wheel when I have an eye patch and can't drive.

God made us to need each other. So if you're stuck or tempted to live in isolation because it seems easier, think again. You need a community to get there, not more time alone. Think bus, not unicycle. The people God has already dropped in your life are proof that God is on your side, that He loves you, and that He's in it for the long haul.

Who in your life is proof that God loves you?

GOD NEVER COMPARES WHAT HE CREATES.

Each one should test their own actions. Then they can take pride in themselves alone, without comparing themselves to someone else.

GALATIANS 6:4

We're born into a world of comparison. We're asked whether we prefer the ocean or the mountains, chocolate or vanilla ice cream, tea or coffee, mild or spicy. We compare prices at the grocery store and football players on fantasy sports teams. We compare sermons and singers and writers. It's hard to imagine a world where one thing isn't better than another.

God doesn't compare what He creates. Sure, we all have preferences, and there's nothing wrong with that. There was a time when Jesus' disciples got into an argument about which of them was the greatest, and do you know how Jesus responded? He pulled a child onto His lap, saying whoever welcomes children welcomes Him. Greatness wasn't rated on strength, wealth, or intelligence; Jesus said it was about humility and a childlike faith. He ushered in an entirely new set of rules. He said if we wanted to be great in His kingdom, we needed to be servants. If we wanted to be rich in Him, we'd identify with the poor.

It's hard to believe we don't have to be better than the person next to us in order to please God. Jesus said, however, He's impressed when we serve the people around us and lift their interests above ours. This is how things work with God. He's not looking at all of us like we're in a horse race to see who's in front. God looks at us and He sees His Son, Jesus. He says we are perfect because of Him and there's enough love to go around.

He loves each of us like we're His favorite ice cream. He loves us like the mountains and the beach—He doesn't need us to be the same. We can stop trying to jockey with each other for position and instead stand shoulder to shoulder, knowing God's eternal love is poured out in equal measure to everyone.

Who are you tempted to compare yourself to?

IT'S EASIER TO TALK ABOUT THE WEATHER THAN ABOUT THE STORMS IN OUR LIVES.

Confess your sins to each other and pray for each other so that you may be healed. The prayer of a righteous person is powerful and effective.

JAMES 5:16

The pace of life and the demands of a day can throw us all. I remember a few of those days when I was a partner at the law firm. I'd come home after a big day in court and plop down in my favorite chair, exhausted. A stay-at-home mom leaves it all on the field and has nothing left. The guy at Arby's is just trying to make rent. If that means slicing roast beef, he'll do it. These can be the hardest moments to stay engaged and connected with the people who are most important in our lives. We just don't have the energy for it. So we keep it shallow.

Needing a little downtime is no crime, but if you string too many of those days together, you create the habit of staying on the surface with everyone. When we stay on the surface, we miss the opportunity to share our fears and insecurities and doubts, and we forfeit the chance to hear the same. We trade the few deep conversations we should be having with the ones closest to us for many shallow conversations with everybody else.

The shallow end isn't always as safe as it looks. We can skate through life without having many vulnerable conversations, and our flaws and fears will remain unexposed. If we're never willing to get real, we'll never really be known, and if we're never known, it's hard to feel truly loved for who we actually are. Try anything you want, but being vulnerable is the only pathway to true connection.

The fix is simple. Identify a handful of people who have gone through hard times and have come out stronger on the other end. Invite those people into a couple of the difficult parts of your life—the ones you don't quite have figured out yet. Sometimes, the only thing worse than going through storms is going through them alone. Invite a few friends to join you.

Who will you invite into your deeper journey?

MOST OF OUR DECISIONS ARE DRIVEN BY EITHER LOVE OR FEAR. WHICHEVER ONE HAS THE KEYS DETERMINES HOW FAR WE'LL GO IN OUR FAITH.

Peace I leave with you; my peace I give you. I do not give to you as the world gives. Do not let your hearts be troubled and do not be afraid.

JOHN 14:27

It seems like a universal constant that if you're running late, you hit all the red lights. There must be a sinister operator cackling as he clicks another button while you pound your steering wheel and check your watch every five seconds.

Fear can be like those red lights. Fear tells us that if we actually tell the truth, the punishment will be too costly. It tells us if we really open up to a friend or spouse, we'll be rejected. It tells us there's not enough in the bank account to give, or the person seems too different and scary, or risking the big move in your career is doomed to failure. Fear robs the world of some amazing things. Your imagination is one of them. What could happen if fear didn't exist? What if we could shut it off somehow? It would be like driving down the road with nothing but green lights.

Don't let fear take the wheel and drive you away from where your faith wants to take you. I'm not saying you should live entirely without fear. Some fears can be helpful and inform our actions with wisdom. Don't miss out, however, on what God has for you because taking the step merely feels too risky. Push out a little farther from shore. Throw the nets in the water. Fail trying; don't fail watching. Don't let fear call the shots in your life.

God is inviting you to floor it with your faith. Don't let fear keep you from where Jesus wants to take you.

Which fear do you have that you need to say no to today?

THE WAY TO HAVE MORE THINGS IN COMMON IS TO DO MORE STUFF TOGETHER.

Where two or three gather in my name, there am I with them.

MATTHEW 18:20

When God laid out His vision for us, He didn't tell us just to be nice to each other. He told us to be a family with each other. He said even the people we don't like are brothers and sisters, and we don't get a pass on learning to love them. If you're like me, it's easy to agree with this but hard to live it out.

One of the best ways to learn how to love people we disagree with is to do more things with them. You don't need to book a trip to Europe together, but maybe just get coffee down the street. Jesus' disciples didn't have much in common when He called them. Peter had a short temper and John was a sensitive soul. Some were tax collectors and sophisticated thinkers while others got their education on fishing boats.

But when Jesus invited them to join His family, they were forced to learn how to love each other. They traveled together and shared meals. They didn't have a plan laid out. They went through storms together, witnessed Jesus' miracles, and experienced tremendous disappointments. Starting out, they didn't have much in common, but the more experiences they shared together, the closer they grew.

Look around your community and find the people you struggle to love. Find something to do with them. Go to the blood bank together. Make them drive. Ask them a couple of questions and learn a few things about them. Invite them into your world and learn to appreciate the perspective they bring. Even if they're wrong. The more experiences you share, the more you'll find you were wrong too.

God didn't tell us to put up with each other; He told us to love one another. Don't miss out on someone you've written off. Grab them by the hand and go do something. I bet you'll find they're worth your love once you do.

Who are you going to do something meaningful with this week?

JESUS ALWAYS POINTED PEOPLE TOWARD A BETTER VERSION OF THEMSELVES, PARTICULARLY WHEN THEY'D FAILED.

"Come, follow me," Jesus said, "and I will send you out to fish for people."

MATTHEW 4:19

It's hard enough having to endure our failures, but the failure itself usually isn't as bad as the story we tell ourselves about it. We'll tell ourselves our worth took a hit because we've tied it to our performance. Our darker angels say we should've known we wouldn't amount to much because we let someone we love down. We say we'll never risk giving our heart away again because it just never works out. The failure isn't where we get roadblocked. Failure's just a part of being human. The problem is usually the story we tell ourselves that keeps us from moving past it.

Jesus saw people's failures as an opportunity to tell them the truth about themselves. After Peter denied Him on the loneliest night of his life, Jesus told him he would become the rock the church would be built upon. After the woman was caught in adultery and thrown at His feet, Jesus told her she wasn't condemned. He said there was hope for a beautiful future if she wanted it. As He forgave people who brought shame upon themselves, He always took the opportunity to say they were more than their mistakes and His grace was bigger than their lives.

Jesus pointed people toward a better version of themselves. He saw their shame and knew the story they told themselves could have a greater paralyzing effect on their lives than the failure itself. He wanted them to know their value wasn't based on their ability to get it right. He wanted them to understand who they were was more than what they'd done. He wanted them to know He saw them at their worst and had never loved them more.

Next time you mess up, don't invent a new plot. Don't tell yourself a story different from the story Jesus has been telling about you. Listen to Jesus instead.

What would Jesus say He really thinks about you?

THE MOST BEAUTIFUL SCENERY IN THE WORLD IS WHEN OUR FRIENDS COME INTO VIEW.

Two are better than one, because they have a good return for their labor: If either of them falls down, one can help the other up.

ECCLESIASTES 4:9-10

One of the greatest miracles of living in the twenty-first century is how extensively we can travel. No previous generation has had the gift of being able to step on an airplane so easily, lean back for a nap, and wake up on the other side of the world. No matter where we are in the morning, by the evening we can lie on the floor of the Sistine Chapel or float in the Dead Sea. Traveling opens our eyes to see beauty in ways our great-grandparents couldn't have imagined.

But after a trip, as the plane touches down and we drive the last stretch home, we're reminded that the most beautiful scenery in the world is when our friends come into view. Even the best moments from our trips don't quite compare to the hugs and smiles we get when we walk through the doors of our homes and into the arms of our loved ones.

Boredom and discontentment spread like germs. They whisper lies to us in our daily routines, telling us we'd be happier if we could be free to go wherever we want, whenever we want. They try to entice us with the freedom we could enjoy if only we weren't tied down by all the responsibilities that come with being invested in a community.

But the strings that tie us to the people we love are the ropes that pull us up when life gets hard. Don't believe the lie that you would experience more beauty if you could only get a break from the people you're sharing your life with. The most beautiful view in the world is the sight of the faces who show up for you no matter what.

Do you need to re-see the beauty in someone in your life?

LOVE FINDS US WHERE WE ARE,
NOT WHERE WE WERE.

"Moses! Moses!" And Moses said, "Here I am."

EXODUS 3:4

If anyone had reason to believe they had blown their big chance to use their influence for good, it was Moses. Moses was a Hebrew boy and was supposed to be killed according to a decree by the pharaoh. But the pharaoh's daughter had compassion and adopted him. After he had grown up, Moses went for a walk, saw an Egyptian beating a Hebrew slave, and killed the Egyptian in a fit of rage. He thought no one had seen it, but when he realized his sin had been exposed, he ran.

Moses fled to the desert and stayed there for forty years. Moses was tending a flock on a mountain one day when he saw a bush had caught fire. Moving closer to check it out, he heard a voice from the fire—the voice of God. God told Moses that he had heard the cry of the Hebrew people in slavery, that He had seen them in their suffering and had compassion. Then He told Moses to go back to Egypt to lead His people out of slavery.

It's easy for us to feel like our mistakes disqualify us, that we've missed our opportunity when we mess up the plan. Shame shackles us. Our failures prepare us. God meets us where we are and uses our stories to bring courage. He's not looking for us back at the place where we made the wrong turn—He follows us down the road and guides us into a better story. Love finds us where we are, not where we were.

What past mistake or failure do you feel
disqualifies you from God's love?

A FATHER'S JOB IS TO GET DOWN ON BOTH KNEES AND WHISPER, "WHERE DO YOU WANT TO GO?"

You did not choose me, but I chose you and appointed you so that you might go and bear fruit—fruit that will last—and so that whatever you ask in my name the Father will give you.

JOHN 15:16

When each of my kids turned ten, I took them anywhere in the world they wanted to go, just the two of us. It sounds extravagant, but I have free airplane tickets like farmers have corn. Lindsey loved tea, so we went to London for a tea party. Richard wanted to summit Half Dome at Yosemite. Adam picked riding motorcycles across the desert.

The only plan was that we wouldn't make a plan. The kids dreamed up exactly what they wanted to do, and we set out for an adventure together. That's how the best adventures unfold for all of us. We decide to follow a passion and bring people we love along with us for the ride.

A father's job is to get down on both knees, lean over his children's lives, and whisper, "Where do you want to go?" Their answers had me flying over sand dunes on motorcycles, huddled together in tents during snowstorms, and lifting pinkie fingers as we sipped tea on the Thames.

I used to think adventures with God meant living in foreign countries alone. I feared I'd have to enter the priesthood or go door to door or do something I didn't want to do at all. But I've learned that God lets us decide what we want, even if it's not the kind of thing He might have picked. He's not trying to manipulate us. He wants to be with us. He hopes we'll trust Him enough to tell Him what our desires are.

God isn't as concerned about where we go as much as about who we become along the way. He wants us to become His. God doesn't force us into things we don't want to do. He's more interested in joining us as we run after our dreams. He leans over our lives and whispers, "Where do you want to go?"

Where do you want to go?

WE ARE A REFLECTION OF OR A REACTION TO THE PEOPLE CLOSEST TO US. CHOOSE WISELY.

As iron sharpens iron, so one person sharpens another.

PROVERBS 27:17

"The apple doesn't fall far from the tree." You hear this when a child or grown kid acts like the parent, and it usually has a negative slant. I've always wondered how you would say a kid was completely different from the parents. "That apple fell in the next county." Or "How did that kumquat come from that apple tree?"

The truth is, we can't get away from the influence our parents had on us growing up. We might be able to turn down the volume on their voices, but we can't do away with them completely. God made us highly impressionable. We pick up phrases and habits from our friends almost without even realizing it. And if you're trying to act differently from your parents or some friends in your life, guess what? They're still the people you're pivoting off of.

We can't choose the families we're born into, but we can choose the communities we'll link arms with for the rest of our lives. Be choosy. These friends will either replace or reaffirm the tapes we grew up hearing, and some might do a little of both.

God doesn't ask us to avoid the people we're trying to be different from. And it's pretty hard to toss out all the old tapes. But God gives us friends to add new voices to the mix. Find friends who sound like Jesus, and keep them on repeat in your life.

Who is the best reflection you've seen of Jesus?

FIND THE VOICES THAT WHISPER ABOUT YOUR FUTURE. DITCH THE ONES THAT SCREAM ABOUT YOUR PAST.

In the past God spoke to our ancestors through the prophets at many times and in various ways, but in these last days he has spoken to us by his Son, whom he appointed heir of all things, and through whom also he made the universe.

HEBREWS 1:1-2

One time my son Richard and I were rushing to the airport with some friends. Once we got past security, he came to a halt in front of a tech gadget vending machine. He needed a new pair of headphones, and he saw the kind that drown out all the noises you don't want to hear. They were at a crazy-low price, so he decided to get a pair for every person in our group. The blood drained out of his face when he realized he'd misread the price tag: $199.99 instead of $19.99. Yikes!

That was a costly goof. But what price would you put on hearing the right voices in your life? What would you pay to drown out the voices of doubt, fear, and insecurity?

God speaks to us through His Word, through our friends, through our desires and dreams. Are you listening to them, or are you giving the microphone to the voices that make you envy what your friend has or fear that the next move will end in total failure? Have you put your head next to a megaphone that screams you back into the person you were?

And what kind of voice are you in the lives of others? Remember that fear calls out our insecurities and doubts. God calls out our names. Listen for His voice and be like it too. Speak of love and beauty, trust and acceptance, grace and forgiveness—and you'll be the voice people are longing to hear.

What kind of voice are you in the lives of others?

THE COST OF FAKING IT IS ISOLATION. VULNERABILITY LEADS TO COMMUNITY.

Confess your sins to each other and pray for each other so that you may be healed. The prayer of a righteous person is powerful and effective.

JAMES 5:16

I have a few friends who have been brave enough to go into recovery programs. They made the courageous choice to quiet the voices in their hearts saying they wouldn't be accepted if they told the truth and got the help they needed.

The battle leading up to recovery can be a lonely fight, I'm told. People hear one voice saying they need help right now while the other voice says, "You can stop after the next one." And the next one, and the next one. After all the next ones, brokenness crashes in where reason couldn't, and the last episode becomes the catalyst someone needs to ask for help. Help comes in the form of people who don't run away.

Plenty of us have our secrets. Bumping into the car. Fudging taxes. Too much alcohol. The relationship. Whatever it is, bad choices have this whiplash effect, causing us to avoid anyone who might discover them. That will cause distance and loneliness. Most of us have something we're afraid to tell the other people in our lives. We tell ourselves we can beat it alone, but our solo struggle against it keeps us isolated.

Don't fake perfection. Go for broke instead. The hidden cost of faking it is isolation, but the payoff of vulnerability is community. Find someone safe and share the part of your life you hide from others. You're going to find the rejection you fear is a myth and lie. People will still love you. Hope will catch you on the other side of your confession.

What do you need to confess today?

JUNE 29

TRUE FRIENDS LOWER US DOWN THROUGH THE ROOF RATHER THAN WAITING FOR PERMISSION.

Since they could not get him to Jesus because of the crowd, they made an opening in the roof above Jesus by digging through it and then lowered the mat the man was lying on. When Jesus saw their faith, he said to the paralyzed man, "Son, your sins are forgiven."

MARK 2:4–5

Once Jesus was teaching a crowd of people—a bunch of religious leaders from all over the region. As He taught, a group of men tried to approach Him carrying a paralyzed friend on a mat. They believed if they could just get him to Jesus, he would be healed.

The crowd was too big for them to get in—the line for this club stretched around the block. So they created a new entrance. They climbed up onto the roof and lowered him down through the tiles. I've always wondered what all the scraping and commotion would sound like to the people inside. I also wonder how far these men carried the guy. How far are you willing to carry a friend on a stretcher? These friends lowered him right to the feet of Jesus, and the Bible says when Jesus saw the *faith of the man's friends*, He forgave and healed the man. Isn't that amazing? It wasn't even the man's faith that moved Jesus to heal him. The faith of his friends was enough. They didn't wait for a more convenient time, and they didn't wait until the guy on the stretcher got all the theology right.

We need friends to have the faith we can't muster up on our own. We don't need theology cops making sure we can recite the Creed correctly. We need people willing to be Jesus in our lives. We need friends who will hope things for us we're too discouraged to dream for ourselves. We need people who will lower us down through the roof rather than waiting for permission.

Which of your friends will carry you to Jesus? Who will you carry?

JUNE 30

WE WON'T BE DISTRACTED BY COMPARISON IF WE'RE CAPTIVATED WITH PURPOSE.

All the believers were one in heart and mind. No one claimed that any of their possessions was their own, but they shared everything they had.

ACTS 4:32

This guy named Shane was in college when he started to make friends with people who lived in poor neighborhoods in his city. Shane could've gone the expected route after graduation—get a job, start building a 401(k), health insurance—you know the drill. But he chose to live with people in poverty instead. He and some friends pooled together enough money to get a house in a struggling neighborhood. Their only goal was to be good neighbors.

At any given point, Shane and his wife have up to ten people living in their home, and they share everything. They put all the money they earn into one pile and spend it as needed. It's kind of like a modern-day version of what you read about in the book of Acts. Their purpose is to show hospitality and generosity to their neighbors, so they're not too concerned with their appearance or net income.

We won't be distracted by comparison if we're captivated with purpose. If we're captivated with purpose, most everything else fades into the background. The pressure to live a particular script or keep up with the Joneses gets exposed for the distraction it is. Look for the people around you who are suffering in some way, and take one of their worries off their plate in secret. You don't need to start a new nonprofit—just step in and relieve a little stress. We won't have time to measure ourselves against one another if we fill our time scheming ways to lift one another up.

What are you willing to share? What are you unwilling to share?

JULY

JULY 1

IF WE ONLY DO WHAT WE'RE FAMILIAR WITH, WE MIGHT MISS WHAT WE'VE BEEN MADE FOR.

Each of you should use whatever gift you have received to serve others, as faithful stewards of God's grace in its various forms.

1 PETER 4:10

Before Walt Disney dreamed up Disneyland, he was fired from his job at a newspaper in Kansas City because his editor said he "lacked imagination." Can you believe it? The editor missed that one in a big way. Whenever I'm at Tom Sawyer Island, I think about what would've happened if Walt Disney had dug in his heels at the newspaper instead. The world would have never met Mickey Mouse. Failure forced Walt Disney to pursue his passion.

Our habits shape our days, and our days make up our lives. Without much thought, we can settle into routines that keep us stagnant for decades. There's nothing wrong with staying put if you've found your passion, but many of us have a dream tucked away inside of us, a dream fear keeps us from pursuing. We fear we don't have the skills or resources to see the project through. We worry we won't be able to weather financial instability as we transition. We tell ourselves there are already other people doing it, and the world doesn't need one more voice to add to the noise.

If we only do what we're familiar with, we might miss what we've been made for. God didn't put those passions inside of you just to give you material for your daydreams. He gave them to you because your gifts and personality uniquely qualify you to do the things God created you to do. Don't get so comfortable where you are that you miss where God wants to take you.

What gifts do you have that God might want to use?

DON'T BE DISTRACTED BY THE POSSIBILITY OF SUCCESS OR FAILURE. BE SOLD-OUT TO YOUR BEAUTIFUL AMBITIONS.

Which of these three do you think was a neighbor to the man who fell into the hands of robbers?

LUKE 10:36

On December 17, 1903, Orville and Wilbur Wright became the first people in history to successfully fly an airplane. At 10:35 a.m., they saw their dream lift off the ground for the first time. But I always wonder: What were they thinking at 10:34? None of us live at 10:35. We don't know if what we attempt will work or not.

The plane had been their idea from beginning to end. They invented it, built it, and got it off the ground. But surely they must have known the odds were against them at 10:34. No one had been able to create a machine that could launch people into the air and bring them back to the ground safely. They must have felt the weight of the risk. They were probably concerned for their physical safety. Even more, they knew if they failed, it would be a big, public face-plant. But at 10:34, Orville and Wilbur chose to focus on their beautiful ambitions rather than all the reasons not to try.

It's always exciting to start a new project, but it's hard to see it through. Distraction shows up in lots of different ways: we're enticed by the promise of easier success elsewhere or scared by the possibility of failure. I've heard a couple of people call this resistance, and they talked about it like it was a constant force of the universe. I agree.

Don't give into the resistance pushing against your vision. Be wholly sold-out and captivated with purpose instead. Like the Wright brothers did at 10:34, keep your eyes fixed on the prize. Will it work? I'll tell you in a minute.

What dream do you need to wholly sell out to?

JULY 3

THE WAY TO FIND YOUR PURPOSE IS TO LOOK FOR WHERE YOUR PASSIONS AND CAPABILITIES INTERSECT.

The work of God is this: to believe in the one he has sent.

JOHN 6:29

At the law school where I teach, there's a sense of huge excitement as we get closer to graduation. But there's also a sense of dread that's subtle but ever-present in the students. It comes in the form of this question: "What's next?" A lot of people act like they have a plan, and a couple actually do, but many times they don't. More often than not, if you ask a student this question at graduation, they will stare back at you in silence. You can literally see the dread.

The best way to find the life you were meant to live is to get started, even if you have to pivot later. Great ideas that don't work out are usually on-ramps to better ideas that do. And every time you put your passions into action, you learn things you couldn't have learned sitting still. We grow on the way.

Jesus' disciples had the same question most of us have: What's our work? Jesus answered, "The work of God is this: to believe in the one He has sent." That's it. Our job is to believe in Jesus. The problem is that we keep adding to it, thinking there's a different "plan" out there. Resist the urge.

That said, where we live our lives best is usually where our passions, our purpose, and our capabilities intersect. We can't miss God's "plan" for us because His plan is for us to use our gifts He gave us to love the people around us. Most of the decisions we make aren't usually between right and wrong; it's more like choosing between a right turn or left. God doesn't force us to go places we don't want to go, and no matter which way we turn, we'll find Him already there if we're looking.

What changes in you when you put God first in your life?

DON'T LET THE PURSUIT OF PERFECTION KEEP YOU FROM WHAT MATTERS MOST: TRUE ENGAGEMENT.

"Martha, Martha," the Lord answered, "you are worried and upset about many things, but few things are needed—or indeed only one. Mary has chosen what is better, and it will not be taken away from her."

LUKE 10:41–42

Sweet Maria knows how to throw a party. My greatest triumph preparing for guests is lining up my shirt buttons correctly, but she has this knack for creating spaces that are comfortable and beautiful and restful. The reason is simple. She pays attention to the details, yet she's learned to let go of perfection when we're hosting friends. She knows turning napkins into swans isn't more important than the right conversations we'll have even if she doesn't. She learned this by listening to Jesus.

There was a time when Jesus joined two of his friends for dinner, Mary and Martha. When He got to their home, He sat down to tell them some stories, and Mary sat at His feet listening to every word. Meanwhile, Martha ran around the kitchen trying to prepare for the evening. She was doing the kinds of things we can relate to: cooking, cleaning up, and setting the table for a nice meal together. It's akin to a young couple hosting their first Thanksgiving dinner for family.

Eventually Martha got fed up with Mary for not pitching in, and she complained to Jesus. But Jesus responded by saying Mary had chosen to do what was most important. Martha's evening was filled with activities, but those weren't the activities Jesus wanted. The goal for Him was just to be with one another.

It's easy to confuse a lot of activity with a purposeful life. Don't get bogged down by the details; choose true engagement instead. Paper plates work just fine.

In what ways do you focus more on being busy than being in God's presence?

QUIT WAITING FOR PERMISSION TO DO WHAT YOU WERE MADE FOR. GO LOVE EVERYBODY.

"Love the Lord your God with all your heart and with all your soul and with all your mind and with all your strength." The second is this: "Love your neighbor as yourself." There is no commandment greater than these.

MARK 12:30-31

When kids are young, parents can seem like the sheriffs stopping all the fun. Kids need to ask permission to do everything. "Can we stay up later?" "Can I go to camp?" "Can I go to the movies?" As our kids grow up, the questions become, "Can I have some money for the trip?" or "Can I borrow the car?" Adults are the gatekeepers of life.

Parents know that healthy guardrails are good for their kids. But these boundaries in childhood conditioned some of us to look to someone else before we took a step as we got older. Even with beautiful things in our lives that bring us happiness and joy, we're conditioned to think our desires will lead us astray, so we're hesitant to fully embrace them. We become suspicious of our hearts and look to people in authority to affirm we're on the right track before we take a next step.

What was once good parenting can cause us to stagnate as adults. God gave us a sense of direction for our lives by creating us with gifts and passions to lead the way. He wired us with beautiful desires that point us toward the next right thing. We don't need to wait for permission to take the next step toward the vision He gave us; we just need a little courage. He's already tossed you the keys to the car. Get it out of the garage, take it out on the road, and see what it will do.

We're past the days of needing to wait for permission. If your plans include loving the people around you the way Jesus did, you've already got all the green light from God you need.

What are you waiting on permission for?

WE CAN BE THE LIGHT OF THE WORLD WITHOUT ANNOYING EVERYONE WITH OUR HIGH BEAMS.

In the same way, let your light shine before others, that they may see your good deeds and glorify your Father in heaven.

MATTHEW 5:16

When Jesus came to be with us, He said He was the light of the world.

Sometimes people of faith try so hard to be a light that they shine a spotlight on their faith every chance they get. They give complicated arguments for their faith or confront people they think are wrong. Regardless of the situation, they always seem to get a word in. Usually they shut down conversations rather than creating a space for light to get through.

There's a difference between a bright light and a spotlight. We can light up the world with our love, making it easier for people to find their way in the dark. When we light up the world, we're a gift to the people around us. We're an encouragement, not an imposition. But when we live with our high beams on, we blind the people around us and ultimately push them away.

We can be the light of the world without leaving our high beams on and annoying everybody. Acutally, how about we give love away like a mighty river, then we can be a floodlight. When Jesus said He was the light of the world, it was to illuminate darkness with His love, not to make everyone turn away. Let's turn off our high beams and light up the world with our love instead.

What have you done this week that demonstrates the love of God?

WE WON'T KNOW HOW IT'S GOING TO END AT THE BEGINNING. KEEP GOING. UNCERTAINTY IS GOD'S INVITATION TO JOIN HIM.

I make known the end from the beginning, from ancient times, what is still to come.

I say, "My purpose will stand, and I will do all that I please."

ISAIAH 46:10

When you read a really good book, it's easy to think it came from the author's head fully formed, start to finish. But did you know novelists usually don't know the end of their stories when they start writing them? They start out with characters sketched in their minds, and they imagine the setting for the story. They have a rough idea of the conflicts. The narrative is driven by the characters and their responses to one another, not the author. The writer is just along for the ride, taking notes.

I've always felt like life works the same way. We don't know the ending of our stories when we begin. We don't even know where a chapter will take us. We all just sketch out a rough idea of who we are and show up with all the passion and whimsy we can muster.

Don't let an unknown ending keep you from beginning. Just start. Uncertainty is God's way of inviting us to join Him. God knows the other characters who will come into our stories. He knows the conflicts we'll face and the ways we'll grow through the process. There's no place we can go where He's not already authoring our story as well as those of everyone around us.

We don't need to have all the information to start; we just need courage to take the first step. Don't worry about next week's potential problems. Give today everything you've got. Our stories are written as we live, so live fully. Our love is refined as we give it away genuinely, so love the people around you authentically. Let the story you're writing be a page-turner.

What's your next step?

GOD ISN'T TRYING TO MAKE OUR LIVES EASIER. HE WANTS TO MAKE THEM MORE MEANINGFUL.

God is faithful; he will not let you be tempted beyond what you can bear. But when you are tempted, he will also provide a way out so that you can endure it.

1 CORINTHIANS 10:13

Whenever I'm in the self-help section of a bookstore, things start to feel a little suspicious. If everyone is telling the truth, I can apparently lose twelve inches in twelve weeks, work for less than half a day a year and make more money, get more friends, increase my influence, have more confidence, and at least a dozen other things by just changing one or two simple things in my life.

I bet some of these books actually work. But the reason I'm suspicious is because the promise of a shortcut isn't how I see the most important thing in my life, which is my faith. Cutting corners in faith can rob us of something important: the challenges we need to face and the relationships we need to make along the way. We need a challenge to grow, to break the plateau of our faith or our routine. The relationships we make add layers of richness and teach us we can't do everything alone. Sometimes the only path to the life you want has to go over some tough terrain.

God isn't trying to make our lives easier. He wants to make them more meaningful. And the meaningful stuff happens when we invest ourselves in our passions and in the people around us. Our best memories are the ones where we overcome adversity at the end of a long struggle. They include people who have seen us at our worst and loved us all the more for it. There are no shortcuts to a more meaningful life and a deeper faith; it takes a lot of love and courage. Will we encounter some setbacks? You bet. Stay the course.

What setbacks have you faced that are discouraging you from progress?

JULY 9

THE WORDS WE USE MATTER.

You are my Son, whom I love; with you I am well pleased.

MARK 1:11

If you're arguing with your spouse, the experts say you should steer clear of two phrases: "you always" and "you never." As in, "You always criticize me," or "You never listen." It's not so much that these *never* and *always* statements probably aren't true. It's more that people who love each other shouldn't use words like weapons.

Some people have lived their whole lives without having a parent tell them they were loved. The words the people closest to you *didn't* say can have as profound an impact as the ones they did say. We are reflections of or reactions to the people who have been closest to us. Be a beautiful reaction.

The words we use—whether spoken or unspoken—have tremendous power in the lives of those around us. Look someone in the eye today and tell them something wonderful and true. Imagine I'm sitting across from you right now: You are brave. You are kind. You are valued. You have what it takes. You have a spark that is unique to you.

Go use your words to build someone up. They won't be the only ones who are changed by these words. You will be too.

**What words could you add to your vocabulary
that would help you be more loving?**

JULY 10

DON'T BE LOUD. BE LOVE.

Dear friends, since God so loved us, we also ought to love one another. No one has ever seen God; but if we love one another, God lives in us and his love is made complete in us.

1 JOHN 4:11–12

One of the most influential people in the civil rights movement didn't give many speeches. Unlike Martin Luther King Jr., Rosa Parks took her stand by quietly taking a seat on a public bus, refusing to give it up for a white man. This quiet act of courage made her "the mother of the freedom movement," according to Congress, and she became an inspiration to young people fighting for justice and equality around the country.

If you aspire to become an influential leader or simply want to create more good in the world, you might be conditioned to think of people on stages or screens as the ultimate examples. The loudest voices don't always deserve to be the most heard. Listen for the truest voices. People like pastors, activists, and leaders, who stay behind the scenes and quietly work for the good of people within their reach, make the most lasting impact. They hand out clothes to the homeless or take the woman just freed from jail to her halfway house. They don't need stages or microphones because their love does all the talking. The reason is simple. Bright lights don't need spotlights.

Words will never move people the way love does. If our actions are motivated by love, we don't have to worry about having big platforms or positions of power, because nothing holds a candle to love that has no agenda.

If you want to change the world, don't be loud. Be love.

What are you going to do today to be love?

JULY 11

MAKE SURE YOU PICK THE RIGHT TARGET BEFORE YOU TAKE AIM.

We make it our goal to please him, whether we are at home in the body or away from it.

2 CORINTHIANS 5:9

There are all kinds of random jobs in the world. Sometimes I'll hear what someone does, and I think to myself, *I didn't even know that existed.* Here's an example: I met these guys who are professional dart players. They travel across the world to compete with other people who throw darts. There are tournaments and sponsorships and jerseys with logos. Who knew? I went to watch one of their matches and was completely amazed. These guys could whiz a dart right into the bull's-eye. They could do it over their shoulder. They could do it with their eyes closed. If they were using bows and arrows, they would have been splitting them down the middle with every shot.

After the match was over, I started thinking about their darts and the importance of knowing your target. I started thinking about all the darts I throw and whether I was aiming at the right stuff. Forget splitting an arrow. I'd be lucky if I hit the tree.

I can find myself waltzing through a day, tossing my darts all over. Finish this project, make that call, do the chores. Remember my quiet time, get to church, don't forget to pray. Even the things that seem like right targets can be wrong if we're only trying to get them off a checklist.

When I look at Jesus, I see someone who lived a life on mission. He lived a purposeful and intentional life. He knew what He was aiming for. Here it is: He wanted to do His Father's will. This didn't seem as elusive to Him as it seems to many of us. He even explained it to someone when they asked. He loved God with His heart and soul and mind, and He loved His neighbor. Go and do the same.

What's your mission today, the problem that deserves your attention and love?

YOU'LL NEVER KNOW IF YOUR FEAR IS TELLING THE TRUTH ABOUT WHAT LIES AHEAD UNTIL YOU TAKE A STEP TOWARD IT.

Jesus immediately said to them: "Take courage! It is I. Don't be afraid."

MATTHEW 14:27

One of the fears common to all of us is fear of the unknown. It's tied to other big fears, like the fear of the dark or failure or the fear of death. What these fears have in common is not knowing what's coming. For some people, uncertainty is like a day at the circus. But for others, if they don't know what's coming, they know they can't control the outcome, and the loss of control leaves them feeling helpless. Understanding the reality of our situation makes life unpredictable and reminds us how small we are.

But fear only has the power we give it. You've experienced this before. The speeches we're certain we'll bomb end up moving the people who hear them. The relationships we fear will become stronger when we drop the act and allow people to truly see us. The stories we tell ourselves about the unknown are always worse than the future that unfolds.

We can only move past our fears by testing them. We can be vigilant and prudent without being reckless. But you won't find out if fear is telling the truth about danger ahead unless you take a step toward it. You might find out you had reason to fear, and then you can use the new information to move in a different direction. But you can't learn anything about the unknown until you walk right up to it, stare it in the eye, and say you're not listening anymore.

One of Jesus' favorite phrases was "fear not." He knew we weren't created to be anxious and stressed out. We were made to live, to engage, to remain open to the people and opportunities we encounter. Fear only has the power we give it, and Jesus said we shouldn't give it any.

What's fear saying to you today? What's God saying to you today?

DON'T LET UNCERTAINTY KEEP YOU FROM PURSUING YOUR PURPOSE. LOVE PEOPLE ALONG THE WAY.

Let your eyes look straight ahead; fix your gaze directly before you.

PROVERBS 4:25

Oprah was fired from her first television job for getting too emotionally invested in her stories. Thomas Edison's teachers told him he was too stupid to learn anything. J. K. Rowling was on welfare when she started writing *Harry Potter*. It seems no good thing or great success comes on a silver platter.

It may seem counterintuitive, but if success came easily, most people would see their visions die—because visions only come to life with a lot of hard work and unwavering persistence. Challenges draw something out of us that easiness could never ignite. If the reason behind our vision lacks purpose, if it's to become famous or earn approval, we'll get discouraged the moment we face rejection. We'll likely throw up our hands and walk away because we'll believe we missed the mark. But if our vision is tied to a clear purpose, we won't be discouraged when times get tough.

Turn the volume down on your doubts and stay focused on your purpose. Set aside the belief that the end goal will come quickly. It's the process, with all the ups and downs and triumphs and misstarts, that will ultimately get you there. In the meantime, surround yourself with people in need and give away love like you're made of it. If it takes a little longer to achieve your goals, you're doing things that last.

What do you need to do today to refocus on your purpose?

JULY 14

EVERYONE'S LEAP LOOKS DIFFERENT.
COMPARISON IS A PUNK.

Am I now trying to win the approval of human beings, or of God? Or am I trying to please people? If I were still trying to please people, I would not be a servant of Christ.

GALATIANS 1:10

When I was in college, my buddies and I didn't know how to have fun unless a little danger was involved. We liked driving to the ocean to explore new spots for cliff diving. We liked having conversations on roofs because there was a chance one of us could fall. Any fun outing became more exciting the moment our lives felt at risk in the process.

Inevitably, someone in our group would be scared of heights. The guy usually tried to play it cool, but you'd see him slide down to a lower ledge to jump or find a safe way to shimmy down. My friends often gave him a hard time about it, but I always had a soft spot for the guy who couldn't quite handle the high places. We all bring different fears with us on our adventures, and his just happened to look different from mine.

Those excursions taught me that even if everyone's leap looks different, we are all in it together. In the end, it doesn't matter whether someone jumps from a high place or a low; what matters is that we make the leap.

We all face different challenges, and those challenges require different kinds of faith. Sometimes faith looks like taking aid to civilians in war zones, and sometimes faith looks like reading bedtime stories to toddlers as they drift off to sleep. God never told us to compare our faith with another's. Comparison is a punk. God told us to be faithful to the path laid out before us and take our next step, not someone else's.

Who have you been comparing yourself to lately? What are you going to do to stop?

JULY 15

SMALL STREAMS DON'T CHOOSE TO BE MIGHTY RIVERS. WE KEEP MOVING IN A DIRECTION AND GOD DECIDES WHAT HE'LL MAKE OUT OF US.

It is the LORD your God you must follow, and him you must revere. Keep his commands and obey him; serve him and hold fast to him.

DEUTERONOMY 13:4

I was on a hike one time and saw a sign to an offshoot trail that said, HEAD-WATERS THIS WAY. I was curious because I had never seen headwaters before, which is the place where a stream or river literally begins. I imagined a massive river coming out of a cave carving its way through the forest. But when I arrived, I couldn't tell if I was disappointed or even more amazed. Bubbling out of the ground, a stream began at the base of a large oak tree and trailed through the forest as a babbling brook. I could hardly believe it. How could this trickle eventually turn into a river?

Small streams don't plan to become mighty rivers. They just run in the direction they were created to move, and their Creator decides what they'll become.

In today's world, we look on with envy as a friend takes the risk to start a business and gets crazy successful. We see the lead guitarist melting people's faces with a solo on his Fender Stratocaster. Or we look up at the stage wondering how that speaker became so influential, secretly wishing we could have the same thing. But I don't think God is wowed by people whose aim is more money or more fame. If those things come through a life of faith, the faithful person knows not to overvalue them. What dazzles God are humble people who use the gifts they have and let God use them any way He decides to.

Don't make following Jesus more complicated than He made it. Don't hand God a list of your expectations about what He'll do with your faithfulness. Start. Figure out what you've got. Move in the direction He sends you and let Him determine what He's going to make out of it.

Have you been making it too complicated?

I USED TO HOPE THE THINGS I DID WOULD WORK. NOW I HOPE THEY LAST.

We fix our eyes not on what is seen, but on what is unseen, since what is seen is temporary, but what is unseen is eternal.

2 CORINTHIANS 4:18

Every year our street has a parade to kick off the New Year. We started it when my kids were young because they were all bored on a New Year's Day and were looking for something to do. I tossed out the idea of starting a parade where no one watched but everyone was in it. About five minutes later, we started knocking on doors and telling our neighbors we needed them to show up. Part of me wondered if people would think we were crazy, but none of us knows what will happen until we ask.

It's a few decades later, and we're still knocking on our neighbors' doors to invite them. Instead of dozens of people, there are hundreds of them. The rule has remained the same. Everybody in; nobody watching. There's a Grand Marshal to lead the way, and we always pick a New Year's Day Queen from the people on the block. The annual event has turned into a celebration of life and community and the power of love without an agenda.

When Jesus told a lawyer like me who was trying to set Him up that the most important commandment included loving our neighbors, it's easy to think this is a metaphor for something else. But it's not. Jesus wants us to love people right where we are. I think He knew that we'd be tempted to go somewhere far away for a week of service and call it good. My hope when I was younger was that I would do things and they would "work." These days, I want to do things that will last. Loving your neighbor will last.

Invest in things that last. If you have to choose between projects and people, pick people every time. Projects work or they don't. Loving people lasts. Of all the things we accomplish in this life, only love remains. Go big on love and let the rest work itself out.

What are you investing in today that lasts?

WHAT WE DO WITH OUR LOVE IS WHAT WE DID IN OUR LIFE. NOTHING ELSE WILL MAKE THE HIGHLIGHT REEL.

Now these three remain: faith, hope and love. But the greatest of these is love.

1 CORINTHIANS 13:13

You know what's great about making new friends? You're invited into stories you've never heard before. When people feel a sense of welcome and safety with you, they begin to tell you where they've come from and who they've been throughout their lives. You get the highlight reel of the major moments, what shaped them into the people they are today.

What stands out in those stories is love. Even in the midst of challenges and trials, we get to hear about the praying grandmother who never stopped believing in them. We get to hear about the coach who took our new friend under his wing and treated him like a son. These stories give us a glimpse into the struggles, but they almost always introduce us to heroes who faithfully loved.

God said of all the virtues we strive to live out, faith, hope, and love remain. And the greatest is love. Not surprisingly, these things that God says remain are the very things the world attacks. Our programs might work, but it's love that lasts. After the curtain falls on our lives and people reflect on who we were and what we did, they won't remember the extra hours we put in at the office or that the house was always tidy. They'll remember the ways our love impacted their lives.

At the end of our days, I'm certain we'll find that what we did with our love is what we did in our life. Nothing else will make the highlight reel. Everything else—our titles, our accomplishments, our books, our notoriety—will end up on the editing room floor. Anything is worth doing if it's done with love, and nothing's worth doing if it comes at love's cost. Hold your priorities up to love's test and do this: throw yourself into anything that passes.

What have you been prioritizing lately that doesn't hold up to love's test?

IF YOU'RE GETTING CRITICIZED FOR LOVING THE WRONG PEOPLE, YOU'RE PROBABLY DOING SOMETHING RIGHT.

Peter began to speak: "I now realize how true it is that God does not show favoritism but accepts from every nation the one who fears him and does what is right."

ACTS 10:34–35

One of Jesus' best friends was a guy named Peter. I love Peter because he got it wrong more often than he got it right. I can relate. Do you remember the time he got into a fight with another friend over which of them was Jesus' favorite? Every one of us does this in less obvious ways all the time. Rather than sidelining Peter because of his shallow behavior, Jesus tapped him to carry on His kingdom movement after He left. I would have bet against Peter, but he obviously got something right about Jesus.

Peter knew he would be misunderstood if he loved people the way Jesus did, and that's exactly what happened. A few years after Jesus left, Peter, who was Jewish, met a guy named Cornelius, who was a Gentile—someone the Jews weren't supposed to associate with. Through his friendship with Cornelius, Peter came to realize the Jews had been wrong to tell an entire group of people they couldn't join their community. And since "Gentiles" meant anyone that wasn't Jewish, that basically meant just about everyone was in.

Peter put himself out there and reached out to the Gentiles, even when he knew his own people would criticize him for it. He said: "I now realize how true it is that God doesn't show favoritism." In other words, we're all tied for first in God's view.

This is what it looks like to follow Jesus. When we're criticized by religious people for sticking up for those who are pushed out, we're probably doing something right. Loving people the way Jesus did means a life of catching heat because of the way you love. If that's happening to you, you're in good company.

Who have you been neglecting to put first when it comes to sharing love?

JULY 19

GOD WON'T TRY TO SPEAK OVER ALL
THE NOISE IN OUR LIVES. BE STILL.

The LORD said, "Go out and stand on the mountain in the presence of the LORD, for the LORD is about to pass by." Then a great and powerful wind tore the mountains apart and shattered the rocks before the LORD, but the LORD was not in the wind. After the wind there was an earthquake, but the LORD was not in the earthquake. After the earthquake came a fire, but the LORD was not in the fire. And after the fire came a gentle whisper."

1 KINGS 19:11–12

Nothing puts a damper on a night out with friends like a restaurant that's too loud. We all know the feeling of leaning in close to our buddies, putting our ears up to their faces in hopes of being able to get the gist of what they're saying.

We can't hear one another when there's too much noise in our lives. We miss our kids' subtle cries for help and our friends' invitations into deeper relationship. As we run from commitment to commitment on autopilot most of the time, we lose sight of all the things that bring us to wonder. We don't see them because we don't hear them. If we can't hear the people around us amid all the noise in our lives, think how hard it is to hear God, who the Bible says often speaks to us in a whisper.

I don't know about you, but I've never heard the audible voice of God. I've asked Him plenty of times to say a sentence to me, or a word. I've even asked to buy a vowel. But it's been crickets. If you want to hear God's words, just read the Bible out loud. He's never answered my prayers with a booming voice or crash of thunder. I understand Him by reading what He said. God also speaks through hunches, ideas, and new desires. For all of these, they will be informed by our faith, our hopes, and our experience. God speaks through invitations that show up just days after I prayed for direction. God's voice often feels like my own thoughts, but wiser and more tenderhearted. Here's the thing: I only hear God when the noise around me fades and it's quiet enough for me to tune in to His soft whispers.

God won't try to speak over all the noise in our lives. Be still. Turn down the volume on the chaos of everyday life. Sit in the silence with expectation, and wait for love to whisper your name.

What environments help you be still and hear the voice of God?

DARKNESS WON'T NEED TO DESTROY US IF IT CAN GET AWAY WITH DISTRACTING US.

Because of the LORD's great love we are not consumed, for his compassions never fail. They are new every morning; great is your faithfulness.

LAMENTATIONS 3:22–23

The sunrise is hands down my favorite moment of the day. Sweet Maria and I like to wake up while it's still dark outside, when the day is so still it almost feels fragile. With a sense of peace and expectation, we wait for the light to burst onto the horizon.

Every time I look out the window to catch a sunrise, I wonder why any of us would ever miss it. Here's the reason why we do. I think we miss sunrises because we get carried away in the night. It might be with work or worry or relationships or sometimes addictions. Darkness holds onto our fears throughout the day too. Dawn waits until there's enough quiet to whisper for us to come back to God. Lies live in the dark. Lies about ourselves, people we love, and the God who's crazy about us. And even if the darkness doesn't destroy us, it can keep us distracted long enough to cause us to miss the hope that comes with the sunrise the next morning. Don't miss it.

Sometimes the greatest threat darkness poses in our lives isn't necessarily what it does to us. It's that it keeps us away from beauty. Good things can distract us from better things, and when they pull us away from the joy of relationships or the hope of our Creator, then they're no longer good things.

Don't be fooled into thinking the darkness is always destructive. Sometimes it's just distracting. Trade in the darkness for a couple of sunrises instead. Hope is always eager to burst onto the scene every single morning, but you need to be there to catch it.

In what ways have you been distracted by the darkness in the past few days?

IT'S EASY TO WANT GOD'S WILL WHEN IT'S WHAT WE WANT. THE REST OF THE TIME WE GROW.

Whoever can be trusted with very little can also be trusted with much, and whoever is dishonest with very little will also be dishonest with much.

LUKE 16:10

I always get a kick out of the way kids love to obey when there's something in it for them. Take a group of boys to shoot BB guns, and they'll be on their best behavior. Promise a treat after the rooms get cleaned, and you're wondering why they don't do it more often. It's easy for kids to get in line when there's a reward after the work. It's a different story when it comes to math class or doing chores around the house. When rules are laid out for an activity we don't enjoy, it's harder to sell us on the beauty of obedience, so we settle for mere compliance. Compliance is just behavior. It's good manners. Obedience is about doing what we don't want even when we don't fully understand.

We like to think we outgrow the grumpy spirit of dissent when we don't get what we want, but I'm not sure we ever shake the tendency. We often just act better. It's easy to follow God's will when He sends us in the direction of what feels fun or exciting or gratifying. But it's not so easy when he keeps us in jobs we don't want or in relationships with difficult people. Those are the moments, however, when our faith is put to the test. It's when we actually find out who we really are.

The mundane tasks, the unpleasant obedience, and the difficult people are report cards on what we've learned about love. If we can be faithful under circumstances we wouldn't choose, people will see what our faith is all about. Hang tight when things get tough. It's training ground for the next adventure. Is God asking you to do something you don't want to do? This is where it gets good.

What's something you need to do that you've been avoiding?

WHAT WE *DO* WITH OUR LIVES IS A GOOD INDICATOR OF WHERE WE *ARE* IN OUR FAITH.

Humble yourselves, therefore, under God's mighty hand, that he may lift you up in due time. Cast all your anxiety on him because he cares for you.

1 PETER 5:6–7

I love going to places like New York City because the city itself is like a constant soundtrack. The honking horns might be overrepresented, but that's okay. I love hearing the city streets filled with the sound of a classically trained violinist or the guy drumming on plastic barrels or the man with the saxophone wailing out the blues in the subway. Musicians play music because they can't help it. The same is true for writers: they write. They get up every morning, and regardless of the size of their audience, they put their pens to the paper. Whether they write to move people or write for therapy, they write. The practice of their art makes them artists.

I think faith works the same way. It's not just a system of doctrines and behaviors and beliefs. It's about what we *do* with the things we believe. People will figure out what we believe when they see how we live. When we actively care for people who have been handed a difficult life, we show people love isn't all talk. When we bring peace to heated debates, our truest beliefs about the value and dignity of other people shine through. When we choose to risk a new relationship or a new business, we acknowledge God is in charge of the outcome, not us.

There is something infectious about seeing someone captivated by their passions. We see it in musicians and artists. We can do it with our faith. When people see this kind of passion in our lives, they'll see more clearly the God who created those desires.

What we do with our love is where we are in our faith.

In what relationship or venture do you need to acknowledge that God is in charge?

SURROUND YOURSELF WITH PEOPLE WHO ADD WISDOM BUT DON'T SUBTRACT LOVE, ACCEPTANCE, AND PURPOSE.

Walk with the wise and become wise, for a companion of fools suffers harm.

PROVERBS 13:20

When I was young and in school, I remember hearing about the president's "cabinet" and assumed he was keeping a secret stash of snacks in the Oval Office. Then I learned the cabinet was a group of people who surrounded the president and offered counsel on how to lead various parts of the government. (I'm still holding on to the idea of snacks too.)

My wife also knew about the president's cabinet and loved the idea so much that she decided to create one of her own. If it works for the president, she figured it would work for her too. Throughout her adult life, she's had an informal cabinet of five or six people. She's pretty choosy about this group and makes sure it's stocked with people who listen and offer advice without forgetting the role of love and acceptance we all need. None of us outgrows the need to get feedback from other people who see the world differently. But a bunch of naysayers can stymie your progress. Cynics are lightweights. Keep them at a distance.

I expected to see Sweet Maria's cabinet members help her make wiser decisions, but I found something more—something maybe a little bit better: they give us emotional support. When we're wrestling with big life decisions, most people want love and acceptance first and information second. When we've failed, we need hugs, not advice. If you happen to be on someone's cabinet, whether they made it official or not, the first purpose of your appointment is to be an terrific encourager.

Who would be in your cabinet?

THERE'S A LOT OF SECOND BEST AVAILABLE. JUST WALK BY LIKE IT ISN'T EVEN THERE.

Blessed are those who hunger and thirst for righteousness, for they will be filled.

MATTHEW 5:6

In-N-Out is a famous burger chain, and there are plenty of locations where I live in Southern California. If you've ever eaten there, you know it may not be the healthiest choice, but they have some of the best burgers on the planet. Which is why, many times, I have faced the temptation to hit the drive-through even when there's a feast with friends or a wedding reception planned hours later. This usually happens when I skip lunch or get up extra early and my body is signaling for more fuel. Our hunger urges us to seek immediate satisfaction, and the apple we brought with us doesn't stand a chance next to a burger with everything on it. It proves a point. We easily settle for second best when a feast is already prepared for us.

We do this in a lot of other ways too. We settle for work that doesn't inspire us because we want some fast cash. We settle for friends who put a wet blanket on our dreams and constantly bum us out, but they're available so we keep inviting them into our lives. We settle for lives that fall far short of our imagination because short-term pragmatism wins out over long-term perseverance.

We don't need to feel ashamed about our tendencies. All of us have settled for second best at some point in our lives. I think it's part of being human. The only thing worse than settling for second best today is allowing shame to keep you there tomorrow.

The good news is this: there are always second chances. If the path you took overpromised and underdelivered, then get back to dreams you started out with, and let today be the day you hold out for your God-given passion. You don't need to settle for second best anymore.

What have you been hungering for lately that isn't God's presence?

NO MAP WILL TAKE US WHERE GOD WANTS TO LEAD US.

As God's chosen people, holy and dearly loved, clothe yourselves with compassion, kindness, humility, gentleness and patience.

COLOSSIANS 3:12

Most people don't know this about me, but I carry a slingshot and a compass with me everywhere I go. They remind me of fun and adventure and also teach a couple of lessons.

When I travel to conferences to speak to a new group of friends, I've got my slingshot. We shoot salt water taffy at each other there. When I go to Iraq to check up on our school and find ways to support refugees in the region, I take the compass with me and we guess where north is. I get a couple of leaders together and instead of talking policy, we knock over a few cans together. I've learned it's hard not to become friends with someone you have some fun with. Try it sometime.

When I first set out to learn how to love people more, I wouldn't have thought to just play with them more. But that's how love works. We set our hearts on building relationships with people, and then we find a way to live into it. We won't figure it out through reading a book. There's no way to chart it out. With compass in hand, we figure out where true north is and keep heading for that. God doesn't give us a blueprint. He just tells us to be humble and connect with people who might not have been our first choice.

No map will take us where God wants to lead us, because He created each of us for a different purpose. He made you the way you are so you could bring your flavor of love and creativity to the world, and your expression of love will look a little different from mine. That's not a bad thing. It's a great thing.

Put on kindness and humility and let love lead the way. You won't be disappointed with where it takes you. And wherever you go, bring a slingshot and a compass.

What have you been "putting on" this week? How can you put on kindness and humility instead?

WHO HAS THE MICROPHONE IN YOUR LIFE? IGNORE THE LOUDEST VOICE; LISTEN TO THE TRUEST ONE.

The name of the Lord is a fortified tower; the righteous run to it and are safe.

PROVERBS 18:10

I was recently at an event, and we tried a little exercise. On the count of three, everyone in the room yelled out the word *sad!* to represent all the sorrows we carry. We did it again, but one guy in the room yelled "hope!" And you know what? Everyone in the room heard the guy who screamed about hope. It sounded like the right note while we all sang something off-key.

We hear bad news almost every day. None of us escapes sorrow completely. But it's amplified by all the negativity around us. Isn't it great to know one positive voice can drown out all the others if we're listening for it? We can be that voice in the world if we don't allow our voices to be drowned out by the people we surround ourselves with.

Be picky about who you give the microphone to in your life. There will always be people who tell you what you can't do. They don't usually mean you any harm—they're just insecure and actually feel like they're contributing something by telling you all that's wrong. Their voices won't carry if you listen to the ones who remind you who you're becoming. They might not be the loudest voices, but they'll be the truest ones.

God already told us we'd have trouble in this world. He prepared us for the grief and the sense of loss we all feel from time to time. We need to feel free to acknowledge our pain with friends who can sit with us in the sadness. But we also need friends who will remind us of the promises of Jesus: that all the brokenness can be mended. We need to give the microphone to people who speak joy and hope into the world. Listen to the people who tell the truth about the grief and the hope in our lives. They're the voices who sound like Jesus.

Who rejoices and mourns with you?

JESUS' PLAN FOR SELF-PROMOTION WAS ALWAYS THE SAME: "TELL NO ONE."

Jesus sent him away at once with a strong warning: "See that you don't tell this to anyone."

MARK 1:43–44

With the advent of social media came this urge we have to essentially market ourselves. We might not do it intentionally, but friends display unwritten rules on social networks. We're subtly invited to curate only the best moments, and we're given filters and tips to make our pictures look better. We know we're telling a story about ourselves, and we don't want to be misunderstood, so the story reflects only the best. It's a misrepresentation of who we are, and we're misunderstood.

I'm sure I'm guilty of falling into this kind of innocent misrepresentation too. Since it's the air we breathe as a culture, it's hard to step outside of it and consider another way of interacting. But it might be easier than you think, because Jesus paved the way for us. Whenever He healed people or worked miracles in their lives, He always left them with the same instruction: "Tell no one." The greatest humanitarian of all time had no marketing pitch and no plan to scale His work. He just loved whoever was in front of Him and wanted to make their lives better. That was enough for Him. He didn't need matching hoodies or a name for what He was doing. He knew love already had a name.

We won't be as concerned about our image if we're more concerned with seeing the image of God in other people. When we love others well, we don't have the energy to worry about what they think of us. If you find yourself wrapped up in trying to present only the best in your life in hopes of winning the approval of other people, dream up a way to make someone else's day the way Jesus would. Here's what He'd do—He would love people with no photos, no expectations, and no announcements. Give that a try today.

What act of kindness and love will you show someone today without reporting about it on social media?

WE DON'T NEED TO KEEP AUDITIONING FOR PARTS WE'VE BEEN CAST FOR. GO LOVE EVERYBODY.

All authority in heaven and on earth has been given to me. Therefore go and make disciples of all nations, baptizing them in the name of the Father and of the Son and of the Holy Spirit, and teaching them to obey everything I have commanded you. And surely I am with you always, to the very end of the age.

MATTHEW 28:18–20

One of my favorite people in the world is a film director named Tom. Tom has a brilliant way of telling stories on the big screen, and he's got an eye for characters who are just the right fit. One of his favorite people to cast was a guy named Jim. They've worked together long enough that Tom knows, as soon as he reads a script, that Jim is the right lead character. He often chooses scripts with Jim in mind, knowing the story will come together magically with him as the lead.

Wouldn't it be crazy for Jim to audition for the part when Tom chose the movie with him in mind? It would be a waste of everyone's time to have Jim show up and go through the motions when the decision had already been made.

As strange as it might sound to you, God already picked you to play a role in the story you find yourself in. He's doing something through you that looks different from the lives of others, and He's not worried about whether you'll fit the part. He had you in mind before the first scene started. He's got the lead in the story.

We don't need to keep auditioning for parts we've been cast for. God wired you with a unique way of giving away love, and then He told you to go play. Embrace those around you, enjoy your story, and give away love like you've got the part. Jesus has written it just for you.

What are you going to do today to align your life with God's mission in this world?

UNTIL WE FIGURE OUT WHAT WE'D TRADE OUR LIFE FOR, WE WON'T KNOW WHAT WE SHOULD TRADE OUR TIME FOR.

Very truly I tell you, whoever believes in me will do the works I have been doing, and they will do even greater things than these, because I am going to the Father.

JOHN 14:12

A few times in my life I have been at a crossroads, unsure of which way to turn. We all come to those from time to time, when life is perfectly okay but we know we were made for a greater purpose. We weren't born to be typical. When I get to those places, I often reflect on a question an older, wiser friend of mine asked. He said, "Bob, if you knew without question you would not fail, what's the one thing you would do with your life?"

It's funny how some can answer that question in a snap, and others just can't. I think I know why it's sometimes hard to answer. Perhaps it's because we get wrapped up in fears and insecurities because we think of all the ways our plans might fail or all the reasons we don't have what it takes. But most of the time our fears lie to us. They keep us from seeing what we were made for and tell us it's impossible before we've even started to try.

We won't know what we should trade our time for until we figure out what we'd trade our lives for. What's the one thing you would devote your life to if you knew, beyond a shadow of a doubt, that you would not fail? Do that. Will it work? Who knows. Try it anyway. Take all the time and energy you pour into worrying about the outcomes and put that energy toward your passions.

Jesus wouldn't have told us we'd do greater things than Him if He didn't think we could. Take Him up on His word.

What's the one thing you would devote your life to if you knew, beyond a shadow of a doubt, that you would not fail?

JULY 30

ALWAYS WELCOME THE STRANGER. GOD MODELED THIS BY HOW HE WELCOMED US.

You are to love those who are foreigners, for you yourselves were foreigners in Egypt.

DEUTERONOMY 10:19

A recurring theme in the Bible is welcoming the stranger (or foreigner). Jesus and His followers tried to live this out and, in many cases, benefited from others welcoming them. Hospitality is always a marker of people who follow Jesus.

Some of us think of hospitality as an industry, like hotels or restaurants. We might think hospitality is cooking a nice meal for friends or someone crashing on our couch when they're in town. But hospitality is much more costly and intimate than we tend to think. A spirit of hospitality is a willingness to open our doors when it's inconvenient for us. It means prioritizing people in need when we might have other projects we'd prefer to work on in a given moment. Hospitality looks like finding joy in creating a place for people we wouldn't naturally choose, people who can be difficult to love.

When my kids visited all those world leaders years ago, you know what we took as a gift for princes, kings, and dignitaries? We took them a copy of our house key. At least a hundred people can just let themselves in if they happen to be in the neighborhood. It's just another reflection of what hospitality looks like when we let it off the leash.

It's easy to trust God's idea of welcoming when it's about people we already know and who are easy to love. It's a little harder when it means an extended stay by someone who dirties up our dishes and borrows the car and returns it on empty. Those are the moments we find out whether we really trust that God knew best when He told us to love one another or if it's just a suggestion we can ignore.

Who's the stranger in your life you can welcome and show love to today?

EMBRACE UNCERTAINTY. SOME OF THE MOST BEAUTIFUL CHAPTERS IN OUR LIVES WON'T HAVE A TITLE UNTIL MUCH LATER.

I will instruct you and teach you in the way you should go; I will counsel you with my loving eye on you.

PSALM 32:8

Do you remember how you felt after you first graduated high school? I remember feeling thrilled and terrified at the same time. The world was thrown open in a way it had never been before. The regimen of the first eighteen years was largely determined by other people—school assignments, meals, bedtimes, and drivers education. We had to sit in classes chosen for us for at least eight hours a day. Our parents decided what meals we would eat and when we'd be home every night, then we'd sleep for the next eight hours. Even though many of us broke some of the rules, there were at least clear boundaries in our lives. As frustrating as they were at times, they provided us a sense of security.

Everything changed once we were out on our own. Whether we went to work or went to college, we didn't know what title the next chapter of our lives would have. We didn't know which group of friends we'd fall into or what subjects would catch our interest. We didn't know if we would soar into great adventures or fall into a sense of hopelessness. We didn't know if we'd lose faith or find it all over again.

It might have felt more intense then, but I think we all revisit those feelings of uncertainty fairly often in our lives, no matter our age. We feel it with moves and job changes, when the kids go back to school, or when we wake up to an unexpected nudge that it's time to move on. Embrace uncertainty. Some of the most beautiful chapters in our lives won't have a title until much later.

Which part of your life feels uncertain?

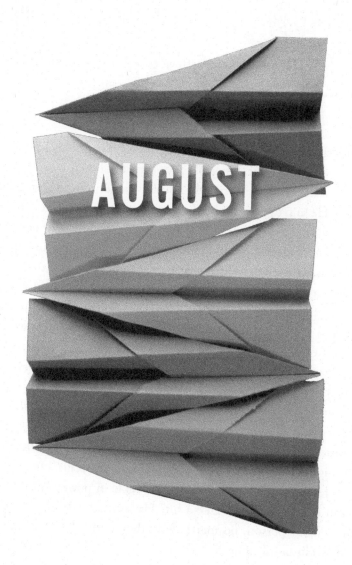

AUGUST

INSTEAD OF TELLING PEOPLE WHAT JESUS MEANT, LOVE EVERYONE THE WAY HE DID.

Dear children, let us not love with words or speech but with actions and in truth.

1 JOHN 3:18

You would think one of the things we could all get behind is Jesus' message of love. Everywhere He went, Jesus told people to love others more than they love themselves. He said if someone asks you for money, give it to them and give generously. He said to do right by those who don't treat you well in return. He lived the message even more passionately than He taught it, engaging every person in front of Him or behind Him like they were His one and only priority.

His message wasn't confusing or hard to understand. But it's surprising how divisive it can be to live out Jesus' message of love. People blast you, saying love actually means rejecting people when they don't act a certain way—they call it "tough love." Or they bring out their Greek and Hebrew words, saying love means keeping people at arm's length until they change their behaviors. Somehow we can turn even Jesus' message of love into a dividing line to determine who's in and who's out.

Jesus was criticized because of who He brought close, not those He sent away. He was scandalous because of who He let in, not those He cast out. Keep it simple. Instead of telling people what Jesus meant, love everyone the way He did.

You might be misunderstood when you love like Jesus, but you're in good company. Jesus was misunderstood. The people in power killed Him. What makes you think you won't take a hit? He was ridiculed because He chose to live like every person, no matter who they were or what they had done, belonged in His family. Do the same.

Don't get bogged down by arguments about what it means to follow Jesus. Lose all the fancy words. Just love everyone the way He did.

What would change today if you chose to love those around you sincerely and without caution?

GOD'S NEVER AS NERVOUS ABOUT OUR FUTURE, OR AS CONCERNED ABOUT OUR PAST, AS WE ARE.

The LORD is my light and my salvation—whom shall I fear?

PSALM 27:1

I have one daughter, Lindsey, who got married to Jon a few summers ago outdoors at our lodge in Canada. Being the dad and walking down the aisle toward Jon gave me a whole new perspective on the way God sees us. My son Richard married Ashley. Like Lindsey, she was stunning and dressed in white. God says we're His *bride* and that our whole story with Him ends with a giant wedding feast. All the sadness we feel will be gone then, all our tears will be wiped away. All the confusion will vanish. He'll bring out the best food and drinks to celebrate the end of strife and the beginning of eternity together.

I think about these family weddings all the time. As exciting as weddings are for the bride and groom, there's also a lot of anxiety they can carry. They're nervous about the future. What will intimacy look like? Will they get on each other's nerves as they'll be together every day for the rest of their lives? They're often concerned about the past. Did their biological families prepare them for life with their new spouse? Will they accept them? We bring anticipation and young love into our weddings, but we also bring fears. It's just part of being human.

The wedding we'll celebrate with Jesus someday will capture all the joy of our weddings now with none of the fear. Since God knows us better than we know ourselves, He's never as nervous about our future, or as concerned about our past, as we are. He can't wait to walk us down the aisle.

What fears are keeping you from joy?

AUGUST 3

IF THE WALLS OF YOUR LIFE ARE CRASHING DOWN, MAYBE GOD HAS A RENOVATION IN MIND.

If anyone is in Christ, the new creation has come: The old has gone, the new is here!

2 CORINTHIANS 5:17

Have you ever asked yourself, "What on earth am I doing here?"

It's a question accompanied by a hollow pit in your gut. If we're not mindful, that hollow feeling can swallow us and make it seem like there's no way out. Fear feels like that. It gets in our system and leaves us hurting for answers and certainty. The whole thing seems like a calamity.

What is God doing here? Is He even here?

I have some friends who are really good at taking worn-down and weathered homes and bringing them back to life. By the time they're done with a project, you can't even recognize the place. From the bones of the house to the finer details, from the light fixtures to the baseboards, they bring brand-new life into a once rickety space.

What if that's what God is up to when nothing seems to make sense? At one level, we're all tear-downs. What if He's fixing up our hearts?

Uncertainty is not a life sentence. We are not forever doomed to wrestle and worry over futures that are a little hazy. What if there's purpose to it, an opportunity to refine ourselves and make positive changes in our lives? The trick is this: don't lose your cool. God uses uncertainty in our lives to remodel our hearts.

When we feel the panic under our ribs, it's our heart asking to be remodeled into something more resilient and beautiful. If we're willing to trust God to bust down some walls and set us up for something restored, our hearts are going to experience quite a transformation. We'll trade anxiety and worry for purpose and confidence. We're being made new.

What in your life is being made new?

DON'T LET UNCERTAINTY TALK YOU INTO PURSUING A BACKUP PLAN INSTEAD OF YOUR PURPOSE.

You need to persevere so that when you have done the will of God, you will receive what he has promised.

HEBREWS 10:36

As college graduation approached, I decided becoming a lawyer was my next step to make the biggest impact. Since I had spent most of undergrad surfing, I didn't feel entirely prepared. My grades were underwhelming; my LSAT scores were even worse. Every application was flat-out rejected. They didn't even put me on their wait lists.

But I wasn't going to let a big load of rejection stop me. My first-choice school was within driving distance, so I hopped in my VW bug and went to the dean's office for an impromptu meeting without notice.

The dean didn't find my argument compelling, to say the least. So after he told me I needed to leave his office, I sat on a bench just outside the door the rest of the day. Every time he passed by, I told him he had the power to let me in. All he had to say was, "Go buy your books" and I'd be in. For six straight days I sat on the bench and waited for the dean to walk past.

"All you have to say is, 'Go buy your books,'" I'd remind him each time, and he'd just smile and move along. Until the day he didn't. Five days after law school started, he approached me at the bench with a smile, and after a long pause, he told me—"Go buy your books."

Every day since, as I've been involved in countless legal cases here and abroad, I've thought about the power of perseverance. Sometimes when a door closes, it's not a sign pointing us in a different direction. Sometimes it's a reminder that we need to knock harder—or maybe try kicking it down.

What doors do you need to keep knocking on?

AUGUST 5

WHEN WE SAY WE'RE WAITING ON GOD, OFTEN HE'S ACTUALLY WAITING ON US.

I wait for the LORD, my whole being waits, and in his word I put my hope.

PSALM 130:5

We've all been in relationships where we've waited for the other person to make the next move. It happens in the exhilarating times, waiting to see if the other will confess their feelings, signaling it's safe to share ours. And it happens in the challenging times, too, when we've been through an argument and we hope they'll apologize so we can say we're sorry too. Insecurity often keeps us from stepping out, so we wait for signs to let us know we'll be okay.

Have you noticed we often do the same thing in our relationship with God? We say we're waiting on Him to show us whether to take the step we're scared to take. We're waiting for a sign to say it's safe to make the move. But just like in our relationships with each other, when we say we're waiting on God, He's usually waiting on us.

It's vulnerable to step out when we're not sure how it'll end. We wait for signs because we want some kind of assurance that the risk won't end in a face-plant. We're scared to misstep and find ourselves exposed and alone. But God already told us He's for us and always with us. Jesus came to live with us so we wouldn't have to wonder how God feels about us. He answered the question about whether there was anything we could do that would disqualify us, and the answer is this: nothing.

We don't need to wait for confirmation any longer. God already drew a circle around us and said we're all with Him.

What are you waiting for?

GOD USUALLY DOESN'T GIVE US ALL THE DETAILS. HE GIVES US A DIRECTION.

The Lord is close to the brokenhearted and saves those who are crushed in spirit.

PSALM 34:18

When my kids were little, we loved scavenger hunts. One of the kids was the designated "hider" and would place objects throughout the house and yard along with clues to help us sleuth them out. At the end, whether we found anything or not, we all got ice cream.

Faith can be a bit like that scavenger hunt. Some things about faith can only be understood by searching for them. In the search lies the building of common experiences, relationships, community. Searching can be frustrating, too, if you need to know the details in advance. It's not a business trip God has invited us on—it's an adventure. God doesn't give us all the details when He tells us to go. Like a series of clues, He sends us in a direction and trusts us to make some moves along the way. We don't know where we'll end up when we start. We just know where to go next, and that's enough.

We don't need to know all the steps or all the answers in order to get started. We just need to know the next step. And after that, the next one. If we're confident the One with the master plan has sent us in a direction, we can relax knowing He'll be faithful to show us what to do when we get there.

God already told us His plan for us is to give away love like we'll never run out. He said He wants us to look for people who are lonely or hurting and hold them close the way He holds us. He said He wants love and grace to be the lens through which we see the world. Take these with you when He sends you out on the adventure, and you'll have all the details you need.

Who in your life is hurting or lonely? What can you do to show them God's love?

THE ONE WHO HAS CALLED US IS MORE POWERFUL THAN THE UNCERTAINTY WE'RE FACING.

Sovereign LORD, you are God! Your covenant is trustworthy, and you have promised these good things to your servant.

2 SAMUEL 7:28

I remember learning an important lesson from my kids when they were first learning to swim. We'd wade into the shallow end with floaties, then I'd go out just ahead of them and hold my arms out to snag them when they jumped from the step. The first leap was always the hardest for them. They could see I was standing tall in the water, they knew I had told them I was there to catch them, but they still couldn't bring themselves to leave the safety of the step. Their uncertainty about the water outweighed their faith in me to catch them.

The memory comes to mind whenever I feel God telling me to take a leap into the unknown. You've probably been there too. We know He'll be there to catch us on the other side, but our confidence in Him doesn't always feel as strong as the security of the step we're on already. We know the deep end has to be more exciting, but the risk of the unknown can be paralyzing.

Those are the times when we can rest, knowing the One who has called us is more powerful than the uncertainty we're facing. Just like a good father holding his arms out to his anxious kids, God's ready to catch us when we're willing to take the plunge. Don't let a little uncertainty talk you out of an adventure with Jesus. Like most adults who were once young, you probably jumped into the water eventually. Why not do it again?

In what ways is uncertainty holding you back? What would you do differently if you had deeper trust in God?

AUGUST 8

THE WAY WE DEAL WITH UNCERTAINTY SAYS A LOT ABOUT WHETHER JESUS IS AHEAD OF US LEADING OR BEHIND US JUST CARRYING OUR STUFF.

Whether you turn to the right or to the left, your ears will hear a voice behind you, saying, "This is the way; walk in it."

ISAIAH 30:21

Some of the lessons I've learned about Jesus have come while I was in the woods backpacking with friends. In college, we brought a dozen high school kids to a remote inlet where my family would end up living many years later. There was a backpacking program there where guides take a group up through the woods to the glaciers and summit one of the peaks.

Halfway through the trip, we got way out ahead of our leader, and all the trees started to look the same. We couldn't tell whether the path went under a log or narrowed to the right of the trees. We took one wrong turn and another and another until we were hopelessly lost. At that point, we were equal parts grizzly food and camper.

We had no map, no GPS, and between us not a lot of brains. The thrill of being independent and exploring had quickly fizzled when we realized we couldn't find our way back. We were entirely dependent on the leader to come find us.

That day we learned we could avoid a lot of anxiety in our lives if we let our guide do his job. His job wasn't to follow behind to make sure no one dropped something or to carry our tents. He was there to guide us safely to our destination. We were headed to a place the guide had been before, and he wanted us to get there too.

When we find ourselves losing our way in life, it's a good time to evaluate whether Jesus is ahead of us leading or behind us just carrying our stuff. There's no shame in acknowledging we got out ahead of Him again, because He will always come find us when we do. He's trying to take us to a place we can't get to alone.

Where is God guiding you right now?

JESUS WAS A LOT MORE CONCERNED ABOUT PEOPLE WHO FAKED IT THAN THE ONES WHO BLEW IT.

Woe to you, teachers of the law and Pharisees, you hypocrites! You are like whitewashed tombs, which look beautiful on the outside but on the inside are full of the bones of the dead and everything unclean.

MATTHEW 23:27

Anyone who's ever raised a teenager, worked with a teenager, or been a teenager knows they tend to have some loose definitions or leaky memories when it comes to telling the whole truth. They're in the stretch of life when they start to feel independent. They can form some of their own opinions about the world. They can drive and get into mischief without adults scrutinizing their every move. They learn how to shade the truth because telling the *whole* truth might ruin the gig.

As adults, we'd always rather our kids told the actual truth rather than several different versions of it. If they messed up, we want them to just get it out there and receive a little grace. Lies build walls that make it harder for love to get through. The reason is simple. People can't receive our love if they think we don't see them for who they really are. The walls our lies create keep us from knowing the people around us are over the moon about us when we blow it just as much as when we get it right.

God feels the same way about us. Jesus was a lot more concerned about people who faked it than He was about the ones who blew it. His response to the ones who acted like they had it all together was to give them a wide berth. He engaged with compassion the people who got real with their mess-ups. And it seemed like everyone around Jesus messed up. This wasn't a coincidence. He seeks out people like you and me who can understand the truth about our absolute need for Him. He wanted people to know He saw them, and there was nothing they could do to make Him love them more. When they messed up, He wanted them to know He loved them in their failure and would be with them in their future.

We all get it wrong sometimes. Don't go into hiding just because you blew it. Keep it real. Let Jesus enter into your failure with you and watch what happens.

**What would it look like for you to fully come out
of hiding and own who you really are?**

AUGUST 10

START FROM SCRATCH WITH JESUS EVERY DAY AND THEN BE CAREFUL ABOUT WHAT YOU ADD TO YOUR LIFE.

We urge you, brothers and sisters, to . . . make it your ambition to lead a quiet life: You should mind your own business and work with your hands, just as we told you.

1 THESSALONIANS 4:10–11

Everyone in my family knows that Sweet Maria is the Queen of the Kitchen in our house. That's how she likes it, and that's how we like it too. But truth be known, I'm always itching to get in on the creative fun.

Have you ever heard the phrase "too many cooks in the kitchen"? That's me. When I'm anywhere near a stove, cutting board, or spice rack, I'm the equivalent of at least three bad chefs in the kitchen. Still, my wife is gracious, and sometimes she'll let me put on an apron and help chop onions. Predictably, it's not long before it gets out of hand and I'm chopping lettuce like Edward Scissorhands and throwing cloves of garlic into the pot like LeBron James. Sweet Maria is kind to remind me that more isn't always better and garlic in the cake batter is definitely a bad idea.

The same is true with Bible study. It's important to know what Jesus had to say if we're going to live like Him. But if we're buried under piles of commentaries, we'll miss out on the opportunity to live Jesus' message.

What I'm getting at is this: in life, we can all go a little overboard with what we add to the mix if we're not careful. We overcommit to good activities and then realize we've missed out on people we value the most in the process. We're devoted to important work, but we skip the even more important work of baseball games and recitals or movie nights. When we add too much to life, we miss out on the most essential ingredient: the people. None of this comes from a bad or malicious place. We're trying to work hard so the people we love can have the opportunities they want. Here's the problem. We can spend so much time trying to provide for our families that we're not providing for our families.

Try this: start from scratch with Jesus every day and then be careful about what you add after that.

What do you need to quit today?

DON'T ROLL OUT SOD WHERE GOD WANTS TO PLANT SEED. HE'S MORE INTERESTED IN HELPING US GROW THAN HAVING US LOOK FINISHED.

Just as you received Christ Jesus as Lord, continue to live your lives in him, rooted and built up in him, strengthened in the faith as you were taught, and overflowing with thankfulness.

COLOSSIANS 2:6–7

Southern California where I live is a desert, so it's difficult to maintain a lawn with actual grass. What's a popular workaround to getting that envious green lawn in the dry desert? You might be thinking of sod, but think weirder. Roll out artificial turf across the yard, of course. The only problem is sometimes you wind up having a house that looks like it belongs at a miniature golf course. If that's your thing, maybe it's not such a bad idea. If it isn't your thing, it is.

Our lives can feel like a desert sometimes, like nothing's coming easy and we're just parched and dried up. We scramble for ways to look like we're the finished product, so we start improvising ways to look like we have things figured out. We throw a fresh coat of paint over our rusted and busted frames, roll out the fake turf, and hope nobody notices the difference.

But God isn't asking us to look like the finished article in our lives. He said Jesus was enough for that. Rather, He's hoping to change us from start to finish, from our insides to our outsides. He's invested in us for the long haul. He wants us to ditch the act of being complete, and He wants to help us grow more desperate for Him.

The miracle is this: when we stop trying to look pristine and perfect, the soil of our hearts becomes healthier and more fertile. Love and grace start sprouting in us, and the desert starts to green up with the real thing. Is it going to take some time? You bet. Will we always get it right? Of course not.

Here's the point. Don't roll out astroturf where God's planting seed. He's more interested in helping us grow than having us look finished.

In what ways is God growing you today, even if it feels slow?

QUIT PLAYING IT SAFE WITH WHAT YOU BELIEVE IS TRUE.

Brothers and sisters, do not slander one another. Anyone who speaks against a brother or sister or judges them speaks against the law and judges it. When you judge the law, you are not keeping it, but sitting in judgment on it.

JAMES 4:11

All of us want to belong. We look for connection in all kinds of places: at churches, on sports teams, in book clubs, and through our jobs. A lot of us get on social media or read blogs to find words that make us feel less alone and more connected to the world. We all want to know we've got a tribe, a place to belong.

The power of community is in its strength to bring us together. But have you ever felt like your group constructed a high wall meant to keep the people you disagree with out? It can be tempting for people to define themselves by who they're against. The problem is, Jesus said He was for everybody. That means you're the guy on the other side of the wall from Him if you've got a list of people God made but you won't talk to because you disagree with them.

When you start to hear friends gossip about people who aren't around to defend themselves, make a stand. If you hear leaders lumping large groups into small and inaccurate definitions, stand up. When the people around you start to divide the world between "us" and "them," listen for Jesus challenging all of us to break down the barriers. Don't let the longing for connection and community keep you silent.

Quit playing it safe with what you know to be true. When the people around us are courageous enough to speak the truth, they remind us who we want to become. When your words invite people in instead of blocking them out, you'll be living the words Jesus whispered in your ear.

Who's on the outside of your friend group, and what can you do to invite them in?

GOD SENT YOU AN INVITATION TO LIVE YOUR FAITH BY GOING BIG ON LOVE.

And now what are you waiting for? Get up, be baptized and wash your sins away, calling on his name.

ACTS 22:16

Every year on the first Thursday in February, thousands of leaders from around the world show up for the National Prayer Breakfast in Washington, DC. The event casts a wide net and brings together different faiths and perspectives to find common ground. For a few days each year, these leaders join hands across faith traditions and denominations to listen to one another, pray together, and find community. It's inspiring to see people who normally stay in their camps come together to pray for justice and peace. They usually find the group they've been avoiding or vilifying has the same dreams and hopes they do.

You only get to attend the event by invitation, and that's not a guarantee every year. But who needs an invitation to get together with friends for prayer and encouragement? Every year I put this gathering on my calendar with plans to attend whether I'm invited or not. I know either way I can stay at the hotel across the street and get a couple of donuts with friends. A lot of us are waiting for invitations to things we're already invited to.

When it comes to breaking down barriers and pursuing peace and justice, we don't need to wait for an invitation. Sure, there might be limited spots in certain places, but there's no limit on the availability or power of love. We don't need permission to bring people together to spread love in the world either.

Stop waiting for an invitation to live your faith. God already asked you to come, and His invitation to love is everywhere, for wherever you are and whoever you're with.

What invitation are you waiting for?

AUGUST 14

WE SHOULDN'T BE SURPRISED WHEN WE DON'T UNDERSTAND WHAT A GOD WHO SAYS HE SURPASSES ALL UNDERSTANDING IS DOING.

The peace of God, which transcends all understanding, will guard your hearts and your minds in Christ Jesus.

PHILIPPIANS 4:7

The traffic where I live in Southern California is world famous for being bad. You can sit on the highway for three hours and go twenty miles. I'm a pilot, so sometimes I'll rent a little plane if I have an engagement farther up the coast. I skip the wait and the traffic, get a terrific view, and have some fun at the same time. Best of all, I skip the feeling of my blood pressure rising and my patience plummeting.

Most of us react the same to gridlock traffic. We wonder, *What's the hold up? Why is everything moving so slowly?* What happens when our life stalls or takes a hard-right turn we weren't expecting? We finally settle down with someone who stole our hearts from the moment we met, then we get bad news from the doctor. Or we pour all our energy into a movement we believed in, only to have it fall apart. As annoying as it is to hit the detours, endure the disappointments, and wait in the stop-and-go traffic life sends our way, these things shape us.

Sometimes the delays in our lives are merely annoying, and sometimes they're devastating. They can even cause us to ask if God is there and if He's good. Don't be surprised when you don't understand what a God who says He passes all understanding is doing. Those are the times when we have to remember He holds all things together, including us. Sometimes we don't see how God was moving until years down the road. For God, a day is like a thousand years, and a thousand years are like a day. Hang tight. This might take a minute to sort itself out.

In what area of your life do you need more patience?

AUGUST 15

GOD DOESN'T BOOKMARK OUR FAILURES.
HE CELEBRATES OUR ATTEMPTS.

I, even I, am he who blots out your transgressions, for my own sake, and remembers your sins no more.

ISAIAH 43:25

One of the best ways to learn about a new friend is ask to borrow their favorite book. Usually it's underlined and dog-eared on almost every page. It's fascinating to see which passages stood out to them—what moved them. It's like we're reading two books at once—the actual one and the one reflecting our friend's experience with it. When it comes to a book you absolutely love, my guess is that you're not highlighting the mistakes, unclear ideas, or grammatical errors. Rather, we focus on the passages that move us, the ones that bring us life and joy.

I think God reads our lives a lot like we read books from our friends. He's not looking for the places we messed up. He doesn't jump on our mistakes and make notes in the margins for future reference. He looks for the ways we're writing passages that move us, the ones that heal the people He made. He's ready to celebrate our attempts to give love and spread hope. He's watching us with an eye for the beauty in our lives.

Jesus had a remarkable way of seeing past people's failures to the heart of the person in front of Him. When the religious people cast judgment and pushed vulnerable people out, Jesus brought them close and saw them for who they were becoming. He knew their stories were still being written and that every story includes a few setbacks and failures. He knew redemption was a process set in motion by love and completed by grace. He didn't see people through a haze of condemnation. He saw people through the gaze of love.

God doesn't bookmark our failures. He celebrates our attempts. Don't let your failures define you anymore. Don't let who you were decide who you'll be.

What past failure or mistake still haunts you?

WHATEVER ELSE YOU'RE AIMING FOR, GOD'S BETTER.

He called a little child to him, and placed the child among them. And he said: "Truly I tell you, unless you change and become like little children, you will never enter the kingdom of heaven."

MATTHEW 18:2–3

If you had asked me what I was aiming for when I was in high school, I would have said I wanted to get out of high school. If you asked me the same question after law school, I probably would've said something vague like, "to make a difference in the world." I wanted to get a job at a good law firm and gain the experience I needed to help people. It hadn't occurred to me to aim for a life where I could have an office on Tom Sawyer Island at Disneyland and be a part of a movement that builds schools for students in Uganda, helps refugees in Iraq, and teaches little girls in Afghanistan how to read when the religious leaders say they can't go to school. I wasn't aiming for these things when I was younger because I hadn't imagined them yet, and we can't long for something we can't already see in our minds.

I think this is one of the reasons Jesus tells us to have faith like children. Kids have wildly creative imaginations. If you ask them what they want to be when they grow up, they'll say they want to be Aslan from The Chronicles of Narnia or Spiderman so they can rescue people in danger. They plan to live in castles and have superpowers. They aim to be helpers and healers and kind. Kids dream big because the world hasn't put their imaginations in check yet.

So why did we let the world stifle ours? Sure, we run into the reality of having to pay bills and make it to work on time, but there are endless invitations to join in a life of whimsy if we'll open our eyes.

God is not limited by the rules we make up, and He doesn't want us to be either. Whatever you're aiming for, God's better.

What are you aiming for?

AUGUST 17

LOVE MORE. FEAR LESS.

There is no fear in love. But perfect love drives out fear, because fear has to do with punishment. The one who fears is not made perfect in love.

1 JOHN 4:18

Our backyard in San Diego spreads right down to the water, and Sweet Maria and I like to sit on our back porch. We meet a lot of new friends out there, and we'll never forget Ryan. He was strolling down the dirt path by the water when he suddenly stopped and started waving.

"Hi, I'm Ryan and I'm in love," he said.

"That's great, Ryan!" I shot back.

Then he continued: "I came here because I was wondering if I could ask my girlfriend to marry me in your backyard."

We shouted "Yes!" immediately. Ryan went big with his plans: he had twenty friends cook dinner for them, then they danced in our backyard and he took her out on our boat to pop the big question. The night ended better than a fireworks show, with water cannons from a Coast Guard boat spraying the stars like they were on fire.

I think about Ryan all the time, his fearlessness to be bold and his willingness to put extravagant love on display. He ran the risk of her saying no or getting embarrassed in front of all his friends. Yet he pushed through the fear that he might look silly with the better chance that he'd get the girl. He did all this because his feelings for his beloved were greater than his fear of what others might think if it didn't go as planned.

When God said perfect love casts out fear, He knew what He was talking about. He knew the only thing bigger than fear was love for other people. He knows love is powerful enough to pull us outside our heads long enough to take risks for other people.

What risks will you take for someone today to love them more?

GOD'S MORE INTERESTED IN OUR HEARTS THAN IN OUR PLANS.

My son, give me your heart and let your eyes delight in my ways.

PROVERBS 23:26

Everyone close to me knows I love surprises. I love surprising others with gift-wrapped bicycles and balloons, and I love when people surprise me—even if it's just sticky-notes in unexpected places like inside grilled cheese sandwiches. Surprises keep life interesting. They let us know people were thinking about us.

My family has managed to catch me off guard, but even more often I've caught them in the act of putting together a surprise for me. Sweet Maria gets as giddy as a kid every year on Christmas Eve, and I'll find a trail of clues I can usually follow. On birthdays, I've occasionally figured out a party was waiting for me before the big day. Even after I discover the surprise, I play along anyway because I know it's a bummer when your surprise gets spoiled.

In truth, it's usually not the event itself that moves us, though the moments with friends can be priceless. We're moved by the love that went into the planning. No one plans surprises for people they feel indifferent about. We plan surprises for the people who have captured our hearts. And when we walk through the door to a big group of friends, or figure it out before the party begins, we imagine all the joy that went into their scheme to make us feel special. It's the heart behind the surprise that moves us.

God feels the same way about us. He doesn't care about the plans we scheme up or the success we achieve. He cares about the heart behind it all. Next time you find yourself too tied to your ideas or the outcome of your efforts, remember God isn't dazzled by the big reveal. He revels in the heart behind the plans.

What plans have kept you distracted from focusing your heart on God lately?

AUGUST 19

GOD'S FAR STRONGER THAN WHATEVER
IS HOLDING YOU BACK.

He got up, rebuked the wind and said to the waves, "Quiet! Be still!" Then the wind died down and it was completely calm.

MARK 4:39

Few things bring me as much joy as being out on the water. Since we live right by the bay, time on the water is one of my go-to activities, and it almost always delivers. But occasionally it backfires. Occasionally I'll get out on the water, sailing in anticipation of a time for a little restoration, and a storm will show up unannounced and knock me around instead.

Every time storms show up when I'm out on a boat, I think about the time Jesus' friends were hit with a similar surprise. I imagine them frantically paddling and pulling on ropes, desperate to get to the shore safely. With no luck after all their efforts, they realized Jesus was fast asleep, and they thought maybe He'd have an answer. They shook Jesus out of a deep sleep, and the first words out of His mouth were, "Don't be afraid." He stood up and told the storm to be quiet, and it was quiet.

We're all a little like the disciples, doing our best to make it through life. But storms happen, and before we know it, we're thrown into a bout with depression or financial pressures or sudden unemployment. The peaceful life we're striving for gets thrown off course. We wonder if God's asleep.

Those are the times it's most important to remember God is far stronger than whatever's holding you back. Jesus wasn't thrown off by thunderstorms then, and He's not caught off guard by the storms in our lives now. It might look to us like Jesus is asleep in the back of the boat, but He's actually fixing the rudder.

What storms are you facing right now?

GOD MADE BEAUTY TO LEAVE US SPEECHLESS. HE DAZZLES US SO WE'LL PAUSE AND LISTEN FOR HIS VOICE.

Come with me by yourselves to a quiet place and get some rest.

MARK 6:31

We all need a place to go and be restored. Maybe it's a family lake home or that favorite trail to hike. Or it could be road trips into the country, riding horses, or baking. My surefire place of rest and refuge is a place called the Princess Louisa Inlet in Canada. It's a place that holds most of my dearest memories.

Every time we return from the inlet, I try to scheme ways to bring the spirit of rest I experienced back with me. Because here's the truth: the real magic in finding rest isn't specific to the places we go. It's about the spirit or rest we return with. We go to a lake or a farm or a favorite river because we want to pause long enough to calm the noise in our lives. We want to tune back in to what's most important.

I think that's one of the reasons God created beauty like lakes and rivers and forests—to dazzle us. They're sanctuaries disguised as nature, reminding us to pause and listen for His voice. We don't need to fly to Canada or take road trips to find them. We can find peace and stillness by tagging out from some of what would normally fill our days and having a picnic in our backyard. We can best tune in to God's restorative voice by sitting silent long enough to hear Him speak.

Don't believe the lie that you have to go away to be restored. Find a way to create a sanctuary in your daily life, because these safe places are within reach if we'll stop long enough to see them.

Where is your favorite place to find rest?

I'D RATHER HAVE A COUPLE OF IDEAS FAIL THAN HAVE A FAITH THAT WON'T TRY.

Do not fear, for I am with you; do not be dismayed, for I am your God. I will strengthen you and help you; I will uphold you with my righteous right hand.

ISAIAH 41:10

One of my favorite sporting events is the Summer Olympics. I love the opening ceremonies and the bright-faced athletes. The event reminds us of our shared history, our shared space, and our shared dreams.

As much as I love the Summer Olympics, it's the Paralympics that capture my heart the most. The Paralympians had to overcome something more than tired muscles or waning willpower. They had to overcome learning disabilities or nonexistent limbs, stigmas, and probably a lifetime of naysayers.

One of my favorite people in the Paralympics is a guy named Lex Gillette. He's a good friend and a blind long jumper. Yep, that's right. He has no sight and yet sprints down a hundred-meter track and flings himself feet first into a sand pit he cannot see.

What strikes me most is how Lex gets from the starting line to the landing. His trainer stands at the end of the sand pit and yells "Fly!" over and over. It's not just motivation—the trainer's voice is a homing beacon helping Lex to run straight as he sprints toward a voice he can trust.

If you're ever wondering if you should take that risk or run toward a big ambition of yours, think about Lex. And I don't mean, "If a blind guy can do it, so can I." I mean, learn from his heart, his courage, and his wisdom. See how he acknowledges the obstacles in his way and chooses to fly over them anyway. Take note of how he has voices in his life he trusts and runs toward. No circumstance will ever be perfectly suited to the big leap you want to make. Lose the fear and throw a little disregard at it instead. Even if it takes the help of a friend or two, make the jump.

What situation do you find yourself in that is inviting you to be more courageous?

FAITH WITHOUT ACTION IS LIKE A SAILBOAT WITHOUT A SAIL—IT WON'T GET VERY FAR.

As the body without the spirit is dead, so faith without deeds is dead.

JAMES 2:26

Whenever I've got a free afternoon at home, the first place you'll find me is on my sailboat. Richard and Adam, my sons who are the dauntless sailors of the family, will raise the sails, and we'll make our way into the bay or into some adventure.

It's the wind that takes a sailboat anywhere at all. So if I showed up one day and told my sons, "Let's not use the sails today," they'd look back at me with scrunched faces and think I had lost it.

Sometimes we operate like faith is one choice or one pivotal moment and then God does the rest. A stationary sailboat isn't much of a sailboat. It's just an extension of the dock. In the same way, belief that doesn't find itself doing much isn't doing much good. Faith that isn't experiencing by doing what it has learned is a boat tied to the dock. It's a sailboat with no sails.

Jesus has a personal revolution in mind for each of us, and it starts with *doing*, not just believing, and certainly not merely agreeing with what Jesus said. When our sails are unfurled, we can't help being moved by the wind. Pull anchor on your beliefs and hoist the sails. Now you're going places. Jesus didn't want us to just be believers. He wanted us to be participants.

It's tempting to think that following Jesus is about learning the right ideas, saying the right words, memorizing a couple of verses, and singing the right songs. It's tempting to think a thumping church service, the right conference, or the right book will validate our faith. Don't get me wrong—there's nothing wrong with the church or the conference or the book. But faith without works is a sailboat without a sail. God is calling you toward the horizon with Him because He knows what can happen with your faith when it unties from the dock and starts to move.

Where is God inviting you to trust the wind of His Spirit more?

LET THE REASONS NOT TO FEAR OUTNUMBER YOUR REASONS NOT TO TRY.

I have told you these things, so that in me you may have peace. In this world you will have trouble. But take heart! I have overcome the world.

JOHN 16:33

Jesus never asked anyone to play it safe. We were born to be brave, and He modeled that for us. He challenged established systems, calling those in power to the carpet, befriending folks on the fringes of society.

It turns out Jesus was trouble, and it's exactly what He guaranteed we would find ourselves: "In this world you will have trouble." Jesus never promised following Him would be easy. Yet it's pretty easy to doubt and wring our hands when the going gets tough.

It's what Jesus says next that makes all the difference: "But take heart! I have overcome the world." Notice Jesus doesn't focus on the trouble. Instead, He highlights *where* we are (the world) rather than *how* we are (in trouble). No matter where you step in the whole wide world, Jesus has us covered. There's no place you can go where Jesus hasn't won the day. You don't need to help Him out. He doesn't need it. You don't need to be His public-relations person putting a spin on things for Him. He doesn't need one. We don't need to try to win arguments He said He's already won.

Adversity isn't going to evaporate anytime soon; however, we can face it boldly with a big, brave, humble love. Aligning with love will earn us weird looks and find us in more than a few tricky circumstances. A glance at the lives of anybody who has followed Jesus can prove this world just doesn't quite get it. Don't get stressed out, and don't become distracted.

If you choose to be brave by choosing love and people give you some funny looks or get mad—if choosing loves gets you into some trouble—it doesn't mean you failed. It more likely means you actually believed what Jesus said and did something about it. Following Jesus means a life of being constantly misunderstood. Get used to it.

Jesus never asked anyone to play it safe.

How have you been brave recently?

IT ALWAYS LOOKS LIKE EVIL IS GOING TO WIN—RIGHT UP UNTIL IT DOESN'T.

Peace I leave with you; my peace I give you. I do not give to you as the world gives. Do not let your hearts be troubled and do not be afraid.

JOHN 14:27

When I was a boy, comic books came onto the scene and started to get big. Characters like Spiderman, Batman, and Wonder Woman lived in a world where evil popped up just in time for another episode. No matter which sinister villain seemed to be giving evil an edge, the hero was always more powerful than the obstacles in front of them. Evil has a way of looking like it's going to win—right up until it doesn't.

While these comics were fantastical, every enduring story reminds us of a truth: even when it seems like hope has lost the lead, redemption is where the story is headed. Just before Jesus went away for a while, He told us we would face trouble in this world. He said there would be times we'd want to give up and seek comfort somewhere else.

But Jesus also told us He would be with us and not even death could separate us from Him. He's living proof that the God of the universe is more powerful than any of the obstacles we face. The obstacles look different for each of us, but we live in a world where fear shows up unannounced and tries to steal our hope. Those are the times we have to remember the power accessible to us.

Are you in a difficult time? Love will show you the way through it. Do you feel like you're up against seemingly unbeatable forces? Remember love will win in the end. Our hope isn't in *our* ability to overcome but in *God's* ability to redeem it.

Don't let the circumstances you're facing do all the talking. Listen to the God who already won it all with His love.

As you listen to God speak into your difficult time, what do you hear Him saying?

GRACE CAN'T BE OUTSMARTED, OUT-WORRIED, OR OUTRUN. THROW BACK YOUR ARMS AND FALL INTO IT.

He has saved us and called us to a holy life—not because of anything we have done but because of his own purpose and grace. This grace was given us in Christ Jesus before the beginning of time.

2 TIMOTHY 1:9

We have the opportunity to wake up to the reality of grace the morning after we've messed up. The morning after the fight with a family member, the negative thoughts or subtle manipulations, the half-truths at work. When we have nowhere to go and no more excuses, grace reminds us we don't need any.

We tend to look for solutions when we mess up. We want to right our wrongs. The world tells us we need to work harder to get back on our feet. As we anxiously try to fix our mistakes, we worry we won't be able to rein in our temper or curb our addictions. We fear we really are defined by our mistakes.

But grace can't be outsmarted, out-worried, or outrun. Our efforts to fix ourselves are pointless because God already told us we don't have to clean ourselves up to travel with Him. He said to run to Him as we are, in the middle of our messes, and He'll be the one to put us back together again.

What if we accepted grace's invitation before we hit rock bottom? Instead of waking up to grace the morning after we blew it, what if we walked in grace the night before? Grace is there for us after we fail, but it's also there to remind us we can grip love tightly instead of spiraling out of control. Instead of falling into old patterns and behaviors once again, what if, instead, we throw our arms back and fall into grace.

What is grace inviting you to today?

WE TRY TO ORGANIZE OUR DAYS.
GOD WANTS TO SHAPE OUR HEARTS.

Be completely humble and gentle; be patient, bearing with one another in love.

EPHESIANS 4:2

One of my good friends is a world-renowned productivity guru. I bet he gets more done in a day than most people do in a week. He's got systems and processes, methodologies and technology. He's like a maestro in front of an orchestra of tasks. To-do lists are the sheet music. He waves his baton and all the objectives are achieved, all the work is done, and no tasks remain. But here's the thing: sometimes his friendships get lost in his efforts at efficiency.

While productivity is a great tool to fulfill our commitments, it's not always the best way to build or maintain the relationships that matter the most to us. I'm not sure how Sweet Maria would respond if I asked her to calendar ten minutes for our morning coffee. What if, in the middle of a rich and needed conversation with her, I announced that I had a "hard stop" in five minutes and we needed to wrap it up. I bet my clothes would end up out on the lawn.

If you want to be remembered for being efficient, getting things done is good. When we're in relationships, we need to remember that people aren't projects with deadlines and deliverables. The same is true in our relationship with God. We want plans and assurances. We would *love* to give God a deadline for the areas of painful growth or for achieving the big dream we're trying to get off the ground. We'd love to send God an agenda and a hard stop date for difficulties. But God wants to shape our hearts, not organize our days.

Next time you're tempted to turn your life into a grand plan, leave some space in your days for God to write more beautiful things into your relationships.

What would change today if you focused more on people than on your projects and deadlines?

GOD DOESN'T GIVE US MAPS TO FOLLOW.
HE GIVES US PEOPLE TO GO WITH.

Turning around, Jesus saw them following and asked, "What do you want?" They said, "Rabbi" (which means "Teacher"), "where are you staying?" "Come," he replied, "and you will see." So they went and saw where he was staying, and they spent that day with him.

JOHN 1:38–39

If you have ever taken a road trip with friends, you probably have found yourself driving in the wrong direction at some point. Perhaps the exit for fast food looped around and put you back on the highway. Maybe you left without a map and sped off in the wrong direction simply because it was Saturday and you had a full tank of gas.

Somehow the wrong turns always turned out all right, didn't they? Even if we didn't have maps, we still had our friends with us. We had someone making the playlist, creating a soundtrack for our inside jokes, and beautiful scenery to enjoy. We had a back-seat driver to help us find our way—someone who drove us nuts most of the time and then saved us some of the time. I'm glad about that.

Life with Jesus feels a lot like those road trips. God doesn't give us detailed maps to follow; He gives us people to go with. It doesn't matter which direction we go, because He's more concerned about who we become along the way than where we go with our lives. And the people around us are the ones who will shape us—they'll remind us who we are and what's most important when we get off track.

Next time you're anxious about whether your plans are taking you in the right direction, call up a friend and go for a drive. No matter where you end up, you'll be better off when you have a friend you can travel with.

Who are the friends you call to ride shotgun with you in life?

CHEER PEOPLE ON WHEN THEY SUCCEED *AND* WHEN THEY FAIL. GOD LOVES IT WHEN WE MAKE THE ATTEMPT.

See what great love the Father has lavished on us, that we should be called children of God! And that is what we are!

1 JOHN 3:1

Surfing isn't for the faint of heart. When I started learning in college, I went to a couple of surf movies at the local theater by the beach and thought I had the form down. But I got doused with reality my first day out in the waves. Here are the steps: you've got to paddle forward, feeling the speed of the wave as you move, then do a push-up on the board—and while you're doing this, land with your feet in the middle of the surfboard.

At the time, I could barely do a push-up on dry land, so my first attempts at riding the waves led to no small number of collisions between my surfboard and the side of my head. It turns out learning to surf is a great lesson in learning how to fail.

Here's something I learned. My friends would paddle out into the waves with me. They gave me a hard time when I fell, but they also cheered me on. They'd swim over to where I was floating face down, get me back on the surfboard, and paddle back out with me. They weren't just there to celebrate my success. They delighted in my attempts.

My surfing friends gave me a little glimpse into how God sees us. He's not surprised when we fail. He knows we're up against a lot in our lives. Jesus didn't come just to offer guidance to us to help us get it right. He's with us, even when we blow it.

Don't believe the lies that you're defined by your successes or your failures. You're defined by Jesus, and He calls you beloved.

How have you been defining yourself this week?

NO ONE WILL BELIEVE OUR ANSWERS IF WE DON'T GET REAL ABOUT HAVING A COUPLE OF QUESTIONS TOO.

What do you think?

MATTHEW 21:28

There are plenty of voices in the world who present their opinions like they're solid fact. People tell us which foods are healthiest, which companies are ethical, and the best way to raise our kids. These same people also are prone to tell us what to believe in our faith. I think that's why so many people hesitate to go to church or start exploring what it means to follow Jesus. The faithful seem to have developed a fear of admitting to having any question marks in their faith. This always seemed strange to me for a religion that says faith is all about finding answers. We should all have a long list of questions. Jesus passed right by the people who acted like they had all the answers and found some fishermen who didn't have any. These are the people He uses to change the world.

Jesus showed us how comfortable He was with questions. He asked more than three hundred of them. He used them when people asked Him things, and it made the religious types squirm. He demonstrated how faith isn't just about subscribing to a doctrine or a lifestyle. What was going on in the heart was just as important as all the information in the head.

When people questioned why Jesus and His friends weren't sticking to a tradition, He shot back one of His own questions: "Why do you break the command of God for the sake of your tradition?" (Matthew 15:3). Don't hold your faith like an answer sheet; embrace what you don't quite get, let people know what you're wondering about, and you'll find more of God there than in any catchphrase. You'll connect with a lot more people that way too.

No one's going to believe any of our answers if we don't let them know we have a couple of questions too.

What questions are forming in your heart today?

AUGUST 30

WE CAN'T GIVE AWAY LOVE FREELY IF WHAT WE'RE REALLY LOOKING FOR IS VALIDATION.

Let no debt remain outstanding, except the continuing debt to love one another, for whoever loves others has fulfilled the law.

ROMANS 13:8

I had a home in Washington, DC, for years, and some of my good friends are involved in politics. They're dedicated to their country. They leave no room for doubt with their commitment and excellence. But when it comes to politicians I don't know personally, like most people, I tend to feel suspicious. I'm sure they're great people, but it's hard to believe they're genuine when you know they're thinking about so many different things. My suspicions make it hard to believe they really care when they show up because they might be working all the angles, and I wonder if I'm just one of those angles.

Politicians are an easy target, but if we're honest, a lot of us do the same thing. Sometimes we compliment other people, hoping to endear them to us. Sometimes we show up for them when they need us because we have hidden motives. We can't give away love freely if we're secretly wanting something in return.

We don't need to be stingy with our love, treating it like currency that buys you something when it's given and makes you bankrupt when it's taken back. When we realize God's already given us His unending love, we can give that kind of love away recklessly.

Let's make it a point to do a check-in with our motivations every so often. It'll be a good reminder that God's crazy about the people He created, and He's using you to show them love with no strings attached. We won't be able to give away love freely if what we're really looking for is validation.

What can you do today to love someone freely without expectation?

AUGUST 31

GOD'S NEVER LOOKED IN YOUR MIRROR AND WISHED HE SAW SOMEONE ELSE.

You, Lord, are forgiving and good, abounding in love to all who call to you.

PSALM 86:5

I saw a sign once that said, "Be yourself. Everyone else is already taken." I loved it because, let's be honest, what choice do we have anyway? The hitch comes when we're trying to be just about anyone but ourselves. We all do this. We want to be thinner or richer. We want to have a better degree or more popular friends. We all have the same basic desires. We want to experience love, purpose, and connection. People try to sell us stuff all the time by tapping into these basic needs.

We want to experience love, so we strive to have relationships that will let us feel loved and accepted. We want purpose in our lives, so we'll join or identify with social groups and issues and begin defining ourselves this way. We want connection, so we buy what it takes to wear the uniform of the social groups we want to fit in with. Most of all, what all of us want are those few authentic relationships—and we'll trade who we really are for who we think we need to be.

God tells us a different story about love and belonging. When He saw His creation, He said it was good, and there were no exceptions. He said you and I were created in His image, with all the wonderful variety that includes. God made some of us sensitive and others analytical, some slender and some burly, some soft-spoken and some rambunctious.

The fact is, we're God's most creative act. If God wanted you to be like other people, He would've made us all the same. God chose to surprise us with different parts of His character and personality by showing part of Himself through you, through me, and even the people who occasionally drive us nuts. Be yourself and let others be themselves—because that's the starting point of God's love. God has never looked in your mirror and wished He saw someone else.

What part of yourself can you embrace more?

SEPTEMBER

WHEN WE REALIZE GOD NAMES US, WE'RE FREE TO CHASE AFTER WHAT MATTERS.

We know, brothers and sisters loved by God, that he has chosen you.

1 THESSALONIANS 1:4

I'm on the cusp of the grandpa stage of life, and I'm over the moon about it. My mind often drifts to the mischief I want to get into with my grandkids. I think about banana splits for breakfast and skydiving on sixteenth birthdays. Rock climbing and motorcycle jumping. And hot air balloons. Several of them. My kids know exactly what kind of grandpa their kids are getting, and I'm sure that scares them just a tad.

I also want to be a wise counselor and help my grandkids chase the things that matter and not get too focused on being popular or rich or famous or good-looking. In other words, I hope to instill a joy in being exactly who God created them to be. Who knows? This might eventually mean they are popular or rich or good-looking, but those aren't the best pursuits. They're secondhand outcomes. I want them to be rich in friendships and people who wouldn't trade being kind and courageous for being merely popular or good-looking.

The pressure to conform starts early, on elementary school playgrounds and at sleepovers with classmates. It gains steam when we're made fun of for standing out, when our shoes are a little worn, or we can't stay out past the street lights. For some of us, it takes a lifetime to unlearn the messaging we received that we'd be more worthy of love if we were a little more like the popular kids and less like ourselves.

What I'm excited to tell my grandkids, every day for as long as they'll listen, is this: other people don't get to decide who they are. God decides who we are. He names us, and He calls us His beloved.

What do you think God feels toward you?

SEPTEMBER 2

IF YOU'RE WONDERING WHAT IT WOULD TAKE TO FIT IN, REMEMBER THAT JESUS SAYS YOU'RE ALREADY IN.

I pray that you, being rooted and established in love, may have power, together with all the Lord's holy people, to grasp how wide and long and high and deep is the love of Christ, and to know this love that surpasses knowledge—that you may be filled to the measure of all the fullness of God.

EPHESIANS 3:17–19

Like most parents, I was determined to be an all-star dad when my kids were born, but I didn't know what exactly an all-star dad looked like. So I turned to parenting books for answers.

After devouring all the books for new parents I could find, I learned there were heated debates raging in the world of parenting styles I had never even thought about. Experts warred with one another about whether to soothe an upset child, how to tuck them in at night, when to quit nursing, how to potty train, how to raise athletic children. By the time I finished my research, I was more confused about raising kids than I had been before I started.

We spend a lot of time trying to live into the rules people set for us. Some of these rules seem wise but others equally arbitrary. None of these rules measure up to the power the love of Jesus has for us. Raising boys, I realized early on it didn't matter if they grew into college football stars as long as they learned to live in grace like Jesus. And my wife and I learned we didn't need to worry about whether our daughter became the president; we just wanted her to walk in love like Jesus.

Not long after the kids arrived, we started getting together with other young families. It's hard not to compare your kid to everyone else's. Ours were learning to walk, and someone else's were running laps on the track. Ours said their first word, and someone else's had just memorized every past president's middle name.

The thing about God is this: He never compares what He creates.

We'll never be like Jesus if it's more important for us to be like each other. Stack up all the pressure you're feeling to be something different, and ask yourself whether the image looks like Jesus. If it does, you're moving in the right direction. If not, then spend some time examining His beautiful life and make Him what you compare everything to.

Who do you compare yourself to? Why?

SEPTEMBER 3

STAND IN FRONT OF THE MIRROR THAT REFLECTS JESUS BACK TO YOU.

I praise you because I am fearfully and wonderfully made; your works are wonderful, I know that full well.

PSALM 139:14

When my kids were younger, we loved going to the pop-up carnivals that would come through town. One day there's a field or an empty parking lot, and the next day there's a Ferris wheel, a Tilt-a-Whirl, really unhealthy food, and a forest of games.

My sons, Adam and Richard, always darted to the most life-threatening roller coaster. My daughter, Lindsey, was in for the games with massive stuffed animals I'd strap to the roof of the car. I was always stopping by the person guessing weight to get the truth of things. Maria just liked to watch all of us with so much joy.

One thing we all loved was the House of Mirrors. Before we sprinted to our favorite spots, we'd all go through together, giggling that Dad was nine feet tall, that Mom's feet looked like skis, that Richard's muscles made him look totally ripped. We had fun with the momentary transformations. But what would happen if we lived every day in front of a funhouse mirror? Would we start to believe we could bench press five hundred pounds even if our arms were as skinny as ski poles? Would we be tricked into thinking we could dunk a basketball even if we were four feet tall?

While it's fun to imagine yourself differently, don't get trapped in a life of thinking you need to be different. God says you were fearfully and wonderfully made. He doesn't want us to be a better version of us. He want us to be a more accurate reflection of Him. God wants you to stand in front of the mirror that reflects a life like His.

What parts of you do you think God likes?

SEPTEMBER 4

IF YOU DON'T LIKE WHO YOU'VE BECOME, HEAD IN A NEW DIRECTION AND GIVE YOURSELF SOME TIME AND GRACE.

Now we see only a reflection as in a mirror; then we shall see face to face. Now I know in part; then I shall know fully, even as I am fully known.

1 CORINTHIANS 13:12

John Newton became a Christian when a storm struck his ship as it was returning from a trip to Africa. He decided to follow Jesus in 1748, and he stepped off his ship in England a new man. You might have heard of John Newton because he wrote the hymn "Amazing Grace."

You would think the guy who wrote this amazing song was as perfect as freshly fallen snow. But Newton was also part of a time in human history when people owned and traded slaves. Even as a Christian, he continued his work as a captain on a slave ship for years and invested financially in slave operations even longer.

Decades after he started following Jesus, Newton woke up to the horror of the slave trade and began working to end it in England. He said his time in the business would always be a humiliation to him, and he joined leaders in the abolitionist movement in his country.

Testimonies like John Newton's always resonate with me because I know my whole life didn't turn around the moment I decided to follow Jesus. It's been a lifelong process of waking up to new things I need to hand over to God so I can grow. What we do right doesn't get us in, and what we do wrong doesn't rule us out.

What I love about John Newton's story and the experience of so many people of faith is this: we are always given the opportunity to become someone new. When you wake up and realize you don't like who you've become, just move in a new direction. Is it going to be easy? Of course not. Do it anyway, and give yourself a little time and grace to get there.

What parts of you have changed already?
Which parts are still being changed?

WE'RE ALL DEEPLY FLAWED AND EVEN MORE DEEPLY LOVED BY GOD.

Be filled with the Spirit, speaking to one another with psalms, hymns, and songs from the Spirit.

EPHESIANS 5:18–19

Doesn't it feel like a bit of a gamble when you invite a friend to church? Even if your pastor is inspiring and the people are welcoming, there's still some risk. Church doesn't always feel like the safest place to take new friends.

Most of us have sat through services where the speaker makes sure every person in the pews knows they a sinner. Many have said it in ways that make us feel like God's an angry dad who wishes He hadn't brought us into the world. And even if we have a pastor with softer tones, many of us never outgrow our anxiety about what we'll hear when we show up.

We already know we're far from perfect. A lot of us live with loads of guilt. We know we miss the mark, and we don't need to hear again that something's broken inside of us, because we live with the knowledge every day.

What we need to hear, more than anything else, is that God sees all our flaws and He couldn't possibly love us more. God knew we were bound to blow it, so He sent Jesus to take care of this inescapable problem for us. We need to hear God loves us so much that He's given us a new identity. We aren't our successes or failures; we are His.

If you're around people who don't emphasize God's love enough, read the stories of Jesus one more time and turn up the volume on His voice. God doesn't love you because you've earned His respect. He loves you because you are one of His unique and creative expressions in the world.

Why do you think God loves you?

SEPTEMBER 6

QUIT ASKING FOR PERMISSION.
LOVE IS ITS OWN GREEN LIGHT.

Whoever has will be given more, and they will have an abundance. Whoever does not have, even what they have will be taken from them.

MATTHEW 25:29

Jesus had a friend named Matthew who was a tax collector. Matthew wrote down things about Jesus so we could learn about Him more than two thousand years later. Matthew told a story about a master who entrusted his money to three servants—ten bags of money to one, five to another, and one to the third. When the master returned to settle accounts with them, the first two managed to double their amounts, but the third buried his bag in the ground and only had the same money to return. The servant was crippled by fear, so he chose not to act at all.

God didn't create us with so much love to give so we could spend all our time calculating the risks of doing something with it. When we do hide it rather than invest it, God's not angry with us. He's not a disappointed dad who scrutinizes our every move, waiting for us to get it wrong. He's a proud dad, eager to celebrate the moments when our passion explodes into acts of love.

I don't think the direction we go with our gifts will matter as much as the fact that we went. We moved. We saw a need in the world—a need in the people around us—and we did what we could to meet their need. We didn't bury our faith or our love.

Next time you find yourself sitting still out of fear, remember God absolutely delights in you. You don't need permission or approval. Don't put in a hole what God wants to put into play. You've got all the green lights you need to do something beautiful with your life and your love.

**What talents do you have that you can
more fully entrust to God?**

SEPTEMBER 7

WE CAN'T BE MORE LIKE JESUS IF WE'RE TRYING TO BE LIKE EACH OTHER.

Holy Father, protect them by the power of your name, the name you gave me, so that they may be one as we are one.

JOHN 17:11

Anyone who knows me for five minutes will hear the two best words in the English language I know: *Sweet Maria*. Anyone who knows her for five minutes will understand why I think those are the two best words around. She is considerate and giving, empathetic and kind, generous and creative. But she's also strong and willing to have hard conversations. She's willing to push her own boundaries and find ways to grow.

Okay, so I adore her. That's not too strange, I suppose. But one of the things I've seen in marriages and other close relationships is that people start to blend into each other. Know what I mean? They start to have the same habits, use the same catchphrases, like the same movies and songs. There's not really anything wrong with that. We tend to become more like the people we spend the most time with. When we got married, the pastor said the two of us would be "one." At first, Maria thought we were both going to become her. But here's the deal. I'm not trying to be like her, and she's not trying to be like me. We're trying to be like Jesus.

This takes all the pressure to be the same off the table. Maria is a homebody. I travel eight days a week. She's thoughtful and measured. I talk first and ask questions later. She plans it, then checks the plans again. I'm more a ready-shoot-aim guy.

We both have a lot of room to grow, but we're making sure it's in the direction of the One person we both want to be more like—Jesus. We won't get there by trying to be like each other. Our target is to be like Him.

Is there someone in your life who replaced Jesus as the target?

SEPTEMBER 8

WE'RE INVITED BECAUSE WE'RE LOVED, NOT BECAUSE WE MEASURE UP.

I have loved you with an everlasting love; I have drawn you with unfailing kindness.

JEREMIAH 31:3

We all doubt God's love for us from time to time. We know ourselves. We know the times we've lost our temper and the mistakes we've made. Since we know God witnesses every moment of our lives, we fear He doesn't love us as much as He would if we were the kind of people who prayed more, the kind of people who didn't have to apologize so much.

Do you ever stop to interview the voices telling you God would love you more if you were better behaved? Find out where the voices came from, because they didn't come from Jesus. When we read about the people Jesus hung out with and the way He loved them through all their failures, we see grace and forgiveness. Even when His disciples asked if they should call fire down from heaven to destroy people who didn't welcome Jesus, He just corrected their crazy idea and then moved on to a new town to make new friends.

Despite all the ways Jesus' friends got it wrong, they were still His people. They were called because they were loved. They were invited because they were wanted. Their value wasn't dependent upon their behavior or performance but in their identity as children of God. The same applies to us.

Our worth isn't tied to our performance. It's tied to Jesus. That truth keeps us humble when we're flying high, and it lifts us up when we've hit a low. Just like the disciples, we are called because we're loved, and we're invited because we're wanted.

What is love inviting you to today?

COMPARISON WILL RIP YOUR SAILS, SINK YOUR BOAT, AND BLAME THE WEATHER.

We do not dare to classify or compare ourselves with some who commend themselves. When they measure themselves by themselves and compare themselves with themselves, they are not wise.

2 CORINTHIANS 10:12

There's this boat race called the Transpac Race that goes from California to Hawaii. I live on the water in San Diego and wanted to sail across the ocean, so one year I was like, *Why not?* It takes about five hours to *fly* from Los Angeles to Honolulu at five hundred miles an hour. So the boat trip at ten miles an hour is pretty long. I wasn't really sure how long it would take, so I bought a bunch of beef jerky, a couple of cases of Stagg chili (bad move on reflection), and a couple of buddies, and I started sailing west.

You can go wild preparing for this race. Charting your course, preparing your boat, buying matching outfits. Sextants and maps of ocean currents and star charts, not to mention all the tech gadgets. Or you can just untie from the dock and go.

While the Transpac is a really famous race, for myself I called it a *trip*. I wasn't in it for the trophy but for the adventure. Too often we turn what should be an adventure with a few course corrections into a race with others where we overprepare, overthink, and assume that winning is the only goal. When I left harbor, it was a chaos of careening boats and guys spinning things to make the sails taut. But once you were out in the wide ocean, it was just you. There was no point in comparing—the goal became somehow finding Hawaii at the end of the race rather than missing it and ending up in Japan.

Hear this: comparison will rip your sails, sink your boat, and blame the weather. Don't buy the lie that an adventure with God is a race with everyone else.

Who do you need to stop comparing yourself to?

SEPTEMBER 10

THE MORE BEAUTY WE FIND IN SOMEONE ELSE'S LIFE, THE LESS WE'LL WANT TO COMPARE IT TO OUR OWN.

One who has unreliable friends soon comes to ruin, but there is a friend who sticks closer than a brother.

PROVERBS 18:24

My friend Doug has been by my side through some of the best mischief. He was there when I used to shoot BB guns as a teenager, including the time he shot me and then tended to my wound with gum and leaves. He's also the friend who introduced me to Jesus. He told me God became friends with messed-up people like him, and I thought if God accepted Doug, maybe He'd accept me too.

Doug and I have been buddies through high school and college, during our years as camp counselors and then as young professionals. We stood by each other on our wedding days, and we've played pranks on each other in the decades since. Doug and I have seen each other at our best and worst and everything in between.

People often ask what makes for great friendships. I think a big part of it is choosing to celebrate one another rather than competing. Every time people around us succeed, jealousy tries to get our attention. It says we deserve the blessings they received. It tells us we should be noticed, too, and probably more. When we stop celebrating with them and start comparing ourselves to them, resentment creeps in and puts wedges between us.

My friends and I see one another as cheerleaders, screaming for the winning goal and encouraging when the inevitable loss happens. The more beauty we find in someone else's life, the less we'll want to compare it to our own.

Who's your greatest cheerleader?

SEPTEMBER 11

WE'RE SAD, BUT WE'RE NOT AFRAID.

The master told his servant, "Go out to the roads and country lanes and compel them to come in, so that my house will be full."

LUKE 14:23

The United States took a devastating hit in 2001 when airplanes flew into the World Trade Center. I remember rushing home from work to explain to my kids what had happened. I didn't want them to hear it from anyone else. As we held hands, trying to process the tragedy together, I told them it was okay to feel sad, but we didn't have to be afraid.

A lot of the rhetoric quickly started to sound like fear. People feared other countries and other religions. Some of us feared refugees who had been driven to the United States by wars in their homelands. Tragedy can incite major fears in us—sometimes irrational fears. I have friends in some countries where a great deal of violence happens. These friends are nothing like the extremists. They're kindhearted and hospitable. They love their kids and they love their neighbors. They're a lot like us.

While our country has recovered from the tragedy in 2001, we tend to find reasons to fear one another still. Some of this is well placed, but most of it isn't. God doesn't want us to live in fear; He wants us to engage the world with love. God's brand of love casts out fear. When we become friends with people who are different from us, love begins to take hold and grow. Love grows as we sit around tables with our neighbors who live across the street or across an ocean, sharing meals and stories. We can't love our neighbors if we don't know them.

Next time you find yourself fearing an entire group of people you don't understand, find a way to connect with them. Figure out an experience you can share with them, no matter how small. This is where the good stuff always starts.

So, who will you reach out to?

WE HONOR THE MEMORIES OF ALL WHO LAID DOWN THEIR LIVES SO WE COULD LIVE OURS.

And do not forget to do good and to share with others, for with such sacrifices God is pleased.

HEBREWS 13:16

When you ask kids what they want to be when they grow up, there's a reason so many of them say they want to be firemen or police officers. It's less about sliding down the poles and riding on top of trucks and more about their earnest desire to be courageous. They know these heroes run toward danger so the rest of us can run away from it, and little kids want to grow up to have big courage.

We see in these public servants a glimpse of Jesus, whether they claim to follow Him or not. They risk their lives to protect us every day, and many make the ultimate sacrifice so we can live in freedom. It's what Jesus did for us. He knew we wouldn't be free as long as death had the last word, and He gave His own life so we could live ours.

These brave men and women who daily walk the path Jesus walked are living examples of the sacrifice He made for us. Let's make sure they know how thankful we are for their service. If you know any local leaders who keep our communities safe, send them cupcakes and thank-you notes. Offer to babysit their kids so they can have date nights. Whatever it takes to make sure they know how much we appreciate the freedom they've given us.

Make it a point to look for the heroes in your everyday life. It's impossible to celebrate them too much.

What simple thing can you do to show appreciation for the servants in your community?

SEPTEMBER 13

GRACE MEANS WE DON'T NEED TO AIRBRUSH OUR LIVES TO MAKE THEM LOOK PERFECT.

All those the Father gives me will come to me, and whoever comes to me I will never drive away.

JOHN 6:37

I was reading the other day about an art exhibit themed around ancient Egypt. One of the centerpieces is a massive statue of this old guy named Ramesses II, a powerful pharaoh from thousands of years ago. On the back of his seven-ton bust are a few lines of hieroglyphics, and if you look closely, you'll see the world's oldest typo.

Turns out, someone goofed. When the original makers were completing the writing on the back, they made a print of the bird symbol facing backward. Apparently they had to stick mud over their mess-up like ancient white-out. Their mistake gets studied by experts, their momentary lapse gets put under a microscope.

Whenever you feel like airbrushing your mistakes, just remember, they probably won't be big enough to be seen thousands of years later. God isn't taking a microscope to your failures. Perfection doesn't need grace, and for misfits like us, we need to understand our need for grace over perfection. Perfection will not give us what we're looking for, and in fact perfection tends to change its definition whenever we think we've attained it. Exposing your flaws gives grace a chance to do the healing instead of covering yourself with false perfection.

When we aren't comfortable with ourselves, it's easy to get tied up trying to be someone else. Grace doesn't want to meet anyone else but you. God tells us every day we're accepted. It doesn't mean God doesn't want us to make moves from where we are. It just means He sees our flaws and loves us no less.

How have you been acting like you're not accepted?

WHEN IT MATTERS MORE WHAT OUR FAITH LOOKS LIKE THAN WHAT IT IS, IT'S TIME TO START OVER.

On the outside you appear to people as righteous but on the inside
you are full of hypocrisy and wickedness.

MATTHEW 23:28

If you follow the news, you'll see the headlines are full of people messing up big in their lives. Sometimes it's even pastors, and we hear about moral failures. When I hear the news of a friend with problems, I get on a flight as often as I can to spend some time with them. Sometimes they're old friends and some- times they become new friends, but either way, I know they need a friend. Some people wag a boney finger when we run toward someone who's messed up. But isn't that what God does with you and me? Forget being right; be Jesus.

Many of the people who have messed up publicly have been struggling privately for a long time, but they were expected to be perfect. They lost the joy in the faith they used to know because their faith was always up for public scrutiny. These friends usually feel a lot of shame, but it's coupled with an odd sense of relief—relief that they can finally exhale and tell the truth about what's going on inside and get some help.

We don't always feel free to tell the truth about our doubts and struggles. But Jesus never asked us to look like we're well behaved or to sound like we're theologically sophisticated. He just asked us to follow Him and keep it real while we do. Just like it did with the disciples, following Jesus will look like getting it wrong a lot and receiving forgiveness every time.

When it matters more what our faith looks like than what it is, it's time to start over.

**How have you been focusing more on
appearances than on reality?**

IT'LL BE HARD TO KEEP OUR EYES FIXED ON JESUS IF THEY'RE ON EACH OTHER. WHO WE WATCH SHAPES WHAT WE'LL BECOME.

Fixing our eyes on Jesus, the pioneer and perfecter of faith.

HEBREWS 12:2

One time I saw this show about a world-famous pop musician who was pretty edgy at the time. And she appealed to a lot of young girls. One part of the show stood out to me. There was this clip of the musician giving an interview after a concert, and then it cut to an interview of one of the girls who was there. This fan dressed the same, talked the same, and was clearly trying to be just like the musician. It showed me that we become like the people we watch.

Maybe you didn't have a superstar for a role model growing up. But think about the star student whose intellect you wanted to imitate. Or the star quarterback or prom queen. We watched them because everyone else seemed to be watching them too. Whether we realized it or not, spending too much time watching them was our attempt to become more like them—and a little less like ourselves.

Our tendency to fixate on people doesn't stop as we get older. Sometimes we do it out of a sense of envy and sometimes out of admiration. But Jesus never told us to be like other people, even the ones who get idolized. He told us to be like Him. It's hard to keep our eyes fixed on Jesus if our eyes are on each other, because who we watch shapes what we'll become.

If we keep our eyes on Jesus and follow in His footsteps, it won't be long before we'll surprise ourselves with the shape our lives have taken.

Who have you been fixing your eyes on?

COMPARISON IS THE ENEMY OF CREATIVITY.

Each of you should use whatever gift you have received to serve others, as faithful stewards of God's grace in its various forms.

1 PETER 4:10

I was recently talking to a young friend of mine who's an artist. She caught me up on her life and told me she had a business online where people commissioned her to do drawings for them. She said she had to scale back a little bit because she was losing a sense of her own style as she threw herself into the commissioned pieces other people wanted her to create.

She said she learned a lot studying famous artists and imitating their styles, but it also had begun to limit her imagination. She missed the days when she had the space to dream up images and then sketch never-before-drawn pictures in her notepad.

I'm not an artist, but I could relate to my friend because I've done the same thing in other ways. There's always the temptation to watch the people around us and try to emulate them in our work. We do it when we start nonprofits or give speeches or go on adventures.

It's okay to learn from other people, and we should all do a lot of that, but we lose the unique ways God created us when we stop using our imaginations to try to copy someone else. It's like copying their art in our lives, and it limits our ability to do the things we do best.

God didn't settle for second best when He created you. You're not a carbon copy; you're an original. Play your own song, write your book in your voice, make your own painting, not someone else's. Keep your eyes on Jesus and let Him fill your imagination with your own unique gifts to bring to the world.

What do you have that you can give to others in love?

SEE INTERRUPTIONS AS OPPORTUNITIES AND YOU'LL BE MORE LIKE JESUS THAN BEFORE.

In humility value others above yourselves, not looking to your own interests but each of you to the interests of the others.

PHILIPPIANS 2:3-4

One of my favorite qualities of Jesus is the way He responded to interruptions. Read the Gospels and try to count how many of the stories involve a couple of interruptions. He and His friends would be on their way to a city, and suddenly a woman would approach Him, desperate for relief from an illness she'd been plagued by for over a decade. Or He would be on His way to heal someone, and He'd get word that He was needed elsewhere—a young child had stopped breathing, and they thought maybe He could help.

Most of us get frustrated by interruptions because we think they get in the way of the real work we're supposed to be doing. But Jesus didn't see it that way. When Jesus experienced an interruption, He saw people in need. Loving people wasn't something on Jesus' to-do list or something to squeeze into His schedule when He had time. His whole life was about loving people, and whoever was in front of Him was the most important person to Him in that moment.

Jesus showed us love isn't something we do; it's someone we become. You'll know this is happening in your life when you see how you respond to the interruptions in your day. What's really happening on our insides comes pouring out when we're tired and pressed and in the middle of something urgent and are interrupted. Those moments reveal what we're made of, and for Jesus, those moments revealed love.

The more we become like Jesus, the more we'll stop resenting interruptions and start embracing them. Look for moments of love in the midst of interruptions, and you'll be like Jesus for someone else in need. Following Jesus means a lot of constant interruptions. Prepare to be interrupted.

Who's trying to interrupt you these days? How can you turn your heart toward them today?

SEPTEMBER 18

GOD MADE BEAUTY SO WE'D KNOW HOW HE FELT ABOUT US.

He has made everything beautiful in its time. He has also set eternity in the human heart; yet no one can fathom what God has done from beginning to end.

ECCLESIASTES 3:11

I like to pop into shops when I travel. I'm always on the lookout for gifts for Sweet Maria. Recently I popped into a jewelry shop just to take a peek into the glass cases. A kind lady casually approached me and asked if I was looking for something in particular. Then she launched into a story about how the concept for the store started.

She said the jeweler and his wife were artists before they were jewelers. Their paintings and sculptures were featured in galleries across Europe. But when the jeweler met his wife, his love for her moved him to try his hand at jewelry for the first time because he wanted to create something that expressed his love for her. The piece of jewelry he made for her was the beginning of the story that now led to all the rings and necklaces in the glass case in front of me.

Art is usually the overflow of beautiful, intense feelings people carry inside them. They want to bring their emotions into the physical world, and out comes a song or a poem or a painting or an engagement ring.

I think God did the same thing when He created beauty. He wanted us to know how He felt about us, so He painted a sunset and put iridescent wings on a butterfly. If you ever doubt God's love for you, remember that of all the beautiful things God created, He said you were the most stunning.

What beauty do you see around you? How does that beauty point you to God?

SEPTEMBER 19

GOD DIDN'T GIVE YOU A DREAM TO KEEP YOU BENCHED THE WHOLE GAME. HE'S CALLING YOU ONTO THE FIELD.

To each one the manifestation of the Spirit is given for the common good.

1 CORINTHIANS 12:7

If you played sports when you were younger, you knew your roles. If you were a parent, you were there to help those young stars become better in practice, and you were there to lift the team's morale. A parent's responsibilities include cheerleading, grabbing water for timeouts, and buying pizza afterward. If you were a kid on the team and were not very good, you probably got to know the bench well like I did. You knew you also would occasionally get in the game when the team had a big lead.

Sitting on the bench gives you a lot of time to fear what might happen. You fear this will be another night of no playing time, where you've suited up and warmed up and then end up shivering on the sidelines. You fear you're letting down the people who came to watch you and who you wanted so badly to impress. You fear you're wasting your time devoting yourself to something you're obviously not very good at. You fear failure. These are the things that go through your mind on the bench.

Most of us still feel like the kids sitting on the sidelines even though it's years later and we've grown up. We remember our dreams to change the world, and now we're just left with doubts. Or we've messed up, and we wonder if we've been benched again.

Remember this: fear calls out our doubts, but God calls out our names. The dreams He put in your heart are dreams He still wants to fulfill through you today. He didn't create any of us to just be practice buddies or water boys—there's no sideline in God's story of redemption, and there's no bench.

What would change if you got off the bench today?

SEPTEMBER 20

DON'T LET WHO YOU WERE NAME YOU, DEFINE YOU, HASSLE YOU, OR CONTROL YOU. GOD DECIDES WHO WE ARE, NOT OUR PAST.

To all who did receive him, to those who believed in his name, he gave the right to become children of God.

JOHN 1:12

If you've been in church long, you've probably heard a lot of testimonies about people who used to be drug addicts or were caught up in destructive cycles. They talk about how they were spiraling out of control, and then they met Jesus, and everything radically changed. It's amazing, to be sure. We hear these stories and remember God can turn around our lives in the most miraculous ways. These stories remind us that who we've been doesn't dictate who we'll become.

But wouldn't it be great to hear more stories from people who were doing just fine, maybe getting a B-minus in life, and then they decided to live a better story? They didn't want their lives to be defined by their jobs, so they started measuring their days by the love they gave away instead of money they made.

We don't hear enough stories of transformation from being people who found their self-worth one day and then did an internal overhaul driven by love. They might've stayed in the same job and lived in the same community, but the way they interacted with the people in their lives changed everything. These stories are even more relatable for many of us.

Many of us might not need to be delivered from a life of drugs and a gambling addiction but from something even more insidious—finding our worth in success or approval. When Jesus invited us to follow Him, He invited us to become new people. His invitation was for all of us to leave behind who we were so we could start bringing loads of love to everyone we encountered.

God decides who we are, not our past.

What do you think God thinks of you?

YOU DON'T HAVE TO BE FAMOUS TO MAKE A DIFFERENCE. WE ALL KNOW WHO JESUS IS, BUT HE TRIED TO STAY UNDER THE RADAR.

Very truly I tell you, whoever believes in me will do the works I have been doing, and they will do even greater things than these, because I am going to the Father.

JOHN 14:12

All the great heroes I know have been ordinary people. They didn't run countries, and they don't have museums named after them. They're moms, dads, and teenagers who saw a need in the people around them and did what they could to meet those needs.

When I think of heroes, I think of people like Dorothy Day, who lived among the poor so she could better serve them, and my friend John, who started an organization to train governments in other countries on how to end human trafficking. I think of Mother Teresa, who held people as they breathed their last in Calcutta, allowing them to die with dignity, and I think of my friend Jeff, who uses his gift with words to make people feel less alone. Even the famous ones tried to stay under the radar.

Heroes come in every age and size. Sometimes they're household names, and sometimes they're unknown. But what binds them together is this: they heard about a need in the world, and they figured out how to use whatever they could to alleviate suffering in other people.

We don't need more degrees or status to change the world. We only need eyes to see a need and a faith that believes in redemption. Jesus wouldn't have said we'd do greater things than Him if He didn't think we could do it. Stop listening to the voices saying you can't make a difference, and start listening to the One telling you He wants you to take your next step.

What's your next step?

SEPTEMBER 22

LOSE THE CAPE.

When you give to the needy, do not let your left hand know what
your right hand is doing, so that your giving may be in secret. Then
your Father, who sees what is done in secret, will reward you.

MATTHEW 6:3-4

One of my favorite movie moments is a scene from the Pixar film *The Incredibles*.
It's the part where the superhero dad is trying to get a new uniform, and he's
really into having a cape as part of the design. His quirky designer gives him
example after example of other superheroes who chose style over function—
with catastrophic results. "No capes," she tells him. I think Jesus agrees. Not
seeking attention gets God's attention.

Anytime Jesus did something miraculous, He would follow it up by saying
to the people nearby, "Tell no one." Doesn't that seem counterproductive if
you're starting a movement? Jesus was introducing us to another way to change
the world—one that doesn't require any marketing taglines, self-promotion, or
capes. He wanted to show us that all those things meant to draw attention to
ourselves can actually trip us up.

God always seems more interested in working through those who don't
need any affirmation outside of His. Perhaps it's because He wants us to point
people toward Him, not ourselves. Being secretly incredible means you've
found a way to be awesome without spinning up a ton of unnecessary attention for yourself. You just do awesome things and are content in knowing God
sees what you've done.

The most interesting people I've met are the ones not trying to look interesting. We don't have to impress to earn the right to be on God's team. He
wants our attention. He's not impressed with our activities. Keep your eyes
fixed on Jesus and just go be awesome. No capes needed.

What quiet act of love will you do today?

LIGHT SHINING IN DARKNESS IS WHAT MAKES THE PICTURE WORTH IT.

The light shines in the darkness, and the darkness has not overcome it.

JOHN 1:5

I know almost all photos today are taken digitally, but when I was growing up, Polaroid pictures were all the rage. You could snap a photo and see it in a couple of minutes. It was *wild*. The thing about a Polaroid picture is that it needed light to develop and it took a little while for this to happen. People ended up shaking the pictures in their hands in the hopes it would develop a little faster. It didn't work with the Polaroid images, and it doesn't work with people either.

If you're going through a hard time or making some bad choices, you don't need to stay cooped up in the darkness. What you need is light to help a better picture come into view. Give yourself a little grace too. The image of who you're becoming isn't going to instantaneously emerge. It's going to take a little time. We don't need to shake people up while we're waiting either. It doesn't speed things up by a second.

It's tempting to keep things hidden. Think about a time when a friend came to you and said they needed help. Did you scoff in their face and walk away? Of course not. You had sympathy and expressed empathy for them. You loved them, and you asked how you could help. Sadly, we don't often extend the same grace to ourselves. Instead, we listen to lies we tell ourselves about how we'll just be a bother if we tell a friend we're having problems. We tell ourselves we don't deserve their presence. We think God is disappointed in us. Don't fall for this.

If you think God might love you more when you act like you have it together, you're believing a lie. God sees you at your worst, and He's nuts about you. God knows life happens to us and it can leave scars on our hearts. He wants us to be patient with ourselves and the people around us. What He's creating in us is going to take a little time and a whole lot of light to develop.

What dark parts of your life does God want to shine in?

SEPTEMBER 24

GOD DIDN'T CREATE THE WORLD AND STEP BACK TO ADMIRE IT. HE PAINTED HIMSELF INTO THE PICTURE.

The Word became flesh and made his dwelling among us.

JOHN 1:14

I saw some artwork a while back where this guy painted himself into scenes of a city. I don't mean he painted a city and disguised himself in it. I mean he went to an actual location, took a picture, went back to his studio, and painted a tight-fitting suit that he would wear and look *exactly* like a spot in the real place. Then he'd go back wearing his city-suit, stand in the same spot, and someone would photograph him like a human chameleon. Trying to find him was like a human Where's Waldo game.

This got me thinking about God and how He saw that we had gotten ourselves into a big mess with wars and factions and hate. He saw us turning on one another and using one another for our own ends when we were made to give ourselves away. Instead of scolding us or sending fire to consume us, God painted Himself into creation. But unlike the artist, He wasn't trying to hide in what He had made. He was trying to help. In short, Jesus jumped onto the canvas and got down into the mess with us.

When you look around you and see something you don't like, try to resist the urge to criticize from afar. Be like Jesus and throw yourself into the situation so you can be a part of the change. It's easy to hide and criticize, to stay hidden and lob your insults or discontent across the fence. I've never met a courageous cynic. Paint yourself into the picture instead.

What have you been criticizing, and when will you stop?

WHEN GOD MAKES SOMETHING, HE DOES IT RIGHT THE FIRST TIME. NO REGRETS, NO MISTAKES, NO DO-OVERS.

My frame was not hidden from you when I was made in the secret place, when I was woven together in the depths of the earth.

PSALM 139:15

There are passages in the Bible that talk about God knowing all these precise details. He made the *entire universe*, and He formed you in your mom's womb. He determined the speed of light and numbers the hairs on your head. When we hear these descriptions about God, it helps us understand His scope and enormity just a little. But there's a hidden point in there too. God, who can see you down to the very core of who you are, is *crazy* about you. I mean, just head over heels about you. Not someone similar to you—actually you.

This makes me wonder why so many people are trying to be like someone else. There are so many comparison traps, from accumulation to success and even to things like sacrifice and service. We look around and ask the question, *Do I measure up?* And if we feel like the answer is no, we get started changing things. In those moments I think God is saying, *Wait, hold up. Why are you moving away from the version of you I created?*

Comparison seems to be a way of life, but what if it isn't God's way? What if we settled into how God made us and celebrated others who did the same? If God is head over heels about you, you should be too. When God makes something, he does it right the first time. No regrets, no mistakes, no do-overs.

**What parts of who you are do you think
God is most happy about?**

JESUS ISN'T GOING TO TRY TO SPEAK OVER THE NOISE IN OUR LIVES. HE WON'T COMPETE FOR OUR ATTENTION. HE WANTS OUR HEARTS.

He passed in front of Moses, proclaiming, "The LORD, the LORD, the compassionate and gracious God, slow to anger, abounding in love and faithfulness."

EXODUS 34:6

Remember elementary school days when we got a little too rowdy for our teacher's nerves? I was that kid, which resulted in a lot of quality time with my principal in his office. Short of sending us out of the room, our teachers had a few strategies for calming us down, and my personal favorite was the silent, confident eye lock. They didn't shout over us or call the troublemakers out by name. The teachers just stood at the front of the class with their hands folded, quietly waiting for us to hush.

I was always struck by the authority of their silence. When they shouted, it kind of brought them down to our level, and when they called us out by name, it made us defensive. But the silent eye lock reminded us of who was in control. It reminded us there was one person in charge in the room and none of us was that person. It calmed us down without shaming us. It brought some order to a load of chaos in our lives.

I've noticed God uses similar tactics to get our attention. He doesn't try to speak over the noise in our lives. He won't compete for our attention. He wants our hearts. He lets us carry on in our often clueless ways until we come to our senses and look to Him. Then, once we've quieted down long enough to let Him speak, He locks eyes with us and gently takes up where He left off.

God is strong, but His strength is often most evident in His tenderness. He won't force us to submit to Him, and He won't fight for our attention. He'll wait for us as long as we need to realize He is in control and then continue talking to us about the things that matter most to Him.

How are you experiencing God's patience?

GOD'S THE GIFT; WE'RE THE WRAPPING.

We are God's handiwork, created in Christ Jesus to do good works, which God prepared in advance for us to do.

EPHESIANS 2:10

I know a guy who wrote a book in which he came up with a way to understand love through five main "languages" we all use. It's actually a brilliant book—you should check it out some time. One of the five is "gift-giving." Some people feel deeply loved when you give them a physical present. Granted, we all like getting presents, but this is different. To them, receiving a gift is like a deep token of true expression—when they receive a gift, they feel more deeply loved and seen.

Sweet Maria and I have a friend who we're pretty sure is one of these people. She seems to love giving gifts as much as she loves receiving them. I think one of the ways you can spot a gift-giver is by how much time and attention they spend on the wrapping. Me, the gifts I wrap are a tangle of butcher paper and tape. There's no mistake that a guy wrapped it. But her gifts are works of art unto themselves. Every fold, crisp. Every piece of tape perfectly placed. Sometimes I don't even want to open these presents because I don't want to ruin the wrapping.

Did you know you're a gift too? We're His masterpiece. God gives Himself away through people who follow Him. We are all special to Him, but we're just packages carrying the real gift, which is the spirit of Jesus. The trick is to try not to make too much of ourselves, because we know we're not the main event at the end of the day. It's all about Jesus. God loves to give gifts, which is why He sent Jesus. But He's also big on the wrapping, which is why He created you.

What keeps you from believing you're God's masterpiece?

COMPARISON IS A THIEF. DON'T LET IT STEAL YOUR PURPOSE.

In all these things we are more than conquerors through him who loved us.

ROMANS 8:37

When I was growing up, my parents were big on me taking piano lessons. Their style wasn't to encourage and compliment me as I tried to get better. Instead, they installed a seat belt on the piano bench and buckled me in for as long as I could take it. Here's the problem. I just wasn't into it, nor was I very good. On the day of a big recital, I had to follow this other kid who played my same piece flawlessly. He had a real gift, and the crowd loved him. As I walked on the stage, I thought, *I'm about to make that kid look even better.*

There's no surprise twist to the plot. I completely tanked, and I felt pretty bad about it afterward. Why? Because our culture thrives on competition. We're told a story from the time we're born that success looks like standing out, it looks like winning, it looks like beating the rest. Nope. Jesus told us success looks like service. It looks like putting other people first even when they play a few bad notes.

Part of loving others means paying attention to how we can best be a gift to others. It means knowing our strengths and serving in ways that make us come alive too. We're not going to get there if we start comparing ourselves. The comparison game always lies to us. It comes from a place of insecurity and says who we are isn't good enough unless perhaps we're a little bit better than the person next to us. Do you want to do something awesome for God? Forget what other people are up to. Go be you.

Who do you need to quit comparing yourself to?

JESUS WOULDN'T HAVE USED MUD TO HEAL PEOPLE IF HE CARED WHAT WE LOOKED LIKE.

After saying this, he spit on the ground, made some mud with the saliva, and put it on the man's eyes.

JOHN 9:6

When I worked as a counselor at a Young Life camp, we used to take teenage boys out to a pit in the middle of the night for some serious mud wrestling matches. We jumped in what felt like a swimming pool full of mud and would dunk each other and sling it around. We didn't care what we looked like—girls could've shown up and we wouldn't have thought twice about our appearance. We were in it for the experience.

Those nights often come to mind when I read about Jesus healing people with mud. One time He came across a blind man, and the Bible says Jesus spit in the dirt to make some mud, then rubbed it on the man's eyes to restore his sight. I always wonder why He spit in the dirt and created mud to bring the healing. He could've just said a couple of words or waved His hand and the healing would've happened all the same. The truth is, we don't really know. One thing we do know for sure is that Jesus never cared about appearances. Just like my friends and I wrestling in the mud pit, Jesus was more concerned about the experience than the appearance. He came to start a movement, not put on a display. He released His Spirit to spread love all over the world, and love doesn't depend on people looking pretty.

The world will try to mislead us about the need to present ourselves a certain way, but God remains unconcerned. He cares about our hearts more than our appearance. If you find yourself consumed with how you look in the eyes of other people, remember this: Jesus could care less. He wouldn't have used mud to heal people if He cared what we looked like.

**Whose opinion about your appearance
matters most to you? Why?**

RESIST THE URGE TO PUT WARNING LABELS ON THE PEOPLE AROUND YOU. THEY'RE GOD'S KIDS, NOT EXPLOSIVES.

It is not the healthy who need a doctor, but the sick. I have not come to call the righteous, but sinners.

MARK 2:17

My favorite label is the warning label. As a kid, I was captivated by power tools and flammable objects. Anything that could create a minor explosion was on my Christmas list. I spent most of my younger years with my eyebrows burned off. My buddies and I saw warning labels as windows into a world of possibilities, while the adults around us reminded us they were there for a reason. We continue to assume the reason was to alert us to the possibility of massive amounts of fun.

When I got older, especially when I had kids, I began to realize warning labels were actually a pretty good idea. I also picked up on a different kind of warning label that creates its own kind of destruction: the warning labels we put on people. We often speak about certain kinds of people as "issues" or "problems." And we're usually referring to people who are different from us, have different beliefs, or rub us the wrong way.

The warning labels are less overt than the ones on heavy equipment, but they nevertheless say we're better off not getting too close to these people. Perhaps we think engaging them in friendship could cause an explosion because we'll be misunderstood for reaching out. When I look at Jesus, though, He didn't seem very concerned about what onlookers might think about Him. He went to the fringes and found the ne'er-do-wells, the dropouts, and the junkies . . . the rejected, the odd, and the disenfranchised, and He drew them in close. He touched them when no one else would.

Loving people like Jesus means doing the unlikely. If people look confused when they look at your life, you're probably on the right track. If they're distancing themselves from you because of who you're getting close to, that's a pretty good sign you're living out your faith the way Jesus did.

Who would Jesus spend time with if He were in your shoes?

OCTOBER

OCTOBER 1

GRACE LETS US HUM THE PARTS OF OUR LIVES WE DON'T UNDERSTAND YET WHILE WE FIGURE OUT THE WORDS.

My sheep listen to my voice; I know them, and they follow me. I give them eternal life, and they shall never perish; no one will snatch them out of my hand.

JOHN 10:27–28

I have a few friends who are great at playing instruments and writing songs. They perform on stages and compose masterpieces on their pianos and guitars. Whenever Sweet Maria and I go to one of their concerts, their music seems so effortless, like the songs just burst out of them.

One time I asked one of these friends what it was like to write a hit song that everybody sang along to. When he told me about his process, I was really surprised. He said his songs usually started with a vague melody or a series of chords. While he drove around, got the car washed, took a walk, or made dinner, he would have these notes in his head and start building on them, thinking about them, humming along without a clear sense of how they might become a song. He wasn't trying to finish the song all at once. He was just living with it.

This reminded me of a time we took hundreds of kazoos to the school we built in Gulu, Uganda, for kids who were the first generation after a twenty-five-year civil war had ended. At the beginning, all the random blowing sounded like the stuff of Beethoven's nightmares, but then the students started suggesting songs for us all to play along to. There are so many languages and cultures represented in the room, deciding on a song would have only solved half the issue because everyone would be singing different words to it in their traditional languages. But with the kazoos, we didn't have to know the words—we just blew a tune we all knew and the music did the translating for us.

Maybe you don't know the words to the song God is creating with your life. Don't sweat it, just give it some time. Drive around with it. Go to the car wash with it, take a walk, make dinner. Live with it for a while, and ask God to give you the words later.

What words is God speaking to you?

THE FAMILY OF FAITH SHOULD LOOK LIKE A REAL FAMILY—A LITTLE MESSY BUT FULL OF GRACE AND ACCEPTANCE.

"Who is my mother, and who are my brothers?" Pointing to his disciples, he said, "Here are my mother and my brothers. For whoever does the will of my Father in heaven is my brother and sister and mother."

MATTHEW 12:48-50

These days it's possible for us to live where we want to live, regardless of where we work and play. We can drive across town to churches, attending the ones we like the most instead of learning to like the ones near us. It's given us the freedom to connect with like-minded people who are far away and the freedom to avoid those who are different from us, even when they're nearby.

We need to give some thought to how much our lives have become tailor-made to our likings. It isn't necessarily a bad thing when we choose to live among people who look like us, or go to church with members who think like us, but we might not realize we've slowly been cutting out the people who are different from us. And those who are different from us are often the ones we need to learn from the most.

Instead of huddling with people who make us comfortable, let's seek out those who are different so our circle of love can expand. If we only love the people who are like us and love us back, we confuse the life Jesus gave us to look more like a buffet, where we just take what we want and disregard the rest. Think of faith like your real-life family instead. I bet there are a few members of your family who get on your nerves a little and a few who are just plain weird. The family of God should look like that, where we go through life with people who drive us a little crazy but we love them nonetheless.

Jesus didn't call us to be picky with one another. He said to love like Him.

Who's difficult for you to love right now?

IF I HAD ONE LAST MEAL, I WOULDN'T SPEND IT WITH THE PERSON I KNEW WOULD BETRAY ME. LOVE DOES.

Very truly I tell you, one of you is going to betray me.

JOHN 13:21

It's always fun to hear people share what kind of meal they'd plan if they knew it would be their last. As friends go into how they'd like their fillet cooked or how many flavors of ice cream they'd want with their Chicago-style pizza, you get a glimpse into the foods that bring them joy. I've never heard anybody say they'd want kale. But even more fascinating than learning about deep-fried Twinkies is hearing about who they'd want sitting around the table with them for their last meal.

Hearing the answers to these questions, you get to know more about who shaped our friends into the people they've become, the ones who were there when they got their battle scars, the ones who were loyal. But we rarely hear about their enemies. It's not surprising. People don't gather around the table with the ones who broke their hearts or crushed their dreams or betrayed them.

Just before Jesus went to a garden to plead with God one last time to provide a way out of His looming death, He invited twelve of His closest friends to have one last meal together. As they passed the wine around the table, Jesus told them He knew one of them would betray Him and one would deny Him. Shocked and dismayed, they all said it wasn't them, but He knew just hours later He would be handed over to be crucified.

A final dinner together, and Jesus could have had anyone there. He didn't send invitations to the most influential or helpful or even the people who had supported Him during His life. He invited the ones He knew would soon wrong Him. If I had one last meal, I wouldn't spend it with the person I knew would betray me, but love does.

Who would Jesus invite to dinner if He were you?

INSECURITY WANTS US TO KEEP TRACK OF OUR FAILURES. GRACE DOESN'T KEEP SCORE.

If you, LORD, kept a record of sins, LORD, who could stand? But with you there is forgiveness, so that we can, with reverence, serve you.

PSALM 130:3-4

I love watching baseball in person. The atmosphere is electric. If a game is tight in the eighth or ninth inning, every pitch and every swing feels more important than the ones in the first seven innings. Everyone is standing or craning their necks to see what happens. The only smart move is to slide your nachos under the seat or you're bound to launch them with a spontaneous leap from your seat.

I always feel anxious for the batters in these late-inning moments. When the game is on the line, all the pressure is on them. Every time they swing and miss, the umpire yells "Strike!" and throws his fist through the air. The failure is amplified as the pressure builds.

While it's fun to experience the pulse-pounding moments of a tense ball-game, I think T-ball games get it right. In T-ball games, there's no umpire to yell strike and no pressure to connect in three tries. You can chop at the ball as many times as needed. No one keeps track of how many times they miss. We just wait for the hit so we can cheer.

A lot of us treat life like a major league playoff game instead of neighborhood T-ball. Instead of rooting for one another to swing for the fences and get a hit no matter how many swings it takes, we keep track of the misses, the failures, the disappointments. We treat life like it's "three strikes and you're out." Jesus says we're all in no matter how badly we've messed up.

When our insecurity wants us to keep track of our failures, remember grace isn't keeping score. It doesn't even start counting.

**What part of your past has God forgotten
but you keep holding on to?**

GRACE IS ONLY HARD TO GIVE IF WE'RE KEEPING SCORE.

The kingdom of heaven is like a landowner who went out early in the morning to hire workers for his vineyard.

MATTHEW 20:1

When Jesus tried to tell people what the kingdom of heaven was like, He knew descriptions would fail, so He told stories. He said God's kingdom was like someone who was lost but then was found. He said it was like a tiny seed that grew into a large tree. In one of my favorite stories, He said it was like a landowner who hired some laborers to work in his field for a day.

The landowner went out around nine o'clock in the morning, looking for workers for his vineyard. He agreed to pay them fifty dollars each for a full day of work. Then he did the same at noon and three and five o'clock. At the end of the day, the workers all lined up to get their wages, and the owner of the vineyard gave each one fifty dollars regardless of when they started.

When the workers who started in the morning saw the others receive the same amount, they started grumbling. I get it. I think I'd be a little miffed too. But I love the story because it reminds us grace doesn't keep track of when you punch the clock. It's ironic that it doesn't bother people who know how much they need grace to see it given without hesitation. It only upsets people who think they need to earn grace with their hard work.

Grace doesn't work if we're concerned about getting our fair share. God's grace is infinite and unending. It's never accurately seen in short supply. Instead of grumbling about someone else getting a little grace, celebrate with them. And be thankful, too, that God gives you just as much grace as you need.

Who around you is receiving grace right now?
How can you celebrate with them?

OCTOBER 6

STAND LIKE A MOUNTAIN, LOVE LIKE AN AVALANCHE.

Bear with each other and forgive one another if any of you has a grievance against someone. Forgive as the Lord forgave you.

COLOSSIANS 3:13

After Nelson Mandela was released from prison in South Africa, he said: "As I walked out the door toward the gate that would lead to my freedom, I knew if I didn't leave my bitterness and hatred behind, I'd still be in prison."

Nelson Mandela knew he had been wronged, but he didn't want to be controlled by the people who had wronged him. He chose the more beautiful path of forgiveness. He knew loving his country meant letting go of his anger, even if his anger was justified. He stood like a mountain and decided to love like an avalanche.

Most of us want to be the kind of people who extend forgiveness, but we can't give it away unless it's genuinely been stored up in our hearts. Forgiveness is an overflow of who we're becoming when no one is watching. If we regularly take time to think about how God has forgiven us for everything we've done (even the things we've managed to hide from other people), our hearts will begin to take the shape of forgiveness. Do this long enough and we'll turn into the kind of people who naturally extend it to others because we've felt its transforming power.

As difficult as it can be, the only way to multiply love in the world is to let go of the wrong done to us. We don't need to minimize it or make excuses for people; we just need to see their failures alongside our own record that Jesus wiped clean. When we become people who extend forgiveness, especially when it's costly or hard, we'll be well on our way to loving like Jesus.

What do you need to let go of?

OCTOBER 7

PEOPLE GROW WHERE THEY'RE ACCEPTED.

God does not show favoritism.

ROMANS 2:11

We care most about the things that cost us something because those things are more valuable by their nature. Love works like this too. We can parade around things looking like love, but they won't last or be worth much to anybody. When love requires us to give something, then it's the kind of love that sticks around. Selfless love has no outs, no disclaimers, no expectation of returns. It just simply gives itself up. The most unnatural thing we can do is act for someone else's benefit. Selflessness is uncanny, almost suspicious. But it can change everything.

Selfless love changes us and our small worlds. Sure, we stand to lose what we've come to know as comforts, but we'll gain the kind of things we've wanted all along—like love and purpose and connection. We'll experience true friendships and community because we'll be a part of a collective larger than one where we're merely looking out for ourselves. Our accounts with fear and pride will go bankrupt, and their once-convincing voices will get smaller and slimmer. It turns out, the cost of selfless love is all the selfish parts of us we grip for safety. Selfless love is always costly. Fear can't afford it, pride doesn't understand it, and friends never forget it.

God said His plan for loving people on earth was us. He said people will know He delights in them when they feel unconditionally loved by those who share His name. Jesus never said anything about tough love. He didn't tell us to push people away so they'd know the pain of the loss of community. Those are just ideas people made up along the way to punish people.

God told us to welcome people into His love. People don't grow where they're merely informed; they grow where they're accepted. Don't cut people off from the source of love when they lose their way. Draw them in close and breathe life back into them like Jesus did when He was here.

Who might God be calling you to welcome?

OCTOBER 8

WE'RE ALL BROKEN. WE DON'T NEED MORE VARNISH—WE NEED A CARPENTER.

Restore to me the joy of your salvation and grant me a willing spirit, to sustain me.

PSALM 51:12

If you've been reading through this book, you probably know by now that my family and I head to Canada each summer where we built a lodge. This magical place didn't happen overnight. For the first few years, we just camped on the property until we could build a little something to get us out of the elements. Over the years, the lodge took shape and housed some of our best memories.

It was the middle of the night when I got the call. The lodge had burned down. We were getting the exterior restained to protect it from the harsh Canadian winters. Some highly flammable, combustible rags were left in a pile, and they spontaneously caught fire and leveled the place. There weren't even ashes left when the fire went out. We lost everything.

How crazy would it have been if I had showed up with a can of stain the next day to keep working on the lodge? There was nothing there. It's an extreme example, but sometimes I wonder when we show up with some varnish for our lives after one of our dreams or ambitions or relationships has burned down, if what we really need instead is a good Carpenter.

God isn't interested in what your faith looks like. He cares about what it is. The next time you're feeling a little broken or burned out, don't go for the cosmetic fix first. Go to God and ask Him to help you completely rebuild. It'll probably take longer, but it will be the only way you can be truly restored.

What does God want to rebuild in your life?

WHEN YOU'VE GOT A GUIDE YOU CAN TRUST, YOU DON'T HAVE TO WORRY ABOUT THE PATH YOU'RE ON.

Fixing our eyes on Jesus, the pioneer and perfecter of faith. For the joy set before him he endured the cross, scorning its shame, and sat down at the right hand of the throne of God.

HEBREWS 12:2

I have a friend named Charlie who has endured some really hard things in his life. As a young Ugandan boy, he was captured by a witch doctor who performed a horrific ritual that left Charlie scarred for life. We became his legal guardians and set out to make him whole again.

Charlie went through a series of surgeries, and his body was in much better shape. The surgeon restored some of the damage caused by the witch doctor, but I felt like something was missing. Charlie needed something to convince him his courage was intact and his heart could be made whole too. So I told Charlie I would take him anywhere he wanted to go for an adventure. You know what he picked? He said he wanted to climb Mount Kilimanjaro. I didn't want to break my promise, so we headed to the famous mountain. We had the gear, the guide, and a dream worth chasing.

People have asked me what the views were like climbing Mount Kilimanjaro. The truth is, I never really looked up to see. I had my eyes fixed on the boots of the guide in front of me. Where he went, I went. He went over a couple of boulders I would have rather gone around, but if he went over them, I went over them. He went around a couple of rocks I would have rather gone over, but if he went around them, I went around them. I didn't need to know where to go next because I was following someone who did.

The next time you're asking God to make you whole, remember that there isn't a straight line to the summit. There will be plenty of switchbacks and hard work. Don't worry about the trail ahead. Keep your eyes fixed on Jesus' feet. When you've got a guide you can trust, you don't have to worry about the path you're on.

Where is the Guide leading you today?

OCTOBER 10

WHEN I THINK SOMEONE OUGHT TO BE MORE LOVING, IT'S USUALLY ME.

Anyone who has two shirts should share with the one who has none, and anyone who has food should do the same.

LUKE 3:11

Airports are a place to build patience. Few things amp up my anxiety more than sitting on the runway a few feet short of the gate while I miss a tight connection one gate away. Or waiting for the last plane out before the storm, then having it canceled at midnight. Airports are a place where babies cry and strangers bump into us with roller bags and all comfortable seats have been removed.

I used to dread airports for all these reasons, but when I started thinking of them as opportunities to give away love, my attitude changed. Now when I interact with a customer-service agent who isn't moving as fast as I want them to, I think about how many people have probably been rude to them that day, and I try to make them smile. When I'm seated next to a screaming baby on a flight, I imagine how tired their parents must feel, and I do my part to make the kid smile.

When I think someone ought to be more loving, it's usually me. The longer I follow Jesus, the more I'm trying to see through the eyes of other people. Don't get me wrong. It's not always easy, and I've got a lot to learn. We come into contact with people every day who need to encounter love. They need to know that whatever they're going through at the moment, they don't have to go it alone.

One word, one kind and understanding nod in the direction of someone struggling, can change everything. When we choose to step in the shoes of people having a difficult time, we usually find they're a lot like us. They just need to know they're loved and valued and that it's going to be okay. Don't leave it to someone else to do the loving for you.

What one word can you share with someone today to show them love?

LET'S LIVE LIKE THE MOST FAMOUS PARTS OF THE BIBLE.

For God so loved the world that he gave his one and only Son, that whoever believes in him shall not perish but have eternal life.

JOHN 3:16

John 3:16 is probably the most famous verse in the Bible. Even if someone has never cracked the cover, they've probably heard this verse a couple of times. This verse boils down who God is and the sacrifice He made by sending Jesus to us. What we heard doesn't stick with us nearly as much as what we see. People who follow Jesus might be the only living version of John 3:16 another person ever sees.

Here's the problem. We're prone to backstabbing and gossip, infighting and pridefulness, and making camps out of opinions to declare on behalf of God who's in and who's out. If God sent Jesus for the whole world, why do we cause so many divisions in what He said He wants to bring together?

Jesus' life started with His coming and ended in His sacrificing. In between, He showed forgiveness and acceptance, grace and truth. He put himself on the hook for our wrongdoings. We need to find a way back to the beautiful truths about our faith rather than telling everyone else what they need to do. Take a breath. Get a puppy. Do whatever it takes to show the kind of love Jesus had for the world to the people next to you.

If you're holding a grudge or putting out a stiff arm to keep someone you disagree with at a distance, step back for a minute. Remember that God gave His one and only Son for us. He didn't do it for just some of the world or just for the people who acted a certain way. He loved the whole world and everybody it it. Maybe we can too. And since you're part of the family, He's invited you to be an ambassador for that truth—not with what you believe but with what you do about what you believe.

**If God gave His one and only Son for you,
what can you do today for someone else?**

OCTOBER 12

QUIT BEING "RIGHT." BE HUMBLE.

What does the LORD require of you? To act justly and to love mercy and to walk humbly with your God.

MICAH 6:8

Have you ever been able to change someone's heart and mind with a compelling argument? Yeah, me neither. I'm a lawyer. I win arguments for a living. Still, what sways a jury won't reshape our worldview. I think there are a number of reasons. One is that we can try to convince someone about what's "true," but we can't make it matter to them, and people will only move forward on things that matter to them. I'm not saying we shouldn't voice our opinions or disagree with people, but I think we need to reboot how we're having the debate. I've learned the power of letting other people have the last word. It won't kill you. Yield the last word and you'll make an impression.

The next time things get a little heated, make it an opportunity to show love and grace, even if you've got a different opinion. Say the truth in love but be willing to concede the last word. When we let other people have the last word, we let them know we're more interested in spreading love than winning arguments. Instead of convincing people we're right, let's be humble. Humble people know when to speak up and when to be silent. People listen to our lives even more than our words, and it will be love that moves them in the end.

In what ways can you be more humble today?

THE WORLD WILL FIGURE OUT WHAT WE REALLY BELIEVE BY WATCHING WHAT WE ACTUALLY DO.

By this everyone will know that you are my disciples, if you love one another.

JOHN 13:35

I've heard a lot of people say something like this: "I'm not big on religion, but I could really get into Jesus." Have you ever heard that? I think it's because people assume religion is a bunch of rules governed by religious zealots who spend their days deciding who's right and wrong. I can't really say I blame them.

Perhaps a more accurate way to see faith is that it's a bunch of ideas and Jesus was a bunch of action. Sure, there are times in the Bible where we see Jesus teaching. But more often, we see Him telling stories or getting down on one knee to look a child in the eye or feeding hungry people or healing the lame.

We all know people who are eager to tell us what they believe—about God, about the poor, about love and heaven and hell. But ideas can only get us so far. If your car breaks down in rush hour traffic, do you want someone to send you a detailed diagnostic of what went wrong? Or would you prefer a pair of jumper cables, a lift, or a call for a tow truck? If you know a single parent who lost their job, do you think that person wants a performance review or a gift card to a local grocery store?

Understanding the Bible is important, no doubt. I spend loads of time discovering the truths in its pages, but the moment we chase knowledge at the expense of loving others, we've missed the point of Scripture. Remember that the world will know what we believe by seeing what we do. Be love, and you can't go wrong.

What will you do for someone today that demonstrates God's love?

OCTOBER 14

FOLLOWING JESUS COSTS EACH OF US SOMETHING DIFFERENT.

Those of you who do not give up everything you have cannot be my disciples.

LUKE 14:33

The Bible tells us about an extraordinary practice in ancient Israel called the Year of Jubilee. This came around once every fifty years, and it was a time when all slaves and prisoners were set free and every debt was forgiven. God set it up for the people of Israel because He wanted to communicate in a human way what His mercy was like, and it looked like freedom for everyone no matter their burden or debt.

Everyone's debts were different. I bet some were only short fifty dollars and some owed what would be millions. The point of the celebration was to say God's mercy wipes all our debts clean, whether we've blown it in big ways or just failed to show up when it mattered. It's all the same in God's economy.

Each of us starts in a different place when we choose to follow Jesus. The debts we owe reflect the different lives we've lived. The cost of discipleship looks different from person to person. Some of us have to give up our need to be the center of attention, and some of us need the courage to find our voices. What feels like a sacrifice to you might come naturally to your neighbor. They're just facing a different kind of battle.

Following Jesus costs each of us something different, but mercy looks the same for all of us. It looks like God letting us off the hook for the ways we've fallen short and a celebration for all of us because Jesus covered the cost.

What is following Jesus costing you this week?

OCTOBER 15

IF YOU'RE WAITING FOR HOPE,
KEEP LOOKING FOR JESUS.

When Jesus saw him lying there and learned that he had been in this condition for a long time, he asked him, "Do you want to get well?"

JOHN 5:6

In the Bible, there's a place called the Pool of Bethesda. The spring was believed to be stirred by angels every so often, and when it was stirred, those who managed to jump in the pool would be healed. Every day, a large number of disabled people would lay next to the pool, getting as close to the edge as possible so they wouldn't miss their shot at healing.

One day Jesus walked up to the pool and met a disabled man who had been lying by the pool for thirty-eight years. Jesus struck up a conversation with the man, wondering if he wanted to be healed. The man told him every time the water was stirred, he tried to hop in but someone else always jumped in front of him and he never quite made it. When Jesus heard his story, He told the man to take up his mat and walk home because he was healed.

We might not have a condition like this guy had, but a lot of us still feel we've been sitting next to the pool. We see hope for a better life, but every time opportunities come, something gets in the way. Some of us know what it's like to hope for something without seeing signs of change. It's tempting to expect more of the same tomorrow.

But grace means tomorrow's always a friend. Grace means Jesus can step into the scene in an instant and bring the healing we started hoping for. Don't believe hope is lost just because change hasn't come yet. Get back in the water.

What do you want Jesus to heal in you?

WE'LL FILL OUR LIVES WITH WHAT WE CULTIVATE THE MOST. PLANT GRACE BY THE ACRE.

Grow in the grace and knowledge of our Lord and Savior Jesus Christ.

2 PETER 3:18

If you have a neighbor with a green thumb who likes to grow vegetables, you've hit the jackpot. It's not unusual for them to stop by in the middle of the afternoon with bags full of tomatoes or some other produce. It's never just a small basket either; it's more than you could eat in a week's worth of meals.

How weird would we look if we took their offering of tomatoes and then asked why they didn't bring us watermelons? Not only would it be ungrateful, we'd also look silly. They didn't bring us watermelons because they didn't plant watermelons. They can't harvest something they don't plant. And neither can we.

I wonder why we ask those questions in our lives though. We tend to grow the virtues we've planted: cultivating grace makes us more gracious, giving away love makes us more loving, practicing patience helps us become more patient. We can't take jabs at people behind their backs and then expect to become more tenderhearted toward them. But we can practice giving the benefit of the doubt to people and watch compassion for them grow in our hearts.

God created the earth with these rhythms of planting and harvesting to teach us about His kingdom. He gave us tools to understand His work of redemption in our everyday lives. We'll fill our lives with what we cultivate the most. Plant grace by the acre.

What are you cultivating in your life? How can you cultivate more grace and love?

DON'T JUST FOCUS ON THE PAGE. REMEMBER TO GET OUT INTO THE MARGINS.

The Pharisee was surprised when he noticed that Jesus did not first wash before the meal.

LUKE 11:38

Jesus didn't do things by the book. He wasn't beholden to the playbook the rest of humanity seemed to be living by. Whenever I'm reading, or writing on occasion, I'm trying to stay inside the lines. I mean, the rule for writing and reading is stay inside the margins where all the words are. The words somebody pored over getting their point across or their poem in perfect meter with clever rhymes. We don't really notice the space on the edges.

When I say Jesus didn't go by the book, I mean that He pretty much spent all His time in the margins. Instead of being enamored by the fanfare and well-formed arguments of the Pharisees and religious people, He went to the places everyone else seemed to forget. What if we decided to fill up the margins with our love instead? What would it look like for you to share a meal with someone who genuinely creeps you out? Or give them hope and a listening ear? That's the stuff we do in the margins.

When I feel a little listless or restless, it's tempting to go straight for the words I know, the ones in the middle of the page that are comfortable and reassuring. But when I look at Jesus, I see someone going outside the lines to the poor, the orphans, the widows, and the prisoners. Those are the ones Jesus set His sights on. Sometimes we need to trade the words we've known for the margins where God calls us.

What rules or expectations can you break to love people on the margins?

IF YOU TELL A STORY ABOUT WHAT JESUS HAS DONE FOR YOU, YOU'LL ALWAYS BE SHARING TRUTH.

He replied, "Whether he is a sinner or not, I don't know. One thing I do know. I was blind but now I see!"

JOHN 9:25

The Bible tells a story about a man who was born blind—the man Jesus healed with some mud and the touch of His hand. When the Pharisees caught wind of the story, they went on a tear to find the guy who had been healed. They wanted to hear his story. You get the sense that the Pharisees were threatened that Jesus was stealing their spotlight.

When they found the man who had been healed, he simply bore witness to the miracle Jesus had done. He admitted he didn't know anything about Jesus. He didn't know where He came from, and he didn't know if Jesus was a sinner or a Savior. He just knew one thing: he had been blind and now he could see. He didn't turn it into a lecture about illness or theology or try to convince the Pharisees they were wrong about the world; he just told them what he had seen Jesus do.

I've come to realize there are two ways of telling stories about ourselves. Our stories can stay focused on us, presenting us in the best light. Or our stories can be an entryway into telling the truth about what God has been doing in our lives, even if we can't explain it.

Instead of telling stories to brighten your spotlight or hold on to power, simply talk about what you've experienced Jesus doing in your life. We don't have to have the answers or look like we have big faith. We just have to be humble and tell it like we've known it.

With whom will you share a story about Jesus' work in your life?

BRIGHT LIGHTS DON'T NEED SPOTLIGHTS.

Let your light shine before others, that they may see your good deeds and glorify your Father in heaven.

MATTHEW 5:16

I've always thought outdoor Christmas trees were magical. Ever since I was a kid, when I passed a Christmas tree in the center of a city, I would stand back to take in the scene. Kids notice Christmas trees with a little more energy and excitement, quick to point out the size of the gifts beneath them, wondering if anyone would notice if one went missing. Even grownups can't help but be grabbed by the sight of a beautifully lit tree. Part of their splendor comes from the way they illuminate the whole block. You don't need store lights or lamps in city centers in December. The Christmas trees shine bright enough.

Wouldn't it be weird if someone decided to draw attention to the tree by putting up construction lights to shine a spotlight on the tree? The tree would lose its magic because the spotlights would get in the way. They would detract from the subtle brilliance of the warm lights on the tree. The tree gets more attention when it stands tall against the backdrop of the night sky with no spotlights adding extra light.

All of this seems so obvious it almost goes without saying, but we don't see it so obviously when it comes to the light in our own lives. Jesus said our love is the light that shines in the darkness. He said people will see our acts of love and see Him in the process. We don't need to draw attention to ourselves; our good deeds will attract all the attention Jesus needs. Shining light on them would only get in the way.

Bright lights don't need spotlights. Just be love and it'll light up everything.

How can you let God's light shine brighter in your life?

OCTOBER 20

GIVE AWAY BREATHTAKING AMOUNTS OF GRACE.

When you stand praying, if you hold anything against anyone, forgive them, so that your Father in heaven may forgive you your sins.

MARK 11:25

Several years ago, a sweet little old lady named Lynn was driving home from her seniors' exercise class when she blew through a stop sign and T-boned me with her car. I was driving a convertible jeep, and the collision catapulted me through the open roof into the middle of the road. They make you pay for those kinds of rides at the state fair. Incredibly, although my car was upside down and totaled, I landed on the street and was just fine.

Lynn was in knots about the wreck for weeks. She was afraid they would revoke her driver's license since this might prove she wasn't fit to get behind the wheel, and she was anxious about losing her independence. She also felt awful about totaling my jeep and about launching me into the intersection. I got to thinking about it and figured out a way to let Lynn know that she was truly forgiven. I called the flower shop and told them to send Lynn the biggest bouquet in the shop with a note saying, "It was great running into you. You're forgiven."

It might sound like a crazy idea, but it actually wasn't my idea; it was God's idea. God responds to us the same way every time we blow it. We hijack His plans and make a mess of things, and He gives us grace in return. There's nothing we've messed up that He hasn't been able to turn into something redemptive and beautiful. There's no sin we've committed that's stopped Him from giving us grace.

Give away a breathtaking amount of grace. We have an endless supply since it comes from an infinite source.

Who needs more grace in your life?

OCTOBER 21

TREMENDOUS LOVE MAKES BIG GRACE LOOK EFFORTLESS.

Dear friends, since God so loved us, we also ought to love one another.

1 JOHN 4:11

My friend Jamie runs an organization that helps connect people who are depressed and addicted to the help they need. It started when he met a girl who believed a bunch of lies about herself, and she turned to heavy drug use and self-harm to try to drown out the lies. When she looked in the mirror, she saw a screw-up. But Jamie didn't see a screw-up; he saw beauty.

Jamie and his friends hung out with her for a whole week of detox, passing the time at concerts, sports games, and scheming new adventures. After the girl went to rehab, Jamie knew there were more people like her who needed a family to fall into when they couldn't fall much farther, so he started an organization to help spread love to them.

Anyone who knows Jamie knows him as someone who always has words of hope and love for people in desperate places. It's not a surprise when they're met with hugs if they show up on his doorstep in the middle of the night. It's not a special occasion; it's just Jamie.

Tremendous love makes big grace look effortless. When our lives revolve around loving people, grace becomes a natural outpouring. People don't have to worry about bothering us or wearing out their welcome. They know we'll be gracious just because it's Tuesday and that's who we are.

Give away tremendous amounts of love and watch grace come along for the ride.

Who do you know who needs to be loved like Jamie's friend?

THINK ABOUT ALL THE THINGS YOU ALREADY TRUST IN YOUR LIFE. THEN ASK WHY YOU DON'T TRUST GOD MORE.

Trust in the LORD with all your heart and lean not on your own understanding; in all your ways submit to him, and he will make your paths straight.

PROVERBS 3:5-6

Since my kids aren't making mischief from home anymore, I'm always working on finding some reasons to hang out with them. My son Adam recently took up skydiving, so I decided to get my skydiving license without telling him. I had this daydream of him freefalling through the air and then I float down next to him. "Oh, hey, Adam. What are you doing here?" I would scream into the wind.

One weekend I drove Adam to the drop zone like I did each weekend. He got out of the car, grabbed a parachute, and got in the plane. This time I got out of the car, grabbed a parachute, put it on, and got in the plane next to him.

"Dad?!" Adam said, shaking his head at me.

"How hard could it be?" I shot back at him.

Sometimes on a weekends we'll still grab some lunch, catch up on life, and then jump out of a plane together. It's fantastic.

The craziest part about the whole skydiving thing is that when you're falling through the air at around 125 miles per hour, you pull a cord connected to a tiny, metal pin that deploys the parachute. Your whole life depends on one piece of metal that is less than an inch long. When it's pulled, the parachute either goes off or it doesn't.

The truth is, I sometimes trust God less than I trust that pin. I don't believe He's going to catch me at the perfect moment. I'm afraid He won't be there when I need Him to be. I think He'll let me plummet if I make a mistake. Or I believe He'll withhold His grace if I mess up one more time.

Sometimes God leads us into difficult circumstances so we'll realize our absolute need for Him.

In what difficult circumstance are you finding it difficult to trust God?

CYNICISM IS FEAR POSING AS CONFIDENCE.

Let us consider how we may spur one another on toward love and good deeds.

HEBREWS 10:24

I was at a coffee shop the other day and overheard a conversation between two young people about to graduate college. I was trying to be polite and not eavesdrop while lobbing over big smiles and positive vibes their way.

One friend, with a twinkle in his eye, was talking about whether he should start a company, join the Peace Corps, or backpack across China. But the other friend chimed in each time about why he didn't think the ideas would work or why they were foolish. It made me wonder why this friend would rain on the other guy's parade. I mean, it's fine to give someone a hand as they take the next step, but this guy was a fire hydrant of negativity dousing enthusiasm, dreams, and hope. I wanted to chime in, but I held my tongue.

I don't know why the negative friend was saying what he said. But it made me wonder if cynicism is really just fear posing as confidence. There are enough voices in our lives, in addition to our own, telling us what we can't do. There's a multitude of people who are ready to say our idea is crazy or irresponsible. Don't let them steal the microphone in your life, and make sure you're not the one speaking discouraging words over your friends.

Next time you're tempted to rain on someone's parade or feel like you need an umbrella from someone else's downpour, remember that cynicism is just fear in disguise. Ditch the fear and go bold with a boatload of encouragement instead. Failure or not, we all need voices that shine light on dreams. The world is desperate for people who do this. Be one of them.

Who needs encouragement in your life?

ANTICIPATE DIFFICULTIES. BANK ON GRACE.

Encourage one another and build each other up, just as in fact you are doing.

1 THESSALONIANS 5:11

Every year in May, our organization hosts a cycling trip called the Love Does Tour. People from all over the country gather together in Monterey, where they start a ten-day bicycle trip down the coast of California. Some of them are experienced cyclists, and some don't even own their own bikes, but they come together because they care about the cause. They want to raise money for kids to go to school in Uganda and make new friends in the process.

These adventurous men and women know they'll face difficulties in the five hundred miles to come. They're likely to get a flat tire or two along the way. They know they might hit thunderstorms or high winds as they ride through the mountains. They expect it to be challenging, with maybe a couple of close calls too. But they also know if they get a flat tire, they can rely on other teammates to pull over with the right tools. And if they hit thunderstorms, they'll huddle under tents and weather the storms together. No one will be left alone.

Life isn't easy. Difficulties and disappointment are real. Here's the thing: we can bank on grace. There's no challenge we can't face when we've got friends who've got our backs. The fact is, nothing has the power to overcome us, because Jesus faced even death head-on and kicked it in the teeth so we would win, too, when it came for us.

The bike tour ends most years down by the bay in my backyard. A couple of times we've had the ones who weren't afraid of a little rust ride right into the water. I love to hear the stories about the uphill stretches where the peddling was most difficult and about the views they saw when they got to the top. Grace isn't always like the view from the top or the downhill coast. It feels like having someone with us on the ride.

Who can you show up for today?

OCTOBER 25

GRACE FEELS LIKE A PAINTING GOD IS STILL COMPLETING OVER OUR TORN CANVASES.

> Jesus did not let him, but said, "Go home to your own people and tell them how much the Lord has done for you, and how he has had mercy on you."
>
> MARK 5:19

I recently learned about an artist whose trademark is painting over old photographs. He gets portraits of families, gathers pictures of landscapes with oceans, mountains, and vineyards, and then turns them into a totally different art form. Sometimes he covers the entire photograph, and sometimes he just adds a little color here and there, but either way, the pictures are transformed.

When I see his pictures, I can't help but think about grace. God takes us as we are, with all our gifts and quirks, and He turns us into people who are altogether different yet still ourselves. Take the possessed man who was living in tombs when he met Jesus. The people in the town said the man couldn't be contained. He broke chains on his wrists and irons from his feet. He cried out and cut himself with stones when people approached him.

But Jesus had compassion on him. He asked the man his name and then delivered him from his torment. When the people from the town showed up, they saw the man dressed and in his right mind. I like to imagine he cut his hair and trimmed his beard and greeted them with a smile as they approached. He was still the same person—they could recognize his characteristics—but he was totally transformed. Like a beautiful painting over an old photograph.

When we decide to live a life following Jesus, God doesn't do away with our old selves altogether. Instead, He points us in the direction of Jesus and says, "Go be like Him." Grace is like allowing God to paint Jesus into our lives.

What would Jesus do today if He was you?

FAITH ISN'T A SERIES OF FLASHCARDS TO REMEMBER. MEMORIZE GRACE.

Always be prepared to give an answer to everyone who asks you to give the reason for the hope that you have. But do this with gentleness and respect.

1 PETER 3:15

As a lawyer, one of the things I'm really good at is memorization. All the codes and rules and laws are a snap for me to access. Lawyers have to memorize a lot to pass bar exams and try cases, so this was a good fit for me.

Sometimes I wonder if we give too much importance to the power of memorization in our faith. Don't get me wrong. I read the Bible a ton and try to find truths God has left for us there. Some of us were told to memorize scriptures when we were young, so we drilled verses into our minds like kids cramming for the big test. We memorized doctrine, too, so we could explain our faith to people. We were told to be ready to give an account for it at all times. What didn't get a lot of airtime was doing these things with gentleness and respect.

When we merely memorize our faith like we're cramming for a test, we download a bunch of information, but the problem is, we're not transformed by it. What if, instead, we memorized grace the way we memorize a song? Here's why. When we memorize songs, we play them on repeat as we go about our days. Years later we can still sing the words. When we memorize music, it becomes a part of us and shapes us. It moves us to reach out to people and makes us feel less lonely. We don't memorize music the way we crammed for tests; we learn from it by allowing it to become a part of us.

Let's memorize grace. We don't need to download doctrine like we prepared for tests with flashcards. God doesn't need a lawyer to defend Him. He's stronger than the whole world. Instead of memorizing a few verses and calling it good, listen to grace and let it transform your whole life.

What part of God's character are you learning these days?

EVERY TIME WE WON'T FORGIVE EACH OTHER, WE ACT LIKE GRACE DOESN'T EXIST.

Do not judge, and you will not be judged. Do not condemn, and you will not be condemned. Forgive, and you will be forgiven.

LUKE 6:37

There's a quote you might have heard that goes something like this: "Unforgiveness is like drinking poison and hoping the other person dies." It made me wonder if we could start this quote: "Forgiveness is like drinking poison for someone else and you both live." Here's what I mean.

If you've been alive for more than a couple of years, someone has probably hurt you in some way at some time. Maybe it was a big way that made your life feel off-balance for a little while. Maybe it was a small way that you just can't seem to get over. Whatever it is, perhaps it left you in a place where forgiveness is hard to come by.

The hardest part about giving forgiveness is when the person who is wrong doesn't ask for it. We should give it anyway. If we don't, we'll have the poison of unforgiveness flowing through our veins and making our whole life feel sick.

It doesn't have to stay this way though. In a sense, forgiveness isn't like drinking poison; it's more like giving you both the antidote. Forgiveness is an invitation to humble ourselves and turn toward the people who have hurt us. It opens the door for grace to come in and surprise us with a renewed sense of love and commitment to each other. But even if that doesn't happen, forgive anyway. Every time we forgive each other, we create a little more space for love, and it's this new space that has the power to change us.

What's keeping you from forgiveness?

GOD DOESN'T ENJOY SEEING US FAIL.
HE LOVES WATCHING US GROW.

He cuts off every branch in me that bears no fruit, while every branch that does bear fruit he prunes so that it will be even more fruitful.

JOHN 15:2

Jesus taught so many lessons with nature as a metaphor, I figured I should learn more about wheat and seeds and trees and stuff. So when I come across farmers or lumberjacks, I do a little informal research to learn what it's all about. In one of these conversations, a lumberjack actually helped me understand the reason behind some of the pain and failure we all go through at some point in life.

He said for trees to be healthy, they have to be pruned on a regular basis. He climbs up the trees, sometimes with a chainsaw, and cuts off all the diseased branches. He also cuts out dead branches and limbs growing in the wrong direction so the other branches can grow in healthy directions.

When I heard him describe the process, it made a lot of sense to me. Jesus talked about trees and branches. He said even healthy trees—the ones that bear fruit—need to be pruned sometimes so they'll bear even more fruit. It makes sense when I think about all the times I've had to cut things out of my life. Sometimes I'm not the one pruning either. Often God will take things away to guide me in a different direction. When He does, I've figured out later it was to help me become more of the person He had in mind for me to be.

God doesn't enjoy seeing us go through the pain of loss and failure, but He loves watching us grow. Sometimes we do the cutting, and sometimes He does. The end objective is for us to grow into the people God sees us turning into.

Who is God turning you into?

GRACE LETS US IMPROVISE WHEN WE'VE FORGOTTEN THE LINES TO OUR LIVES.

Nothing in all creation is hidden from God's sight.

HEBREWS 4:13

I'm a big fan of all the plays and performances little kids put on. Whether it's a ballet recital, Christmas pageant, or school play, what's better than watching a bunch of little kids do their best with whimsy and joy and without any self-consciousness?

You know how the scene goes. Jane is fidgeting with her fingers on the left side of the stage while Johnny is staring at the ceiling on the right. The ones in costumes in the middle of the stage are tripping over their tails. And two best friends are playing patty-cake to the side when they should be making a big entrance. The kids speaking from the stage don't even care if they mess up their lines. They just keep going, and the crowd gives them a standing ovation in the end.

Don't you wish adulthood could be like that? When we grownups trip up or forget our lines in speeches or business deals, we're mortified. We fumble around to find something to fill the silence and then beat ourselves up about it the rest of the day. But not kids. When kids forget their lines, they either improvise or completely ignore the mess-up.

What if we saw moments when we forget our lines as opportunities to improvise or just walk away like it never even happened? What if, like kids, we put a premium on joy rather than obsessing over whether things go according to the plan? God already told us that the people He made are more important than our projects and productions we put on. God is less concerned about you looking polished and perfect like a Broadway star than He is about you knowing that neither your successes nor your gaffes define you.

The next time you do something that makes you feel like disappearing, remember God sees you and loves you just where you are and just as you are. Grace lets us improvise when we've forgotten the lines to our part.

What part of your life do you feel tempted to hide from God?

WE CAN CONFRONT PEOPLE WITH THEIR FAILURES OR SURROUND THEM WITH OUR LOVE. EITHER WAY, WE'LL BE REMEMBERED.

He lifted me out of the slimy pit, out of the mud and mire; he set my feet on a rock and gave me a firm place to stand.

PSALM 40:2

Close your eyes and take ten seconds to remember one of the most embarrassing moments of your life.

Got it?

Okay, if you're anything like me, that moment was something that happened in front of someone else. Embarrassing moments in private usually make us chuckle at ourselves. Embarrassing moments in front of other people, well, that can be cause for a lifetime of unnecessarily beating ourselves up. If that weren't true, why is it so easy to remember our failures?

I think it's because we've been exposed. Sometimes it's just a blooper, like our pants splitting when we bend over in public, but sometimes it's a moral failure, when we're embarrassed in our relationships. In those moments, it can feel like our whole fragile selves sit in the hands of the people who witnessed our failure. We wait for their response. Will they tell other people? Will they scold us the way we've scolded ourselves? Will they use us as an example to the rest of the world, making a mockery of what little dignity we have left?

We never forget the way people respond to us in our failures. Will they show us empathy or forgiveness, or will they kick us while we're down? The moments when people are most exposed are the times we can have the greatest impact on their lives, for better or worse. We can confront people with their failure or surround them with our love. Either way, we'll be remembered.

Who do you know who's been experiencing failure lately?
What can you show them about who they are instead?

OCTOBER 31

WHEN WE RATION OUR LOVE, EVERYONE GOES HUNGRY. THE MORE EXTRAVAGANT WE ARE, THE LESS IT'S WASTED.

Though the mountains be shaken and the hills be removed, yet my unfailing love for you will not be shaken nor my covenant of peace be removed.

ISAIAH 54:10

The best holidays are the ones with open invites to all the people who have nowhere else to go. When strangers come through the door from all corners of our communities, and they leave as friends. These are the potluck dinners when we tell people to bring whatever they can, but most of all their authentic selves.

When we celebrate holidays potluck-style with an open-door policy, we always end up with more food than we could possibly eat. The more guests we have, the more leftovers we send home, and no one spends the holiday hungry or alone. Love works the same way. We tend to think we should limit the number of people we let in because we think love is a finite resource. We think there won't be enough to go around. This just isn't the way love works.

The more people we let in, the more those people fill us and energize us, the larger the potluck dinner. You walk into the living room and see old friends engaging new friends. You hear new stories about traditions and trips, books and recipes. Each person, each conversation is another main dish for us. It's no different than what Jesus did when the potluck consisted of a couple of fish and loaves of bread. They brought what they had to Jesus and let Him decide what to make of it.

When we ration our love, everyone goes hungry. But the more extravagant we are, the less it's wasted and the better we're fed. Love isn't a limited resource. It's like a potluck where everyone who comes brings what they've got—and there's more than enough for all of us.

How have you been rationing love?

NOVEMBER

WE DID NOTHING TO EARN THIS LIFE. ALL WE CAN DO IN EXCHANGE IS TO GIVE IT AWAY.

What is your life? You are a mist that appears for a little while and then vanishes.

JAMES 4:14

Most of us have gone on vacation before and asked a college student down the street to house-sit while we're away. The house-sitters know they don't own the place.

How wild would it be if we returned to our house to find they had knocked out a wall to begin renovations? We might not have explicitly told them not to renovate or throw block parties, but we bring them in with the understanding that the house isn't their playground. They didn't buy it and it's not their place to do whatever they wish. They're overseers until the owners come back, that's all.

I like to think of our lives the same way. We didn't earn this life. We don't own our bodies or the world in which we find ourselves. Out of the overflow of God's love, He created us and gave us the opportunity to take care of a small space in the world for a while. He gave us gifts and bodies and belongings, all entrusted to us for a time so we could give love to more people. It's actually a huge responsibility when you think about it. We were entrusted with God's precious creation so we could preserve what's beautiful and welcome more people into a life of abundance.

If you find yourself giving in to a sense of greed and entitlement, remember the world isn't ours for the taking. We're just stewards meant to pass it on better than we found it. We've been given a gift to be built upon and shared. All we can do in exchange is give it away.

What can you do today to leave something better than you found it?

WHATEVER YOU HAVE TO GIVE, DO IT LAVISHLY. THE AMOUNT DOESN'T MATTER TO GOD, BUT THE HEART DOES.

Whoever has will be given more, and they will have an abundance. Whoever does not have, even what they have will be taken from them.

MATTHEW 25:29

There's a story in the Bible about a widow who gave a small amount of money, and Jesus said she gave more than those who gave a lot. To Jesus, the widow's "mites" were worth more to the kingdom of heaven than all the gold bars in Fort Knox. Why is that? It's probably because God cares more about the heart of the giver than the actual amount.

How should we give our "time, talents, and treasure" to the people around us? How should we give our love? These are real questions we all have at some point. If we're being honest, most of us live with the fear that there isn't enough to go around, and we have to fight to get what's ours. In a culture that thrives on consumerism, we're suckers for believing we don't have enough of whatever someone is trying to sell us. We start to believe we need more money, more education, more dish soap, or more attractive qualities than the person next to us, and it's easy to give way to these fears and store up, save, and withhold.

Without realizing it, this affects the way we give our love away too. We love people by giving away our time, our attention, our money, and our personal space. And in a world where we're told to store up and gain more in order to get ahead, it's easy to slip into fear that we'll run out if we're not careful.

Whatever you have to give, give it lavishly and generously. Be a little reckless with your love. We're rivers, not reservoirs. God sees the golden heart that gives sacrificially, no matter the amount.

What reckless act of love can you do today?

WE SHOULDN'T SAY EVERYONE'S INVITED IF WE'RE GOING TO ACT LIKE THEY'RE NOT WELCOME WHEN THEY COME.

A certain man was preparing a great banquet and invited many guests. At the time of the banquet he sent his servant to tell those who had been invited, "Come, for everything is now ready."

LUKE 14:16–17

We've all attended a holiday with friends or family when we knew we weren't really wanted. The moment you walk in the door, you see forced smiles and hear the fake tone of voice that sounds like a news anchor trying to convince you they care. We know we're a nuisance before we sit down at the table. We all know what it's like to be invited out of a sense of obligation. It can be spotted in an instant.

The same thing happens in our churches too. People feel like they're supposed to invite everyone because perhaps they read a story in the Bible about a wedding feast and inviting everyone to it. Here's the problem: they don't know what to do when people take them up on the offer. We don't know what to tell the kids about the person who uses salty language because they don't know the Christian speak or the one who expresses their love in ways we don't approve of.

We tell people to "come as they are," but only if they'll change enough to make us comfortable once they arrive. That's not how love works. Love says we need you even more if you're different from the rest of us. Love says everyone has something to teach us, and God will use people from the edges to expand our understanding of His grace right in the middle of where we live. Love says everyone who's invited is truly wanted.

We're meeting people at the starting line, not the finish line. We shouldn't say everyone's invited if we're going to act like they're not welcome when they come.

Who have you been treating like they're not welcome?

NOVEMBER 4

PICKING A FIGHT IS EASY. LOVING EACH OTHER WHEN WE DISAGREE IS HOW WE GROW.

Love your enemies, do good to those who hate you, bless those who curse you, pray for those who mistreat you.

LUKE 6:27-28

We have a family friend who exploded our understanding of love with her baking. She read Jesus' words about loving your enemies, and she started praying about what it might look like for her to love enemies in her everyday life. She knew enemies aren't like villains in the movies; they're the ones we gossip about because we're jealous or the ones who disagree with us about things close to our hearts.

She decided to start baking things for people who got under her skin. She baked cookies for the woman who made her feel like a bad parent. She dropped off a cake for the neighbors who did loud yardwork at seven o'clock on Saturday mornings. She baked fresh bread for a family friend who posted offensive comments on social media.

No one knows she bakes things for people who get under her skin, because she doesn't announce it. It's not a passive-aggressive statement where she gives baked goods and everyone knows what she really means. It's just her quiet way of actively loving people she would be quick to write off if she wasn't intentional.

Picking a fight is easy. Loving each other when we disagree is how we grow. When Jesus told us to love our enemies, He challenged us to draw close to the people we're tempted to push away. He knew nothing would change hearts and minds more than selfless love for other people.

Go for the ones who get under your skin, and experience the kind of love Jesus talks about.

Who gets under your skin? How can you treat them differently today?

DON'T LET YOUR ASSUMPTIONS ABOUT PEOPLE KEEP YOU FROM ENCOUNTERING JESUS IN THEM.

You are no longer foreigners and strangers, but fellow citizens with God's people and also members of his household, built on the foundation of the apostles and prophets, with Christ Jesus himself as the chief cornerstone.

EPHESIANS 2:19–20

Over the years, I've become friends with a lot of people who are or have been in poverty. Some of them live in other countries, and some live here in America, but all of them ended up in poverty for reasons outside their control. They were given a poor education or no education at all. Some were arrested for small crimes as teenagers, and their records made it difficult to get a job for the rest of their lives. There are a lot of reasons people end up in a rough place, but all of them need the help of a community to get them back on their feet.

It's easy to have opinions about people who need help. You hear people from a relational distance say that "helping hurts," or they wonder aloud why unemployed people don't work a little harder to get a job. But when you come alongside people and walk with them for a while, you learn that helping actually helps.

Relationships have the power to transform us in ways opinions never will. If we talk about a group of people without developing a relationship with them, we're bound to get it wrong. But when we make new friends, we find we're changed in the process. We might help them by connecting them with a job, and they might help us by exploding our preconceived notions about the disadvantaged so more love can get in. We find out we need grace for all the ways we had mischaracterized people.

If there's a group you've made some assumptions about, go make some new friends. You'll meet Jesus in one another.

Who have you made assumptions about? How can you reach out to them in friendship?

LOVE IS KIND. TREAT ONE ANOTHER LIKE WE'RE GOING TO BE SPENDING ETERNITY TOGETHER.

Love is patient, love is kind.

1 CORINTHIANS 13:4

There's a scene in movies when someone leaves a job they hate and smashes all the office supplies on the way out. If they're architects, they take a bat to all the models. If they're administrative assistants, they smash copy machines and steal a stapler. Usually some screaming or soapboxing is involved.

It's always exaggerated in the movies, but we do these kinds of things in our lives too. We hear about the "tell-all" book after a disgruntled executive leaves an organization. We see a friend hurt in a relationship turn to social media to slander the person who did it. We live with the illusion that we can cut ties with people without it affecting anyone for the long term. We think we can leave and build a different life with people who are easier to get along with and easier to love.

We've forgotten to live like we're going to be spending eternity together. When Jesus talked about the kingdom of heaven, He wasn't talking about a place somewhere up in the clouds with harps and chubby angels. He said heaven was coming to earth and invited us to put His teaching into practice. When we love the way He loved, forgiving our enemies and including those who have been pushed out, we bring a little more of heaven into the world.

When you think about it, if eternity is all the time *ever*, we're already a part of eternity. Love is kind. Let's start treating each other like we'll be together for eternity, starting now.

Who would you treat differently if you had an eternal perspective?

WE DON'T NEED TO MAKE AN ACCEPTANCE SPEECH TO RECEIVE GRACE OR A KEYNOTE WHEN WE GIVE A LITTLE. JUST LIVE GRATEFUL LIVES.

Give thanks in all circumstances; for this is God's will for you in Christ Jesus.

1 THESSALONIANS 5:18

A friend of mine was confirmed for a government position in which he would lead the initiative to curtail human trafficking in the United States and around the world. I was lucky enough to attend the swearing-in ceremony. As amazing as that was, my favorite part was the end where my friend was given the floor to say a few words. It wasn't an acceptance speech he made. It was one filled with genuine gratitude. He reflected on the cast of people who helped him get to that point and how they shaped him. It was really beautiful.

I'm sure we can all think of times when someone has done us a favor, maybe helped us get a job or loaned us some money. We call them in tears to say they'll never know how they changed our lives. Then we call them again.

I'm always a fan of sending cookies, but most people don't want others to feel indebted to them. We simply help each other out in life because we recognize that we need each other. We do what we can, hoping the person we help will do what they can. When we give people a hand up, nothing would bring us more joy than seeing them take advantage of opportunities to do the same for other people. We don't need to hear praise as much as we want to see them multiplying that love.

We don't need to make an acceptance speech to receive some grace or a keynote when we give a little. Living grateful lives and giving away what we received in equal measure is enough.

What are you grateful to God for today?

NOVEMBER 8

WHERE JOY IS A HABIT, LOVE IS A REFLEX.

We are therefore Christ's ambassadors, as though God were making his appeal through us. We implore you on Christ's behalf: Be reconciled to God.

2 CORINTHIANS 5:20

You don't have to even think about your first moves every morning. You turn on the coffee or pick up your cellphone from the nightstand. You feed the cat or crack open the door to see your kids. We do these things ritualistically because habits become hardwired into our brains and our bodies respond. It's the reason we can dial a friend on the phone without even thinking of the numbers we're pressing or pull out of our driveway and into our parking space at work without remembering much of the drive at all.

We're usually familiar with our physical habits, but how much thought do you give to your spiritual habits? I don't mean habits like praying or reading the Bible, though those are great. I mean habits of finding joy, hope, and peace. Jesus said we could have peace even if there's chaos all around us. He said we could be hopeful even when life looks pretty bleak. These are characteristics that take some practice to get right.

Jesus knew the habits of our hearts would lead to changes in the way we live. If we find peace within ourselves, we'll naturally become peacemakers in the world around us. When we pray with hope and look for it in the little things, we begin to walk in hope, and it spreads to the people around us. Where great joy is a habit, extravagant love is a reflex.

We won't love well if we're in the habit of being negative or cynical. Maybe you're thinking *I'm just a realist*. Just remember that God sees what is and what will be, and it usually starts with the hope we have inside. Practice plenty of that.

What habit of joy, hope, or peace can you start today?

NOVEMBER 9

FILL YOUR LIFE WITH GRATITUDE AND
YOU'LL SPILL OVER WITH LOVE.

I will praise God's name in song and glorify him with thanksgiving.

PSALM 69:30

They say you can divide the world into two types of people: those who see the glass as half full and those who see it as half empty. But I don't see this optimism or pessimism. To me, it's more about gratitude. Instead of one or the other, I tend to think, *Wow, I've got something in my glass.*

I have a friend who wakes up every day and lists ten things he's grateful for. It could be the sunrise or his family or the cup of coffee he's about to drink. It could be health, his spouse, or his favorite flavor of ice cream. Whatever is on the list is less important than making the list itself. When we take a moment to be grateful, we realize how much we have, and it leads to thankfulness.

Now, I'm not a Pollyanna. There are hard days, difficult circumstances, and tragic moments. We've all had them and been with friends through them. But I believe those are outnumbered by the things we can be grateful for.

Remember the time in the Bible when the disciples were trying to rank themselves and figure out who was going to sit closest to Jesus in heaven? "How full is my glass?" and "Is my glass better than the next guy's glass?" is what they were asking. Instead of giving in to our tendency to focus on what we don't have, Jesus simply says to us, "You have Me." And if that's not enough to fill you, nothing will be. Let's be grateful people, and the love of Jesus will spill out of our lives.

What's your outlook on your life right now?
How can you be more grateful?

THE WAY WE TREAT THE PEOPLE WE DISAGREE WITH THE MOST IS A REPORT CARD ON OUR FAITH.

You have heard that it was said, "Love your neighbor and hate your enemy." But I tell you, love your enemies and pray for those who persecute you, that you may be children of your Father in heaven.

MATTHEW 5:43–45

I've started a new practice that has revolutionized the way I see people I don't agree with. If I hear a pastor or politician say something really offensive, I send them a cake pop. I just scribble a note to say I was thinking about them and thought maybe they would enjoy a cake pop as much as I do. It's not a passive-aggressive thing. I can't lie, I just love cake pops. If someone lets it rip on social media, I send them a few Jolly Ranchers and tell them to have a great day. I love those too. It takes about five minutes. I figure people who attack others are probably pretty unhappy, and cake pops and Jolly Ranchers might brighten their day.

When Jesus told us to love our enemies, He wanted us to apply the term broadly. I know this because He also told us to love our friends and neighbors. Between our friends, neighbors, and enemies, that should include just about everyone. The problem is that we scoot around His command by just being "polite" to people who annoy us. They're not necessarily our friends or our enemies—they're just people we keep our distance from. They're watchdogs in a world where we all need a little more grace. They're the cynics where we need champions. They're just hard to be around.

It's a true statement that the most difficult people to love are usually the ones who need it most. Love doesn't dishonor others; it finds a way to lift them up even when they actively push you down. The way we treat people we disagree with the most is a report card on our faith. It's hard to know where to start, but we need to begin anyway. Why not send someone who's been difficult a cake pop? It couldn't hurt.

Who do you know who needs a cake pop?

WHERE LOVE FINDS US, IT WILL LEAD US.

Let your eyes look straight ahead; fix your gaze directly before you.

PROVERBS 4:25

When my friend Alice started following Jesus, she had no idea the path would lead her to a position of leadership at a company with thousands of employees. But she took her faith into her leadership role, and now she tries to make all her employees feel loved and wanted at work. A lot of these people would never go to church, but they get to see Jesus every day because they see how Alice treats everyone around her. The same can be true for all of us, no matter what role we find ourselves in.

Following Jesus looks different for each of us. A lot of people think they'll have to move across the world to become a missionary or start homeschooling their kids if they get serious about following Jesus. But He didn't create us to fit into molds that would have us all turn out the same. He created us with special gifts and passions that are uniquely suited to meet different needs in the world. We don't need to compare different paths to decide which one's right, because God already said He wants us on the ones that lead to Him.

Don't let the path of other people's lives make you second-guess your own. There are millions of people, from all walks of life, who God wants to meet with His message of love. If you take Jesus to the people around you, and I take His love to the ones around me, we'll cover a lot more ground.

**In what ways have other people's paths
distracted you from your own?**

THE MEASURE OF THE GOOD GOD IS DOING IN OUR LIVES ISN'T ALWAYS HOW WE'RE FEELING ABOUT IT.

My Father is always at his work to this very day, and I too am working.

JOHN 5:17

If you've ever walked with someone through recovery from substance abuse, you know detox is one of the hardest and scariest parts of the process. When people first stop turning to their addiction, they go through withdrawals, and it can cause them to feel paranoid, angry, anxious, and depressed. Some people sweat profusely, and others can't sleep a wink. No one ever feels better the week after they enter recovery, but enduring the pain is the only path to life. It means toxins are leaving the body so it can begin to heal.

When we try to measure our spiritual health based on how we feel, we usually end up with a wrong diagnosis. We've all tried to find our identity in the wrong places, whether it's success or money or performance or approval. And when we take Jesus up on His offer to put Him above everything else, we go through a sort of detox.

We have to give up some things we've come to depend on. It means we're being nurtured back to spiritual health because we weren't created to find our worth by comparing ourselves to other people, but it takes some time to get used to God's way of love.

The measure of the good God is doing in our lives isn't always how we're feeling about it. The pain might be a sign of progress, and if we stick with love long enough, we'll find out the fruit of it is life.

What good is God doing in your life right now?

NOVEMBER 13

WE OUGHT TO BE FIGHTING TO GET THE WORST PARKING SPOTS AT OUR CHURCHES.

A generous person will prosper; whoever refreshes others will be refreshed.

PROVERBS 11:25

There are few places like parking lots to bring out the worst in us. It's the only place where teenagers cut off elderly people without a second thought. People throw their arms up and signal out their windows, exasperated at the thought of someone else getting ten feet closer to the building. Parking lots show us what we're made of.

There's several churches I've been to where the people seem to be fighting over the worst parking spots. The staff, the pastor, the people all park as far away from the building as possible so another person can get a little closer. They don't make a big deal out of it either. In fact, no one really even knows. It's a beautiful picture of what the church is really about. These small acts signal a larger decision so many have made to follow Jesus' teaching of becoming servants, being the first to sign up to be last. Most of us will never face a choice to physically give our lives for another person. But we can die to ourselves by making small sacrifices, day in and day out, to put other people first.

Life becomes an adventure when we start to view every moment as an invitation to celebrate other people. If you make it a point to find opportunities to put others first, you'll never run out of chances. In a world where everyone competes for the best spot, sign up to be last and watch what happens next. And here's the best part: if we do it right, nobody will ever know.

Who can you celebrate today?

THE RIGHT THING WITH THE WRONG MOTIVE IS THE WRONG THING.

In everything, do to others what you would have them do to you, for this sums up the Law and the Prophets.

MATTHEW 7:12

When my kids were in junior high and high school, I got flashbacks of what it's like to be in an environment with an invisible scoreboard always keeping track of who's popular and who's not. Who has a date to prom and who will be at home watching television game shows with their parents. Who has a new pimple or who scored the winning basket. There's no tenure track to being accepted. Kids in those ages are trapped in a game where they're constantly wondering if they are in or out.

We might shrug it off when kids do it, chalking it up to immaturity, but we grownups are just as guilty of transactional relationships. People seek out those who are more successful or attractive and identify with them because it makes them feel better about their own image. Or we trade shallow flattery or professional connections in hopes of advancing our careers. Sometimes people give money simply so their names will show up on donor lists and they'll look more generous.

The right thing with the wrong motive is the wrong thing. When Jesus told us to love people, He wanted us to give ourselves away simply because other people are worth it. Jesus befriended people because He valued them, not because He wanted something from them. He gave to them because they were in need, not because He wanted anyone to notice. He knew real love was about lifting other people up so they could flourish, not so we'd look good in the process.

Don't be tempted by the allure of transactional relationships. God approached us with arms open wide, asking nothing in return, so we could show that same love to the people around us.

Who have you been treating like a transaction recently?

NOVEMBER 15

WE DETERMINE HOW MUCH INFLUENCE WE'LL HAVE WHEN WE DECIDE HOW AVAILABLE WE'LL BE.

The Word became flesh and made his dwelling among us.

JOHN 1:14

A lot of people don't know this about me, but I typically don't set meetings. As in, you can try to schedule a meeting with me and I probably won't put it on my calendar. There are a few scheduled things I didn't miss, like my wedding day or the groundbreaking ceremony for one of our Love Does schools. Beyond that, though, there's a reason I don't set meetings. It's because I want the people in my life to know they can have my attention anytime they need it. I just tell them to get ahold of me whenever it's good for them.

We can't love people unless we make it possible for them to get ahold of us. With all the technology we have, it's become easier to insulate ourselves. We can like a photo or make a comment and go months (or years) without having a real conversation.

But Jesus showed us another way by welcoming interruptions. Most of His interactions with other people happened when He was on his way somewhere else. He was usually stopped by someone in need, and rather than shrugging them off to keep up his pace, He always took the time to listen. He showed them they were important enough to take a detour from His plans.

If the God of the universe could stop what He was doing to hear the needs of other people, we can answer our phones. Go for a week without sending anyone to voicemail. It'll change your life.

We determine how much influence we'll have when we decide how available we'll be. Don't get so focused on your to-do list that you neglect those who cross your path along the way. Every time you answer the phone and say hello, you've just answered most of the questions people have about how much you care.

What will you do today to be more available to others?

JESUS JUMPED OUT OF HEAVEN FOR THE CHANCE TO SAVE YOU.

Give, and it will be given to you. A good measure, pressed down, shaken together and running over, will be poured into your lap. For with the measure you use, it will be measured to you.

LUKE 6:38

I read a story about a young girl diagnosed with a rare disease. Her days quickly went from going to school and playing in the yard to lying in hospital beds tangled with tubes. The doctors ran test after test and concluded she needed an extensive blood transfusion to survive. But finding a matching donor was going to be tough. The parents were tested, but the results came back negative. She had a little brother, and he was a match because they were family, which made him the best candidate. The parents kept this information to themselves until there were no other options.

One night while tucking him into bed, they told him. They didn't ask him directly if he would do the procedure, since that would be too much pressure. But he could read between the lines and said, "Can I have the night to think about it?" The next morning, he told his parents he would do it. The siblings were soon sharing a hospital room with tubes running between their beds. As the transfusion was about to begin, the little boy waved the doctor over.

"Yes?" the doctor said. The boy asked, "How soon will it be before I die?" You see, the little boy thought that by helping his sister, he would have to give up his own life. And he said yes anyway.

Few of us will ever have to face this kind of choice. But all of us will get the chance every day to do what it takes to get people what they need. Will it be hard? You bet. Will it be uncertain and sometimes scary? Of course. Jesus must have felt the same way. Yet when God gave Jesus the chance to give everything for us, He didn't hesitate. He jumped out of heaven to do it.

Who are you willing to sacrifice for?

EVERY TIME I TELL GOD ABOUT MY OPINIONS, HE ASKS ME ABOUT MY HEART.

That person is like a tree planted by streams of water, which yields its fruit in season and whose leaf does not wither—whatever they do prospers.

PSALM 1:3

When we have friends up to the lodge in Canada, sometimes everyone recognizes someone as an artist or a mystic or a poet. They're thoughtful and quiet. They listen and rub their chins a lot. Because I wake up waving my arms, I'm thankful for the contrast that is apparent when we have an artist-mystic-poet with us. We'll do these devotionals overlooking the inlet, and I'll ask this person to read a poem or a passage of the Bible. When they do it, it feels more meaningful and engaging. They make us all feel at ease and drawn into deeper waters. I have no idea how, but I'm grateful.

Because of people like this, I decided to spend some time in the psalms. David was a poet, and he kept it incredibly real about his hopes, fears, doubts, and questions. The psalms say things we're often too afraid to say out loud or too busy to notice. The psalms give us a vocabulary for sharing secret thoughts and teach us what hope looks like when we're having trouble finding it.

I think God gave us the psalms to remind us our hearts matter. In a world where ideas, doctrine, busyness, and success get so much recognition, we forgo an "inner life," and in doing so, we neglect our emotions. God wants a relationship with us. And relationships involve an emotional connection.

If your life is feeling wrung out and a little empty, turn to a poet or a musician who has tuned into the deeper things. Open up the psalms. They can help us feel our way back to God.

How can you nurture your inner life today?

NOVEMBER 18

LOVE BIG. PACK LIGHT.

A certain ruler asked him, "Good teacher, what must I do to inherit eternal life?"

LUKE 18:18

A well-off guy approached Jesus and asked him what it would take to get eternal life. He thought he had the means to earn his ticket, but Jesus surprised him: "Sell all your stuff, give to the poor, and follow Me." It sounds demanding, but Jesus was showing this guy the value of traveling with a light backpack.

If you were to take the backpack of your life and dump it onto your bed, what would you find? Is your job something you couldn't give up? What about that girlfriend or boyfriend? Or the house or city you live in? I know, this is a tough exercise. I really feel for this guy who was so bold to ask Jesus the question. He didn't get an easy answer—and I don't think we'll find easy answers either.

As followers of Jesus, we're invited to leave everything behind and follow Him. To travel light. But our nature and the world tug us back. Our insecurity loads us up with a bunch of things we don't need. We don't carry these because we need them; we pack them around because we have a hard time putting them down. I'm not suggesting that God wants us to explode our lives as we know them . . . but I also think He wants us to blow a couple of things up. I think He wants us to offload and walk away from anything that's keeping us from Him.

To follow Jesus, we should learn to love big and pack light. The less we carry of our worries, stuff, personal vendettas, and poisonous relationships, the freer we'll be to explore the frontiers of love.

What do you need to get rid of so you can travel lighter today?

LOVE CARES MORE ABOUT WHO'S HURTING THAN WHO'S WATCHING.

He looked around at them in anger . . . deeply distressed at their stubborn hearts.

MARK 3:5

We often talk about Jesus as the Savior or an extraordinary teacher, but we rarely talk about Jesus as a first-class troublemaker. The truth is, Jesus was always in trouble. He slipped away from His parents when He was young for a couple of days and got in trouble for it. The religious people in His day followed Him wherever He went, eager to catch Him in a lie or to witness Him breaking Hebrew laws. The reason they were trying to set Him up was simple. The Israelites had expanded on the original Laws God gave them directly. I'm pretty sure Jesus could pull rank, but He didn't.

On seven different occasions we know about, Jesus healed people on the Sabbath. It might not sound controversial to us now, but back then working on the Sabbath was punishable by death. Jesus didn't care. He did what His Father told Him to do. Sometimes in order to obey God you need to disobey Pharaoh. One day Jesus walked into the temple and saw a man with a withered hand, and He asked the religious leaders if it was better to do good or evil on the Sabbath, to save life or kill it. After He healed the man, the religious leaders went out and plotted how they would kill Him.

Jesus was an affront to the Pharisees because He was more concerned about people who were in desperate need than how the religious leaders were feeling about it. He was more concerned with helping people than staying in the leaders' good graces.

It can be tempting to base our behavior on the approval of the people around us. But love calls us to be more concerned about the vulnerable than other people's opinions about us. Love cares more about who's hurting than who's watching.

How is fear of others' opinions holding you back from living love like Jesus did?

NO ONE CAN TAKE FROM US WHAT WE'RE WILLING TO FREELY GIVE.

Give to everyone who asks you, and if anyone takes what belongs to you, do not demand it back.

LUKE 6:30

I love books. I love looking at them on my shelves and thinking about the lessons I learned from authors I respect. They're not like trophies—they're beautiful reminders. Lots of them have been signed by the authors, which makes them even more special to me.

I refuse to loan people books. I just give them to them instead. When I loaned books, I spent a weird amount of time worrying about whether I'd get them back. The person would move or accidentally lose it or use the paper to line the bottom of a bird cage. The fix was simple. Instead of fretting or asking about a book a few months later, I just tell them it's all theirs and ask them to give it to someone else when they're done. It's been one of the single most freeing things I've done.

Here's the thing: no one can take from us what we're willing to freely give. This is what Jesus was getting at when He said if someone tries to sue you for your shirt, hand over your jacket too. Instead of fighting back, trying to preserve what's rightfully ours, Jesus urged us to hold our possessions loosely because people are always more important—even people who wrong us. I don't think He wanted us to be distracted by keeping track of so many things—who owes us, who wronged us, who ignored us.

Truth be known, it's easy to hold things loosely when it's just books we've read, but it can be harder to give freely of more valuable things people take from us, like our reputation. When someone publicly does wrong by us, it's hard not to tear into their character in response or log the incident away to think about often. But Jesus said if someone slaps us on the cheek, offer the other one as well. It's more important to be like Jesus than to remember all who owe you a book, an apology, or more time.

In these situations, God knows what's going on, and He'll be the one to set things straight someday. Maybe we'll know about it; maybe we won't. But that's not the point. Our character will speak for itself, and love will drown out everything else. Our part of the deal is as easy as this: keep letting go of whatever is distracting us from Him.

What distractions are keeping you from Jesus?

LOVE DOESN'T NEED TO BE LOUD. IT JUST NEEDS TO BE MORE IMPORTANT TO US THAN OUR OPINIONS.

A time to be silent and a time to speak.

ECCLESIASTES 3:7

I was traveling for an event and had the television on in the morning while I was getting ready to leave the hotel. One of those sports talk shows was on, and some guys were passionately arguing about a quarterback's stats or a coach or whatever. I thought, *I wonder if this is how they talk all the time?* I imagined these guys at their homes around the breakfast table and the kids saying, "Dad, could you please just tone it down? You're ruining my Cheerios."

These people we see on television or in the news or on viral videos who seem to scream over everyone else—there's got to be a different side to them. I got to test this theory when I had the chance to get to know someone who does one of those news talk shows. Talk about opinionated. As we became friends, though, I realized my hunch was right. He was more nuanced, dynamic, personable, and kind than he often came across in his job. Once we became friends, I realized there was a lot more to him than the opinions he shared with the public.

Love doesn't need to be loud. It just needs to be more important to us than our opinions. Jesus had strong beliefs and He vocalized them often, but love was always His priority. We can afford to be wrong. We can even be loud once in a while. But keep it about love, not all the other noise in the world.

How can you use actions instead of words today?

WE TRY TO BARTER AND BARGAIN FOR LOVE. BUT GOD SIMPLY SAYS, "FREE HUGS."

Give to the one who asks you, and do not turn away from the one who wants to borrow from you.

MATTHEW 5:42

I have a good friend who I respect a lot. He goes downtown with a sign that reads "Free Hugs." He isn't kidding around. Every person who walks by him and wants one, gets one. He's polite, but even with the people who try to dodge him, if it's appropriate he'll give them a hug too. He probably knows they needed a hug the most.

It got me thinking about what happens when we decide our love isn't for everybody. What if our sign said Free Hugs and then had a list of qualifying conditions underneath it? What if the list had on it entire groups of people? What if it said no hugs for people who hold a particular view or behave in a way we disagree with? That wouldn't be so heartwarming, would it?

Are there people in your life who are counting on your unconditional love? When they see you, do they see you reading an unspoken list of requirements they have to meet to receive love and acceptance from you?

What God will do for us, if we're willing, is break down every barrier between us. He's demonstrated the kind of love that erases all the lists. He didn't hold anything back, and we shouldn't either.

God's not holding a sign that says Free Hugs, but He is calling out to us with a promise of freedom, acceptance, and love. As followers of Jesus, we can do the same for the people around us. The love we've been given is too big and too beautiful to be held back by our inhibitions or our old ways. Everyone gets a hug.

Who can you surprise today with unconditional love?

EVERYBODY'S INVITED TO MOVE TO THE KIDS' TABLE, WHERE JESUS IS.

Truly I tell you, unless you change and become like little children, you will never enter the kingdom of heaven.

MATTHEW 18:3

A holiday can hold a lot of conflicted feelings. It's a time of warmth and celebration, but sometimes the experience doesn't match the hope. We bring out the china that's gathered dust in our cabinets since last year's holiday gathering, and we cook old family recipes that make us nostalgic for a time when things seemed simpler than they do now. Sometimes, however, they can be just as complicated as they've always been.

While we're stressing out at the adult table about the weird relative or family dynamic, have you noticed there's no tension over at the kids' table where they've got paper cups for lemonade and plastic forks for mac and cheese? No one there wishes things were different, because cousins and apple pie are close by. Kids always bring an innocence to the party. They show us how to look past the mistakes people made this morning so we can have fun together in the afternoon.

If Jesus were at our holiday celebrations, I bet He would be at the kids' table. When He was asked complicated questions, He would pick up a child and place them on His lap, then tell everyone to have faith like them. It's how He responded to questions about heaven and how He responded to a fight about who was the greatest. He always pointed to the kids to lead the way.

We're all invited to move over from some of our big arguments to the kids' table, where Jesus is. We can choose to look past the rules we make up as we grow up. We can go past the surface conversations. We can say we're sorry, if that's needed. Do whatever it takes to get there. There's a small chair waiting for you.

How can you act more simply like a child today?

START WITH GIVING YOURSELF AWAY AND LET GOD TAKE CARE OF THE LOGISTICS.

They all ate and were satisfied, and the disciples picked up twelve basketfuls of broken pieces that were left over. The number of those who ate was about five thousand men, besides women and children.

MATTHEW 14:20–21

Because my family and I spend most summers in Canada, I thought it would be good to learn a little bit about the country. One of the fun tidbits I found is that Canada has the world's northernmost inhabited village. It's called Alert, and it's five hundred miles below the North Pole.

Imagine throwing a big party or concert in a place like Alert. It would be hard to figure out how to get there, but I'm sure we could all find our way. Then imagine trying to feed all the people who showed up. They might be able to bring enough oatmeal and dried fruit for the first few days, but at some point we'd need to refill. The logistics would make it tough to pull off.

This is what Jesus was up against when He and his friends got off a boat in a remote village and found more than five thousand people in need. It wasn't as remote as Alert, but the transportation challenges were fierce, and when it came time to feed them, the disciples opted to send them away. They couldn't problem-solve this kind of need. They wanted someone else to deal with it.

But Jesus had a different plan in mind. He told them to fix the problem. You know the story. From a pretty small start, and a kid who just brought to Jesus what he had, God got everyone fed with baskets of food to spare. Sometimes it seems too complicated or inconvenient to give love away or meet people's needs with the little we have. But God's not asking you to figure out all the logistics; He's inviting you to give yourself away. Just bring what you've got. He'll take care of the rest.

What do you have right now that you can give away?

NOVEMBER 25

GOD DOESN'T TRY TO MOTIVATE US WITH LOVE. HE MOVES US WITH IT.

Esau ran to meet Jacob and embraced him; he threw his arms around his neck and kissed him. And they wept.

GENESIS 33:4

There's a story in the Bible about two brothers, Jacob and Esau, who had a falling out after the younger one (Jacob) stole his older brother's inheritance. After doing the deed, Jacob ran away to start fresh somewhere else. He got married, had kids, and acquired a bunch of livestock and land. And after a few decades passed, he and his family had to move on to another land.

But there was a problem. He would have to pass through where Esau and all his people had settled. He would have to face his brother. Jacob did what any of us would: he worried and planned and tried to appease his brother. He sent cattle, donkeys, sheep, goats, and camels ahead of him as a gift. He hoped the hundreds of animals might help smooth things out.

Shortly after, he received word from his servants that Esau was on the way with hundreds of men. Uh-oh. Jacob went back to the sketchbook to come up with a battle plan. This is where the plot twist happened. When Esau finally reached him, he ran to Jacob, threw his arms around his neck, and kissed him. They held each other and wept. Esau didn't want his brother's stuff. He just wanted his brother back.

This story gives us a taste of God's heart for you and me. God doesn't want to motivate or manipulate us. He wants His love to move us toward Him. Much like Esau, who wanted his brother back more than he wanted his stuff, God wants us to be His.

How hard is it for you to believe that God wants you? If you really believed it, how would you move toward Him?

FRESH IS BETTER THAN FROZEN. GIVE AWAY LOVE LIKE IT HAS A SHORT SHELF LIFE.

I will rain down bread from heaven for you.

EXODUS 16:4

The Bible tells how the Israelites wandered in the desert for forty years. I bet you know the narrative already. It's a story about obedience and disobedience, trust and dependence. The part that always stands out to me is the food God sent every morning called *manna*. Plenty of scholars have argued about whether it was more like saltines or pancakes, but I'm more interested in the shelf life.

When the manna came, God said to take only as much as was needed for the day. But some would fill their pockets after filling their baskets. *A little more won't hurt, just in case.* But God made the manna to be eaten, not stored. Any extra would go bad, but the next day, new manna would come again.

When God expressed His infinite love through Jesus, how many of us take as much as we can? But love isn't meant to be stored up. It's only real love when it's expressed in the lives of others. We can fill our lives with things like attendance at church, prayer breakfasts, and Bible studies. We can fill our lives with clothes, money, and possessions. God's not keeping count because He knows these things can't be stored up either. These things either find a way to express themselves in love or they go bad too.

Don't slip into a posture of receiving and accumulating. Don't stuff your pockets with things that will eventually go bad. Instead of scheming to get more and keep it, look at Jesus. Ask Him for enough love and resources to get to the next day. He has plenty more to give. When Jesus gave Himself over to death, that was love too. He invites us to depend on Him one day at a time and to give love away like we know more is coming tomorrow.

Take a moment to focus on being filled with God's love. What changes for you?

YOU CAN'T CLIMB YOUR WAY TO GOD'S FAVOR. JESUS CATAPULTED YOU THERE.

A man was there by the name of Zacchaeus; he was a chief tax collector and was wealthy. He wanted to see who Jesus was, but because he was short he could not see over the crowd. So he ran ahead and climbed a sycamore-fig tree to see him, since Jesus was coming that way.

LUKE 19:2-4

I've spent a lot of my life trying to be righteous. But there's a difference between being righteous and being like Jesus. If you only try to be righteous, you miss the big picture. Try to be like Jesus and you get righteousness as a by-product.

You know the story of Zacchaeus, that little guy who climbs a tree so he can see Jesus? He was a despised tax collector. He felt like he needed to get above the crowd to get noticed by the Savior—or maybe get out of slingshot range from his neighbors. Thankfully the story of Zacchaeus didn't end with him dangling in a tree, nor does mine or yours. Jesus pushed through the crowd, walked right up to Zacchaeus, and told him He would be his houseguest. The crowd grumbled at this favor shown to a tax collector, and I bet Zacchaeus nearly fell off the top branch.

Zacchaeus knew he was a cheat and his money was ill-gotten (a behavior he changed, by the way). You might think the point of the story is to be the opposite of the thieving Zacchaeus, but it's not. Instead of trying to stop a few bad behaviors, Jesus is more interested in our transformation—in helping us become more like Him.

Jesus freed us from the game of trying to earn His attention or favor. We've got it already. We can stop auditioning for a part we already have. When we accept how loved we are, we stop climbing, stop striving and pretending. When we become more like Him, we'll find righteousness comes with the deal.

In what ways have you been transformed this year?

CHOOSE FORGIVENESS AND GRACE BEFORE YOU NEED TO GIVE IT, AND PEOPLE WILL KNOW THAT, WITH YOU, THEY ALWAYS HAVE IT.

The LORD your God is the one who goes with you to fight for you against your enemies to give you victory.

DEUTERONOMY 20:4

When my daughter was still young, I tried to think of how I could encourage her when things went bad. When something goes wrong in our lives, it's hard to accept words of encouragement in the moment. We're too stuck on beating ourselves up when the disappointment is raw and fresh. Then I had a eureka moment. I decided I would write her letters in advance covering as many bad things that might happen as I could and bury them under a tree in our front yard for her to find later.

For instance, on one of the notes I wrote, "I forgive you for wrecking my car." It seemed odd writing it when Lindsey was as tall as my kneecaps, but guess what? It happened! So we dug up the note, and she knew I really meant it was okay because I had forgiven her more than a decade before.

Instead of waiting to pounce when people make mistakes, what if we geo-cached some grace? In a world where everyone is constantly told how they screwed up, what if we were the ones telling people, "Whatever happened, I still love you."

When people think of Switzerland, they think of peace and banks and yodeling sheep. Whenever countries go to war, they sign the peace treaty there. Switzerland cornered the market on being friends with the whole world.

When people think of me, I want them to know they can bank on grace. I want to be more like Jesus, who already wrote the letter saying I was forgiven no matter how big the mistake.

What encouragement from God do you need today?

THE BEST WAY TO EXPERIENCE OUR FAITH IS TO DO WHAT JESUS DID.

Now you are speaking clearly and without figures of speech. Now we can see that you know all things and that you do not even need to have anyone ask you questions. This makes us believe that you came from God.

JOHN 16:29–30

When I first started following Jesus, people started trying to teach me things about faith. They said phrases like "Jesus died for your sins so you could be saved." I didn't really know why He had to die or what it meant to be "saved," but I figured it was an extraordinary act of love nonetheless. I've certainly learned a lot over the decades about Jesus and Christianity, but I'm not trying to become a theologian. I'm trying to be more like Jesus and follow the example of His life.

I find most of the big Christian words thrown around in some faith communities distracting, so I don't use them. I try to speak as plainly as I can so I can understand what I mean and so everyone else around me can too.

I think God understands that we need more than mere book knowledge and insider phrases to understand Him. He gave us the Bible, and then He became a living example of it. He chose to be born and experience toothaches and fatigue, exclusion and oppression, homelessness and poverty. He also experienced joy and laughter and rich friendships.

Through all His human years, Jesus showed us how to live. He modeled love for us in a way we couldn't grasp just by reading or studying. He didn't come just to talk to people about heaven. He came to heal people in the here and now too.

Love found His way to us so we could find our way to one another. He said to follow His example of laying His life down for His friends so other people would come to understand what it's like to be held and protected by love. His life tells us everything we need to know about love. Our lives can teach us a bunch about our faith. Learn as much as you want about faith, but don't overlook the joy that comes from living it.

**What can you do today to change your focus
from mere words of faith to action?**

THE WAY WE LOVE DIFFICULT PEOPLE LETS EVERYONE KNOW THE BABY IN THE MANGER ISN'T JUST A DECORATION.

If you love those who love you, what reward will you get? Are not even the tax collectors doing that?

MATTHEW 5:46

When my kids were little, we used to pile into the car around Christmastime to take a tour of the lights around our neighborhood. We poured hot chocolate into thermoses and grabbed our favorite Christmas music. At a top speed of about five miles per hour, we rolled by homes that lit up the sky like the northern lights.

We always loved the nativity scenes. It's not every day you get to see baby Jesus in a front yard, so we delighted in the season that put Him front and center. After the tour, we always had a family chat about what it meant to show Jesus to people at Christmastime. Sure, He made an appearance in our Christmas pageants and decorations, but we knew decorations didn't start to tell the story.

We knew the way to show Jesus to people was to love the way He loved. When He went away, He said He was leaving His Spirit with us so we could become like Him and act like Him. It means we can love people who are excluded and alone during the holidays. It means we can love people who don't love us back, the ones who seem to find joy in antagonizing us.

The way we love difficult people lets everyone know the baby in the manger isn't just a decoration. When we look for opportunities to celebrate people who have wronged us, we show people a God who gave His life for those who wouldn't receive Him.

Who is on your list of those difficult to love this year?

DECEMBER

DECEMBER 1

LATER IN HIS LIFE, I BET THE INNKEEPER WISHED HE HAD MADE MORE ROOM FOR JESUS.

While they were there, the time came for the baby to be born, and she gave birth to her firstborn, a son. She wrapped him in cloths and placed him in a manger, because there was no guest room available for them.

LUKE 2:6–7

Right before Jesus was to be born, His soon-to-be parents had to make the trek from Nazareth to Judea to register for a national census. The trip had to have taken them a while, especially since Mary was nine months pregnant. When they arrived in Bethlehem, eager to find a place to stay the night, the innkeeper said there was no room for them. So Mary and Joseph spent the night in a stable, on haystacks next to donkeys and sheep. And that's where the Savior was born.

I often wonder how long it was before the innkeeper knew what he had missed. When he heard about the Messiah from Nazareth, who brought dead people back to life and healed lepers of their disease, I can't help but think he regretted his choice to turn them away. He had to have relived the night in his mind, coming up with ways he could've made room for the Savior of the world.

As busy people in the twenty-first century, we can point to a lot of reasons to explain why we don't make more room for Jesus and the people He loves in our lives. We've got bills to pay and kids to raise and responsibilities pulling us in every direction, but there's only one thing God has asked us to do: to love Him—and in doing so, love the people around us.

Let's avoid the innkeeper's mistake. Let's do some renovations to make room for the Messiah while we still have time.

**What do you need to move out of your life
to make more room for Jesus?**

DECEMBER 2

THE ANGELS EXPLAINED THINGS TO JOSEPH AFTER HE'D TALKED TO MARY, NOT BEFORE. BE PATIENT WHEN YOU DON'T UNDERSTAND.

Suddenly a great company of the heavenly host appeared with the angel, praising God and saying, "Glory to God in the highest heaven, and on earth peace to those on whom his favor rests."

LUKE 2:13-14

Do you ever feel like it would've been so much easier to follow God if we had been alive when the Bible was written? We sit in silence for long periods of time, hoping God will say something, but we're often left wondering if we're just hearing our own thoughts. We go on retreats at cabins in the woods and fill up journals, but it's hard to know when you've heard from God. It's easy to wish you could have been one of the people in the Bible who God spoke to through angels or thunder or burning bushes or clouds or even a donkey once.

A relationship with God has always required faith. Sometimes we re-imagine the stories in the Bible, and it seems easier to follow Jesus in our revised version. But think about what it must've been like to be Joseph. When Mary told him she was going to have a baby, he hadn't heard anything yet from the angels. There was no sign from God that the virgin birth was all God's plan, no awareness of the miracle to come. I bet it just felt like a great big mess to Joseph. Be patient when things get weird. Joseph held on for the ride when things didn't make sense, because he loved Mary and he trusted God.

Unfortunately, life is full of open loops. We never have all the answers we want when we need them (or think we need them). Trusting in God when you don't have all the answers is exactly how Joseph welcomed Jesus to the world. We can welcome Him every day in the same way—with patience.

What are you trusting Jesus for this season?

IT'S EASY TO GET WRAPPED UP IN HOLIDAY EXPECTATIONS. REMEMBER THAT LOVE IS ON EVERYONE'S WISH LIST.

Do not store up for yourselves treasures on earth, where moths and vermin destroy, and where thieves break in and steal. But store up for yourselves treasures in heaven, where moths and vermin do not destroy, and where thieves do not break in and steal. For where your treasure is, there your heart will be also.

MATTHEW 6:19–21

Here's how a Christmas list shifts over a person's life: when we're young, we make the list; when we're middle-aged, we fund the list; when we're old, no one can figure out what should be on the list.

I think for all of us, the first phase is the best. When you're a kid you know exactly what you want for Christmas. You make different categories to show Santa which gifts are the priority and which ones he can cut if he needs to get to the next house. Eventually we graduate from the list-making stage right around the time we fund Santa's list.

But as we get older, we don't really value stuff on Christmas morning. Sure, it's fun to unwrap a present, but what we want is more availability, connection, and more love. As gifts decline in value, things like time together and family traditions become the real present.

None of us wants to get to the finish line and realize all we're carrying is a bunch of stuff. That all goes to Goodwill anyway. As Christmas approaches, don't get bogged down in the shopping list. Don't get lured by advertisements saying you'll find happiness buying one more thing or that there is a toy your kid "has to have." Get weighed down by the impressive weight of love instead. That's the real doorbuster. Show the people around you what they mean to you. Give a lot of love and ask for nothing in return. That's a gift worth giving. It's on everyone's wish list.

What gifts of love can you put on your shopping list for the people in your life?

DECEMBER 4

GO BIG ON LOVE.

Remember this: Whoever sows sparingly will also reap sparingly, and whoever sows generously will also reap generously.

2 CORINTHIANS 9:6

I know a guy named Rich who runs an organization that came up with one of my favorite ideas for Christmas. They know most of us already have more than we need, and we don't need to add to the clutter in our closets. But kids all over the world don't have basic necessities like clean water or heaters in the winter. So they came up with a gift idea where, instead of swapping gifts with close friends, people can buy gifts for kids around the world in a loved one's name. You can buy a sewing machine for a woman in Rwanda or medical supplies for kids in Aleppo.

Rich is a genius because not only does he help meet the needs of people in the world this way, he also reminds us all kids are God's kids. I see Rich loving like Jesus because he sees the whole world—people near and far, known and unknown—as people worth loving. The holiday season is not just a time for giving, which is definitely good. But it's for stretching our comfort zones in how we give and who we give to. If we want to love like Jesus, think about those struggling in other countries or other neighborhoods in our own cities.

Jesus didn't tell us to just love the people who are close to us or to love when it's convenient. He told us to love everybody, always.

No one has to go without if we're all generous with what we've been given. Go big on love.

What are you going to go big on this season?

DECEMBER 5

GETTING ANNOYED OR LOSING PATIENCE IS NORMAL. GIVING AWAY LOVE REGARDLESS IS HOLY. BE LIKE JESUS THIS HOLIDAY SEASON.

Anyone who loves their brother and sister lives in the light, and there is nothing in them to make them stumble.

1 JOHN 2:10

As the year winds down and the holidays wind up, parents everywhere are planning their road trips to see family. Those who have braved this trek know what it's like to hear timeless phrases such as, "Are we there yet?" and "I'm not touching you," and "I have to go to the bathroom." (This last one usually happens five minutes after the last stop.)

When everyone in the car is hungry and patience runs thin, we're all reminded about our limitations on love. Yes, there's a deep-rooted, unshakable love in theory. But when the milk spills on the new upholstery, it's hard to remember.

In the weeks ahead, a lot of us will find ourselves with family. Some you might like *a lot*. Others you might trade for a set of golf clubs if you could. No matter where we go, a few people will get under our skin. And guess what—we're those people too.

Don't let minor details make you veer off course. God has an unending, deep, abiding love for you, even when you spill the milk, drop the special plate, knock over the vase, or miss the turnoff. Go into this holiday season ready to show a deep love for others that doesn't get irked by the little stuff. If you want to go big, decide you won't let the big stuff bug you either. And remember, just like a real human family, when you become a part of God's family, you'll be around people who are on a trip. They might be in a moment of anticipation, they might be in a moment of dread, they might be dealing with crippling self-doubt. Jesus came to show them love in every moment—and it's often through us.

What commitments will you make to love the people in your family well?

WHO WE ARE AFTER CHRISTMAS MORNING SAYS A LOT ABOUT WHO WE FOUND IN THE MANGER.

You will seek me and find me when you seek me with all your heart.

JEREMIAH 29:13

Christmas Day might just be my absolute favorite day of the year. All my kids are within arm's reach, Sweet Maria is happy as a clam getting preparations ready, the house is warm and festive and smells like cookies out of the oven. But more than the traditions, Christmas has this special power in my life where the invitation to encounter the Savior feels especially fresh and new. Every year, without fail, a few of my friends are in a tough spot during Christmas though. A loved one died, or a relationship ended. A job was lost, or a project failed. I've had a few hard Christmases, too, so I understand. I bet you can relate as well.

But here's what I've come to learn: if we see Christmas as a season of nostalgia, we'll be disappointed. If we only want warm fuzzies, presents, and stuffing, the satisfaction won't last. But if we encounter the Savior, everything changes.

A lot of people thought Jesus was a good teacher and He had great insight about how to live. But if Jesus is just a great teacher or a cultural identity, your life probably won't change much. Others thought He was a really kind man, and He was, but this alone wouldn't have the power to reshape history or your heart.

If, however, you find a Savior in the manger, you'll leave with a sense of purpose. If you find a God who gave up everything to come live with us and die for us so we could finally get a taste of grace, you'll want to give that grace to everyone you encounter. Who we are after Christmas morning says a lot about who we found in the manger.

What will you do to focus on Jesus this month?

FOR GOD TO GIVE AWAY LOVE, HE HAD TO UNDERSTAND SADNESS. IF THIS TIME OF YEAR IS HARD, LEAN INTO A SAVIOR WHO KNOWS WHAT IT'S LIKE.

Rejoice with those who rejoice; mourn with those who mourn.

ROMANS 12:15

Somehow, this time of year makes it easier to be happy and easier to be sad. It just depends on what's happening in your life. If you find yourself in a hard spot right now, I want to remind you that love still wins and God does not overlook those who mourn.

Maybe you lost a loved one this year or one of the headlines splashing the evening news actually happened to you. Maybe you lost a home or a job, or you're praying for a child to end the straying and come back home. Perhaps it was a relationship that went sideways, and you're feeling terribly lonely. Those are real hurts.

In those circumstances, God says evil will not win.

God wants to remind us we're remembered even if our circumstances are folding in over our heads. God says He's near to the brokenhearted. He says He surrounds those who mourn. When we're down, God understands our sorrow and kneels down next to us.

It's okay to be sad. In fact, mourning is a brave thing to do. It means we're holding our hurt rather than hiding from it, putting it in our cupped hands for God to hold with us. Mourning is a bold stare-down with evil while God declares evil cannot have another inch. That's why He sent Jesus to fight for us, to protect us, to take the brunt of evil's sting.

Our strength is made up of stuff stronger than threats, disease, and loss. If something is weighing you down, hope in Him can set your eyes upward. Let His love wipe away your tears.

What do you need to mourn this year?

IF YOU DON'T STOP, YOU CAN'T CONNECT. WHATEVER YOU'RE WORKING ON, BE SURE TO SET IT DOWN EVERY ONCE IN A WHILE.

May these words of my mouth and this meditation of my heart be pleasing in your sight, LORD, my Rock and my Redeemer.

PSALM 19:14

It seems like Christmas comes earlier and earlier every year. When I start to see holiday garland shelved with the Halloween candy, I'm wondering if we've gone too far. The day after Thanksgiving is when everything explodes. People fly out after the turkey is eaten, apparently to bust down some doors. If you work, the weeks in between Thanksgiving and Christmas are all about hitting numbers and landing all the planes so you can end the year in peace.

To put it mildly, the Christmas season can be *busy*. I think we all feel the busyness rob us of the true purpose lying underneath. It's supposed to be a time of rest and connection, a time to reflect on who Jesus is and how much He loves us. Don't shuffle past the manger like they do with visitors seeing the *Mona Lisa* at the Louvre. Christmastime should feel more like the Sabbath than shopping sprees.

God created us to live with certain rhythms. He made day and night, a season to plant and a season to harvest, a time to work and a time to rest. When He told us to take a Sabbath just like He did, He wasn't making up rules to try to steal our joy. He knew the fruit of rest was joy. He knew breaks from work would give us more time to connect with one another. Rest is the soil where love grows.

Getting things done is necessary. But if you have more checklists than times with friends, you're probably missing something.

How will you slow down this month to spend time focused on what matters most to you?

WHEN JESUS MADE CHRISTMAS, HE DID IT FOR A BUNCH OF BEGGARS LIKE US.

All they asked was that we should continue to remember the poor,
the very thing I had been eager to do all along.

GALATIANS 2:10

I know a lot of families who use the holiday season to introduce their kids to people in need. They serve at a soup kitchen or hand out socks at the homeless shelter. I think it's terrific that people get more attuned to the needs of others during the holidays. It reminds me a lot of Jesus. Before He came, God could look down on us and see a bunch of helpless beggars, people who couldn't possibly pull it together in order to become friends with Him. Instead of avoiding us all, God decided to jump right in.

Don't avoid people who look like they've been on the streets for a while—go to them instead. I don't know if it's our fear, or discomfort, or a sense of helplessness, but the people who need human connection the most are often the ones we avoid.

Jesus spent His whole life engaging the people most of us have spent our whole lives trying to avoid. He spent His time with the people who cheated others out of money, with those who smelled bad and didn't have a permanent home. Even when He knew they would betray Him, He sought their friendship.

During the holidays, we'll scurry around town buying lots of stuff and making new memories. But we'll pass a lot of people who don't have access to that kind of holiday experience. Expand the circle of generosity, and you'll have the kind of Christmas Jesus made for us.

What will you do this month to intentionally love the down-and-out?

USING WORDS AS WEAPONS IS EASY WHEN WE DISAGREE. CHOOSING TO LOVE INSTEAD IS THE LIFE JESUS POINTS US TOWARD.

You have heard that it was said, "Love your neighbor and hate your enemy." But I tell you, love your enemies and pray for those who persecute you, that you may be children of your Father in heaven.

MATTHEW 5:43–45

Unfortunately, negativity happens naturally in each one of us. And what happens naturally is usually the easiest thing to do. It's easy to form opinions that validate our experience, surround ourselves with voices that confirm them, and take shots at those we've decided are wrong.

But Jesus invites us into a different way to live. He tells us to *love our enemies*. When I first started following Jesus and saw that, I was like, *Wow. Okay. Um, how do I do that?*

In calling us to love our enemies, Jesus challenged us to resist our natural tendency to separate the world into people like us and not like us. We might not see those we disagree with as "enemies," but they fire us up the most. They're the ones we're prone to slander and harbor negative thoughts about. We might not be going to literal war with those on the "other side," but we do battle when we tear down rather than build up. We wage war with words rather than weapons.

True Christianity is not easy. It's more straightforward to follow a certain standard of behaviors. But following Jesus is about transformation, not mere compliance—and when Jesus said "love your enemies," He knew only transformation could get us there. Will we do this perfectly? Nope. When we ask God to show us how, though, He'll always point us toward His Son and say, "Just do what He did." The best way to love your enemy is to lay down your words and pick up the love of Jesus instead.

Who's on your list of "enemies," and what can you do to draw closer to them in love?

DECEMBER 11

FROM A MANGER IN BETHLEHEM, GOD LEANED OVER THE WHOLE WORLD AND SAID, "IT'S YOUR MOVE."

For God so loved the world that he gave his one and only Son, that whoever believes in him shall not perish but have eternal life.

JOHN 3:16

I was in college when I first laid eyes on Maria. I knew the moment I saw her that she would be my wife. The only problem was, she hadn't spoken to me yet. My task was to get her attention so she could get to know the man who would become her husband.

Luckily, Valentine's Day was around the corner. My plan was to turn several door-sized cardboard sheets into an oversized Valentine's Day card that said, "Maria, will you be my Valentine?" Then I showed up unannounced at her work to make the ask. She was mortified—not even a little impressed. It took about six months to win back her respect, but at least I had been clear. She knew my feelings about her and my intentions toward her. The ball was in her court.

When Jesus was born, God made His love clear. When He chose to live with us, to experience life as one of us and suffer alongside us, He was telling us in the flesh about a love for us that's stronger than fear, stronger than death. And then it was up to us to decide how we would respond to His love.

It's as if, from a manger in Bethlehem, God leaned over the whole world and said, "It's your move." Just like the ball was in Maria's court once I made my intentions clear, it's now up to us to decide how we'll respond to God's expression of love for us. We can go on like it never happened, or we can step toward the love that set the whole world in motion.

As you take a minute to reflect on God's love for you, what changes in you?

DECEMBER 12

GOD GAVE THE WISE MEN A DIRECTION, NOT A BUNCH OF INSTRUCTIONS. IT WASN'T A BUSINESS TRIP. IT WAS AN ADVENTURE.

The angel said to her, "Do not be afraid, Mary; you have found favor with God."

LUKE 1:30

The story of Christmas tells us a lot about how God rolls. When the angel came to Mary to tell her what would happen, that message didn't come with a playbook of everything that would come after. When Joseph learned about his coming son, the angel didn't sit him down to explain the miracle or how to navigate the situation. Joseph and Mary were asked to trust, no more and no less. The same goes for the wise men. God showed them a star as a compass, but that was about it.

In our age of on-demand instructions, it's hard to accept the vague sense of direction we get in our spiritual lives. God doesn't give us the play-by-play of what's to come when He tells us to go. He just reminds us to pack light and take a lot of love.

God gave the wise men a direction, not a bunch of instructions. They knew the prophets had said the Messiah would be born in Bethlehem, so they knew He had come when they saw His star hanging just above the place of His birth. They didn't hear the voice of God, and there were no angels telling them what to do next. They just had a star to point them toward the Savior.

Don't get discouraged just because you don't have all the answers. God isn't sending you on a business trip. He's inviting you to join Him on an adventure. It always leads you to Jesus.

How do you sense the adventure Jesus is calling you to as you look toward the new year?

PRAY LIKE NOBODY'S LISTENING. GIVE LIKE NOBODY'S WATCHING. LOVE LIKE NOBODY'S COUNTING.

Do not conform to the pattern of this world, but be transformed by the renewing of your mind. Then you will be able to test and approve what God's will is—his good, pleasing and perfect will.

ROMANS 12:2

No matter how old you are or where you live, there's one thing I've found to be true: the world is pushing us to conform. I know we should not be like the world, which is true, but I'm thinking of something different. Wherever we are, the people around us are trying to figure out whether we fit in or not. Sadly, all of us are being nudged toward acceptance, and that often looks like sacrificing some things we shouldn't.

I think this is most apparent in junior high where everyone walks through the doors hoping they don't get noticed, just wanting to fit in. As we grow, we're not much different.

One aspect of living more like Jesus is getting comfortable with being different, with living outside the norms and risking a life of love. Here's where it gets confusing. The world tells us if we give our possessions away to those in need, we'll have nothing left. Jesus tells us whatever we do for the least of us we have done for Him. The world tells us if we give our love away freely, we'll be taken advantage of. Jesus tells us to love our enemies and give them the clothes off our backs.

If you want to move toward a life that looks more like Jesus, be weird. The world has enough of the same ol' same ol' going on. God is waving you on toward something different, something that will catch the world's attention with His love.

**In what ways are you willing to be different
for the sake of loving like God loves?**

FAITH WITH DOSES OF LOVE AND COURAGE WILL KNOW WHAT TO DO WHEN THE TIME COMES.

Esther sent this reply to Mordecai: "Go, gather together all the Jews who are in Susa, and fast for me. Do not eat or drink for three days, night or day. I and my attendants will fast as you do. When this is done, I will go to the king, even though it is against the law. And if I perish, I perish."

ESTHER 4:15–16

One of the strongest leaders in the Bible is a Jewish woman named Esther. She was an orphan who lived with her cousin, Mordecai, until she was chosen to marry the king of Persia. The king was a decent guy, but like a lot of people in power, he was surrounded by some bad guys. One of the bad guys had it out for Esther's cousin Mordecai, and he manipulated the king into ordering all the Jews to be killed.

As you would assume, Esther was devastated when she heard the news about her people. She prayed and fasted, hoping God would show her a way to rescue her people. And would you believe it? God showed her His plan to rescue her people—and she was the plan. She chose to risk her life by revealing her identity to the king because she believed she had been placed in her position by God just to make this one courageous decision.

When we see people make courageous decisions like Esther, it's clear their faith isn't just a set of principles they recite to stay in some kind of club. Their faith is the air they breathe to make it through the day. People who give away love in secret when it comes at a cost are motivated by a faith that runs deep.

Our actions show us the difference between what we really believe and what we just know. Faith with a dose of courage and love compels us to give ourselves away for the sake of other people.

**How do you sense God wanting to use
you for His purposes this week?**

DECEMBER 15

WE'LL BECOME WHAT WE ACCUMULATE
THE MOST OF. GATHER LOVE.

Do not be deceived: God cannot be mocked. A man reaps what he sows.

GALATIANS 6:7

In the decades I was a lawyer, I had the chance to see a few new, optimistic, eager lawyers turn a little sour. I think I know why. I've learned we become what we accumulate the most. These young guys thought they needed to argue with everyone like it was what made them valuable. They somehow believed if they got in enough disputes, they would be good enough advocates and make all their hard work worthwhile. Actually the opposite is true. What they had done over time is accumulate a boatload of people with hurt feelings and a sour attitude. They were around or had been the cause of a lot of pain, and bitterness had begun to consume them.

But the people who gather love throughout their lives become kinder, more gracious, more hospitable, and full of whimsy. The more love they gather, the more their loads lighten. Their response to the failures of others is always grace because the seeds of forgiveness they planted when they were young have grown with time.

The people we become are cultivated by small choices we make along the way. Plant forgiveness and grace like you'll never run out of seeds, and you'll never run out of love.

What are you sowing this month?

WE'RE BOUND TOGETHER BY LOVE, NOT A BUNCH OF OPINIONS.

God is love. Whoever lives in love lives in God, and God in them.

1 JOHN 4:16

When some buddies and I first started getting together for Bible Doing a few decades ago, we didn't know exactly where it would lead. We had been in Bible studies for years, and those were predictable and honestly not very inspiring. It felt a lot more like school or a self-help group than the life-changing adventure Jesus invited His friends into. It was predictable because it was familiar.

A few years into our Bible Doing, we felt like family. We got together every week and read the teachings of Jesus for a while. Then we went and did what He said to do together. We probably didn't agree on every controversial issue, but our group wasn't about agreeing on everything. It was about loving people together. We found our love for one another went deeper as we joined each other in loving other people.

Sometimes it's implied that you need to think like a group to be considered part of it. You have to go through classes about doctrine and sign statements of agreement in order to belong. But Jesus didn't walk by fishermen and say, "Drop your nets and come away to agree with Me." He told them to drop their nets and follow Him. He invited them to join Him in scheming ways to spread love across the globe.

We're bound together by love, not a bunch of opinions. Don't waste your time trying to convince people to agree with you. Band together in spreading love instead, and you'll find that the arguments that can tear us apart don't matter that much anymore.

How can you build deeper bonds with people in your life by loving others together?

THE BIRTH OF JESUS MEANS THAT FEAR LOST ALL ITS POWER. WHY DO WE KEEP GIVING BACK WHAT THE MANGER TOOK AWAY?

After Jesus was born in Bethlehem in Judea, during the time of King Herod, Magi from the east came to Jerusalem and asked, "Where is the one who has been born king of the Jews? We saw his star when it rose and have come to worship him."

MATTHEW 2:1-2

Right after Jesus was born, some wise men from the east went to Jerusalem to find Him. They saw His star and knew it meant the Messiah had come. Herod, the king, was furious. He felt threatened by Jesus because he knew this baby was more powerful than him. He ordered the wise men to go find Jesus and then report back with His location. Herod had evil plans in mind to put an end to Jesus' life.

The wise men were under the king's orders to share this information, but when they got to the manger where love lay fast asleep, everything changed. They knelt to the ground and offered gifts. Any fears they brought with them went away once they saw the face of love. The wise men tricked the king to save the life of Jesus. They went back to their home country by an alternate route. Sometimes in order to obey God, we need to disobey Herod.

Most of us will never have to fear for our lives the way the wise men did, but we still let fear get the best of us. Fear keeps us from following our passions because we're afraid we might fail. It keeps us from giving love away because we're afraid of vulnerability. We fear judgment and disapproval. We fear the unknown.

But just like the wise men who changed when they came face-to-face with love, we can put fear in its place. When we love people more than we fear failure, disappointment, and even death, love wins. We don't have to fear less. We need to love more.

**What can you do today to place the fears
you have at the feet of Jesus?**

THE FUTURE VERSION OF YOU IS BETTER AT SAYING NO AND EMPHATIC WITH SAYING YES.

We all, who with unveiled faces contemplate the Lord's glory, are being transformed into his image with ever-increasing glory, which comes from the Lord, who is the Spirit.

2 CORINTHIANS 3:18

The end of the year is a great time for reflecting on all that's happened during the last twelve months. If your life is like mine, it's a mix of unexpected surprises, milestones crossed, a few disappointments, and swinging at some curveballs. In addition to what did or didn't happen, think about what you did or didn't become . . . and whether that's the version of you that you're aiming for.

I like to think of my past self as last year's model, and my next self is the new and refurbished version of me. I might look the same, but I've changed a ton since Bob versions one through four. Along the way, I made sure I was always preparing the way for the next version too. I'm still doing this. And you know what that next version always includes more of? Love.

If you're paving the way for the next version of yourself, you'll never go wrong with adding more love to your heart and life. To do that, sometimes you need to make a little more space. Maybe you need to quit something. Sometimes being a quitter is exactly what we need, and the healthiest thing we can say are these two words: "I quit."

The next version of you is going to be amazing—the best one yet. To get there, you'll have dole out a lot of nos, but there's only one yes you need to be sure of. Say yes to the kind of love Jesus lived and died talking about.

What's the next version of you going to be like?

BE CAREFUL WHO YOU LISTEN TO.
BE CAREFUL WHAT YOU SAY.

As iron sharpens iron, so one person sharpens another.

PROVERBS 27:17

Whoever we are today, we didn't get here on our own. All the joy and whimsy or frustration and sadness we embody come from the influences of the people who have been in our lives along the way.

As you gather for the Christmas holiday, take a look around. Be honest. Did a relationship with someone leave some gaps in your life? It's okay—it's normal. What are those gaps, and do you need to have a conversation or find a friend to help you fill them? What if it's the opposite? Is there someone in the living room who played a big role but you've never told them the impact they've had? Put down the pumpkin pie, and go say thank you. Of all the people in your life, your family is the one group you don't get to choose. God's family is kind of the same way. Those who follow Jesus are a part of us whether we like it or not. What voice will you choose to have in others' lives?

We become whoever we trust the most says we are. If the people we look up to tell us we'll never amount to anything worthy of love, shame will fuel our interactions for most of our lives. But if the people we admire tell us our Creator is crazy about us, we'll grow into people who carry extra love with us everywhere we go. Be loud with your love and trust God will put the right people in your path.

How did people shape you this year?

WHAT WE DO IN LOVE WILL LAST. ALL THE REST WILL BLOW BY LIKE IT NEVER EVEN HAPPENED.

Let no debt remain outstanding, except the continuing debt to love one another, for whoever loves others has fulfilled the law.

ROMANS 13:8

The last time it snowed where I live in San Diego was December 13, 1967. There's been one other time since then when they said you could see snow flurries at seventeen hundred feet, but it's hard to make snowmen at seventeen hundred feet. My family always got excited when we traveled in the winter because we thought the odds for snow were improved. We would check the weather to see our chances and pack our hats and gloves in case. We were all disappointed when the flurries didn't stick to the ground.

A lot of the things we do in our lives don't stick either. We spend our time trying to get ahead in our careers so we can make more money so we can get more stuff, which won't hold our interest for long. We use our energy trying to win the approval of people who still don't know what it's like to be unconditionally loved and won't remember us. We spend most of our waking hours trying to make life safe, predictable, and comfortable, yet what we really want is adventure. We strive and chase and spin our wheels for things that won't last.

Love is the only thing that will last. Instead of using our time and energy to gain more attention, control our world, or get more stuff, let's spend it all on love. We don't want to reach the end of our lives and realize all our efforts melted away in an instant. Leave a legacy of love. The rest will blow by like it never even happened.

How will you invest in love these last few days of the year?

THE TRUE MEANING OF CHRISTMAS IS PUTTING OTHERS FIRST. DON'T GET SWEPT UP IN THE HYPE. STAY FOCUSED ON THE HELP YOU CAN GIVE.

Be devoted to one another in love. Honor one another above yourselves.

ROMANS 12:10

If you've ever worked retail during the holidays, you know stores become madhouses that look like a cross between cage fighting, professional wrestling rings, mosh pits, and the carpool pickup line at an elementary school. Everyone gets so caught up in the Christmas spirit that they forget to be kind to the people who make their lattes and refold the clothes they throw in a pile on the shelf. If you're one of the millions of people who serve customers caught up in the Christmas spirit, you probably struggle to find Jesus in the midst of the gift-giving rage.

Don't get me wrong—gifts are great. Who doesn't love to watch kids unwrap the lightsaber they asked Santa for in July? But all the gifts and carols and pageants won't point people to Jesus if we steamroll over them in our quest to construct the Christmas we see in catalogues.

Christmas is the time of year we set aside to remember the incarnation of Jesus. It's a time to celebrate God's decision to show His love for us by coming to live among us. And since He started in such a humble place, in a stack of hay surrounded by donkeys, I bet He would want us to strip away some of the hoopla to get back to the basics of Christmas.

If we make the holidays about parties and presents alone, we'll miss Jesus on His birthday. Let's celebrate Christmas the way Jesus would want us to: by putting people first and being generous with our love.

Who are you putting first in your life?

WE'RE LIVING LETTERS. EVERY TIME WE LOVE PEOPLE WITHOUT AN AGENDA, WE ADD A PAGE.

Above all, love each other deeply, because love covers over a multitude of sins.

1 PETER 4:8

There's a movie called *Stranger than Fiction* where the actor Will Ferrell plays a workaday guy who gets stuck in the rut of his routine. He's quite meticulous, too, which doesn't help. He times how long he brushes his teeth (and sub-times the tops and bottoms of his mouth). His closet is never disorderly—everything has its exact spot. He takes the same route to work, clocks in and out at the same time, and never *ever* deviates from the routine. Until . . .

One day he starts hearing a voice. It's not a voice in his head—it's an audible voice. Spoiler alert: this voice is the narration of a fiction writer whose book somehow has him as the main character. Without his permission, she starts writing his life—*his real life.*

It's a fun plot device, especially if you love books. But it puts on display, I think, the fact that we don't live our story in isolation. You and I may not have some faraway writer typing out the steps we take. But the steps we take are influencing the stories other people are writing with their lives.

When people look at followers of Jesus, they see us as a team living in a combined story. When someone does something lovely in the name of Jesus, they've just added another page to the story we're telling about Him. The truth is, we're living letters. Every time we love without an agenda, we're telling the story of Jesus' life all over again.

What story are you telling about love these days?

IF YOU THINK YOUR FAILURE IS BIGGER THAN GOD'S GRACE, THAT'S YOUR SECOND MISTAKE.

If we confess our sins, he is faithful and just and will forgive us our sins and purify us from all unrighteousness.

1 JOHN 1:9

Christmas morning might just be my favorite moment all year. When the kids were young and still in the house, we'd wake up as a family, huddle in the upstairs foyer, pray together, and head down to celebrate Jesus and have fun. Those moments are some of my favorite memories.

Christmas offered up some chances for mischief too. Like most kids, mine were dying to know what presents were under the tree. A few days before Christmas they would head to the living room, and like expert surgeons with razor-sharp scalpels, they would wriggle under the tree and make incisions on the tape, just enough to see the gift underneath. Then, like sewing in sutures, they'd retape the package. We learned this years later once the kids were confident they wouldn't get in trouble.

Of course, we wish they hadn't done it, but we had to give them credit for covering their tracks. Here's the problem: we spend so much of our lives figuring out how to cover our tracks when we mess up, we get really good at it. You might fool your mom and dad, or even a couple of friends, but you won't fool God. He knows what we've been up to and into. And you know what? He's not holding it against you. So why try to hide it from Him?

God always has plenty of grace for us. It's a gift we can unwrap every day. All it takes for us to access it is to get real enough that we realize our need. Remember this: if you think your failure is bigger than God's grace, that's your second mistake.

True confession: In what ways do you need God's help right now?

THE WAY WE TREAT PEOPLE WHO DON'T HAVE A PLACE TO STAY IS THE BEST WAY TO DESCRIBE WHAT THE MANGER MEANS.

If anyone has material possessions and sees a brother or sister in need but has no pity on them, how can the love of God be in that person? Dear children, let us not love with words or speech but with actions and in truth.

1 JOHN 3:17–18

Have you ever stepped into a full elevator and faced the people inside instead of the door? Even for a guy like me, it's an uncomfortable social experiment. We like our space. We're suspicious of strangers. We're threatened by strangers who enter our space.

In one sense, this is natural. We can hug a new acquaintance as a gesture of warmth. There are creepy hugs too. But what about when we go too far in the other direction? What if we don't let anyone close? What if we never seek out people we typically don't let in? If that's you, be cautioned.

If I've learned anything in life, the people I'm tempted to turn away are usually the ones who teach me the most about love. Whether it's homeless people showing a few nights of grime or friends who call when I'm too busy, the people who infringe on my private space humble me. They teach me things I would have missed otherwise.

We forget Jesus didn't have a place to stay. He was a homeless man at the mercy of hospitable friends. He said when we take in people who don't have a place to stay, we're doing it to Him. If we want to love Jesus, we'll welcome people who are displaced like He was.

The way we treat people who don't have a place to stay is the best way to describe what the manger means.

How are you treating people who don't have a place to stay this Christmas?

FIX YOUR EYES ON JESUS. IT'S OKAY TO STARE.

Let the message of Christ dwell among you richly as you teach and admonish one another with all wisdom through psalms, hymns, and songs from the Spirit, singing to God with gratitude in your hearts.

COLOSSIANS 3:16

Imagine what it must've been like for Mary in those first moments after Jesus was born. Like any mother of a newborn, Jesus would have been pulled tight against her chest, wrapped in a blanket for warmth and comfort while mom looked tearfully and exhaustedly down on the miracle that just happened. (I wouldn't think less of Jesus, either, if He was squealing like most newborns do.) Now imagine what the host of angels must have been doing as they saw God now as a child. If angels drop their jaws at anything, this would have been it.

Last, imagine what God the Father must have been doing. His precious Son, who was with Him before all things, just became the most fragile, tender, totally dependent thing in all creation: a newborn baby. God must have looked on with profound love at the One who would bring His creation back into relationship. He must have swelled with affection knowing the mission He sent His son to accomplish.

When was the last time you gawked at God? Staring at Jesus is a perfectly natural reaction. All of creation did it when He was born, and we've continued to do it for thousands of years. As you think about this God-made-man, shake yourself out of the familiarity that's layered on top of Him over the years. Let your heart be warmed by the traditions, the garland, the candle-lighting service. But be shocked—be in awe of the baby in the manger.

What commitment will you make the rest of this year to meditate on Jesus and His love?

LIVE PEACEFULLY. LOVE FURIOUSLY.

If it is possible, as far as it depends on you, live at peace with everyone.

ROMANS 12:18

One of the great heroes in the Bible is a guy named Paul. Paul was a bad guy in his youth. He was a powerful religious leader who felt threatened by followers of Jesus, so he spent most of his time trying to shut down Christianity. He oversaw the murder of some of the greatest Christian leaders at the time, and he was proud of his oppressive ways. Until he met Jesus.

When Paul met Jesus, his entire world turned upside down, and he was never the same. He devoted himself to spreading the love of God to those who would listen and those who had no interest. Because of his zeal, he was flogged, beaten, stoned, imprisoned, and shipwrecked out at sea. He spent much of his life on the run because he risked it all to tell people about the life-changing love of Jesus.

Paul wrote more than half the New Testament, so he left a lot of wisdom behind, but one of his greatest pieces of advice was this: as far as it depends on you, live at peace with all people. This is from the guy who was beat up and pushed down more than most of us could ever imagine, and still his message was peace.

He reminds us sometimes total peace isn't possible. Sometimes other people choose to battle no matter how much kindness we extend. But as far as it depends on us, let's live peacefully with other people. We can't always control the outcome, but we can love furiously in the process.

How can you extend peace to people in your life today?

NO ONE LEADS PEOPLE TO JESUS; HE LEADS PEOPLE TO HIMSELF. ALL THE PRESSURE IS OFF. JUST GO LOVE EVERYBODY.

And I, when I am lifted up from the earth, will draw all people to myself.

JOHN 12:32

If you had high school friends who happened to be star athletes, you got a front-row seat to the college courtship process. College coaches would sit in the stands for big games, make home visits to spend time with families, and fly the athletes out for first-class visits in hopes of persuading them to join their team.

But the best programs don't have to apply much pressure. They still go through some of the motions to attract the best talent, but they know their program speaks for itself. Young athletes want to play for the best teams, so top-notch programs don't have to overextend themselves trying to convince kids to join. They're attractive because they're good.

Thinking about this process makes me think of Christians who see following Jesus as a kind of recruitment strategy. They see the world in two camps: who's in and who's out. Anyone who has experienced the love of Jesus wants everyone to be "in." But sometimes I wonder if God sees the world in two different groups: "in" and "on the way." If you're spending time with people in order to recruit them, it might already be a lost cause. Being with people to love them is what Jesus did.

No one leads people to Jesus. He leads people to Himself. All the pressure is off. All we have to do is give away all the love He's poured into us. Give of yourself without an agenda, and His love will speak for itself.

How are you lifting Jesus up to others around you?

IT'S EASY TO CONFUSE BUSYNESS WITH PURPOSE. DO WHAT LASTS AND LET THE REST FALL AWAY.

What do you want me to do for you?

MARK 10:51

Every December as the year comes to an end, I set aside time to reflect on all the highs and lows of the last twelve months. I try to honestly evaluate things I got right and identify areas I hope to improve. And almost every year, my regrets aren't about the things I did; I regret the things I didn't do.

We regret trips we didn't take in order to get more work done back home. We regret the kids' soccer tournaments we missed. We wish we'd spent more time with close friends or reading and less time watching TV. We hoped we'd be further along in our writing projects and more involved at the homeless shelter.

It's easy to confuse a lot of activity with a purposeful life. If we let our feelings determine our commitments, we'll probably spend more time on the internet and less time on the adventures we long for. It's nothing to feel guilty about; it's just our natural response if we're not clear about where we want to invest our time. We need to know what we want and why we want it.

What do you want to be remembered for? What things would you like to accomplish if you knew you wouldn't fail? Who would you want to share life with, and where would you like to go? There's a good chance there's not much standing between you and those adventures, accomplishments, and relationships. You just need to get clear on what you want and make sure you want it for the right reason.

We never regret following through on the commitments we're passionate about and the activities that last. Figure those out and let the rest fall away.

What do you want to be remembered for?

JESUS LIVED IN THE MARGINS, AND HE WROTE THE BOOK ON LOVE. COPY A FEW PAGES FROM HIM.

I needed clothes and you clothed me, I was sick and you looked after me, I was in prison and you came to visit me.

MATTHEW 25:36

Jesus definitely didn't do things by the book. When the religious leaders said He needed to play by their rules, He showed them He was listening to His Father's voice. He spent His whole life engaging the people most of us have spent our whole lives trying to avoid. He made loving the marginalized look easy while we find them the easiest to ignore. He had meals with them, He helped make their daily lives better, and He taught them about hope beyond what they could see. He held them.

What if we decided to make it easy to find room in our lives for loving those without? What would it take? What would you quit? It's easiest for us to find margin for others in our lives when we get something in return. You would have never found Jesus going for the photo op; most of the time He spent with the marginalized was in secret. He actually avoided credit multiple times by disappearing in a crowd or saying, "Don't tell anyone." How crazy is that?

When I struggle to decide what I'm supposed to do next, I try to remember those folks left outside the lines: the poor, orphans, widows, and those in prison. Those are the ones Jesus set His sights on. After all, I want to be remembered for what I did outside the lines rather than the stuff I filled in between. Let's go fill up the margins with our love. It will mean more to the world than pages and pages of words.

What can you do these last few days of the year to love those on the margins?

DECEMBER 30

REMEMBER THAT "GOD WITH US" IS POINTING TO THE END OF THE STORY, WHERE YOU HAVE A CHANCE TO BE WITH HIM.

> The Lord himself will give you a sign: "The virgin will conceive and give birth to a son, and will call him Immanuel."
>
> ISAIAH 7:14

This time of year, we hear a lot about the name Immanuel, which means "God with us." Jesus embodied the phrase so well that as He wept for His friends, He made breakfast for them, and He allowed them into His quiet places. Jesus made Himself vulnerable, and He listened when others opened their personal lives too. In Jesus, God kneeled down and said, "I'm with you." He didn't let death be the end of it. Instead, it was the starting line to a relationship we can encounter today.

I think that's what heaven is all about. The tomb wasn't a dramatic explosion. Jesus hadn't come so He would be recognized as a king or a rock star. Jesus came to show all of history that God is here to be as close as a friend.

For people who follow Jesus, we know that Christmas is like the opening act of a play. The hardest part we remember comes a few months later when we reflect on Jesus' sacrifice for us on the cross. This holiday season, as you celebrate "God with us," remember that He chose to come even when He knew the story would take an awful turn that would end His life. The full manger points to the empty tomb. God came to life with the mission to defeat death.

Whenever you hear people talk about "Immanuel, God with us," remember that He did it so you could be with Him.

What will you do today to experience Immanuel?

WE CAN'T CHANGE MUCH IF WE WON'T RISK MUCH.

Commit to the Lord whatever you do, and he will establish your plans.

PROVERBS 16:3

The passage of time is an unstoppable force. It happens to all of us the same. A year ending might stir some frustration for the things left undone, or you might be high-fiving strangers. It all depends on how much you were willing to risk. A year beginning might bring a sense of anticipation, or you might see another lather-rinse-repeat coming. It all depends on how much you are willing to risk.

When God gives us dreams, He wants us to change as we chase them. We achieve our dreams by bravely facing the lopsided odds. We might think achieving a dream is the point, but I think for God it's more about seeing us become more like Jesus with each step we take forward. Of course, He celebrates with us too.

If you've been living with a stirring in your soul, it's time to test your limits. There's no fast-forward to change. Time grinds slowly forward the same way for all of us. The question is, as a famous poet once said, "What do you plan to do with your one wild and precious life?" Because that is what it is. And that is how God sees you: precious and wildly capable of amazing things.

The sidelines aren't a place for you anymore. Take a risk. Be bold and courageous. Dream of something only God could accomplish. Decide you're going to risk much . . . so God can lead you toward your dream and toward Him.

What dreams are stirring in your soul?

ACKNOWLEDGMENTS

Every book is a collaborative effort. This one is no different. What made this effort particularly fun is involving many of my favorite people in the work. Immeasurable thanks to my friend Bryan Norman for giving leadership and direction to this entire project. Julie Rodgers and Hoke Bryan, you worked tirelessly to give life to these words and daily reflections. I respect both of you immensely. Thank you to Webster Younce and the team at Thomas Nelson—Janene MacIvor, Karen Jackson, Rachel Tockstein, Belinda Bass, and everyone else—for your immeasurable patience. Brian Hampton, without you, none of my books would have ever happened. You will remain a hero in all of our lives forever.

Special thanks to the entire team at Love Does and Dream Big. Dae, Jody, Ashton, Catherine, Haley, Tatave, Becky, Savannah, and our teams in so many war-torn countries, without your daily help and support there would be no books. You're so busy getting things done, you don't stop to realize what I've asked you to do is impossible. And yet you pull it off with grace and poise and love.

Finally, to my beautiful family: Sweet Maria, Lindsey, Jon, Richard, Ashley, Adam, and my dad. I love you. Without you, I would be without any words. You are the kind of people I aspire to be some day.

ABOUT THE AUTHOR

Bob is the longest serving volunteer at Love Does and is its chief balloon inflator. He calls himself a "recovering lawyer" because after practicing law for almost thirty years, he walked into his own law firm and quit in order to pursue encouraging people full time. Bob is driven by a desire to love people and to motivate others to do the same. These days, you'll find Bob in an airport on his way to connect with and encourage people or, more likely, on his way home for supper with Sweet Maria.

A few years ago, Bob wrote a book called *Everybody Always*. Before that, he wrote one called *Love Does*. He gave away all the proceeds from that book to help change the lives of children in countries where armed conflicts had left them vulnerable. Today, Love Does is an organization dedicated to helping kids in these areas including Uganda, Somalia, Afghanistan, Nepal, and India. You can find out more about Love Does at www.LoveDoes.org.

CONNECT WITH BOB

Bob's passion is people. He'd love to hear from you if you want to email him at info@bobgoff.com.

You can also follow him on Instagram and Twitter @bobgoff. Here's his cell phone number if you want to give him a call: (619) 985-4747.

Bob is also available to inspire and engage your team, organization, or audience. To date, he's spoken to more than one million people, bringing his unique perspective and exciting storytelling with him. He also puts on seminars called Dream Big. If you're interested in having Bob come to your event, check out bobgoff.com/speaking.